BICYCLE RIDES
Los Angeles County

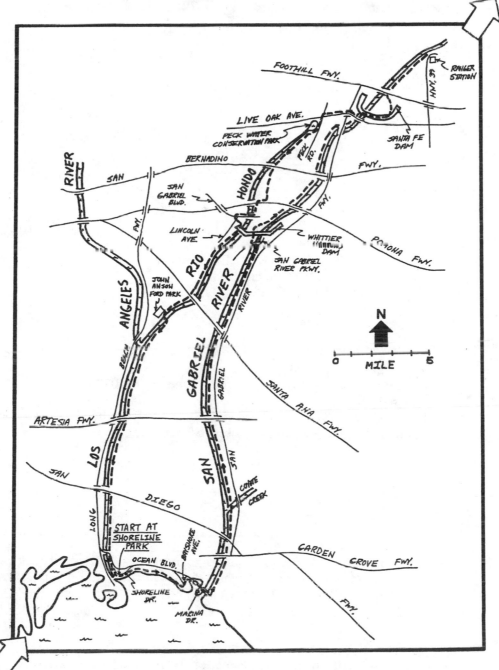

BY DON AND SHARRON BRUNDIGE

Other Books by Don and Sharron Brundige:
Bicycle Rides: Los Angeles and Orange Counties
Bicycle Rides: San Fernando Valley and Ventura County
Bicycle Rides: Orange County

Printed by Griffin Printing & Lithograph Co., Inc.
Glendale, California

Published by B-D Enterprises
122 Mirabeau Ave
San Pedro, California 90732

Corrections and updates will make this a better book and are gratefully
appreciated. Publisher will reply to all such letters.

TABLE OF CONTENTS

(50 Trips ------- and ------- 62 Rides)

IN MEMORIUM

To our dear friend Nels M. Ostrem
the eternal optimist
who already had devised a thousand ways to sell this book

ACKNOWLEDGEMENTS

We offer our thanks to family, friends, and bicycling acquaintances who gave us ideas, advice, and plenty of encouragement while developing this biking book. This includes a "thank you" to the state, county and city agencies and individuals who offered their services and publications. We show particular gratitude to the folks that were kind enough to review and comment to our manuscript: Jill Morales, Al Hook, and Walt and Sally Bond. We also thank our brother Rich Davis for his Pomona area trip ideas and Larry Pirrone and the Cyclesport Olympic crew for their review of our Diamond Bar area tours.

We specifically wish to acknowledge the following individuals and/or organizations who provided some excellent ideas for bicycle trips: Joel Breitbart of the City of Los Angeles, the folks at CALTRANS District 07, the Department of Transportation of the City of Los Angeles, Al Kovach of the City of Torrance, the Recreation Department of the City of Arcadia, the Public Works Department of the City of Pasadena, the Parks and Recreation Department of the City of Burbank, the Cities of Glendale and La Mirada, and Noelia Chapa of the City of La Habra Heights.

We also acknowledge getting some nifty ride ideas from the following sources: *Gousha Weekend Guide to California Bike Tours* published by the H. M. Gousha Company; and *Southern California Bicycling* published by the Automobile Club of Southern California.

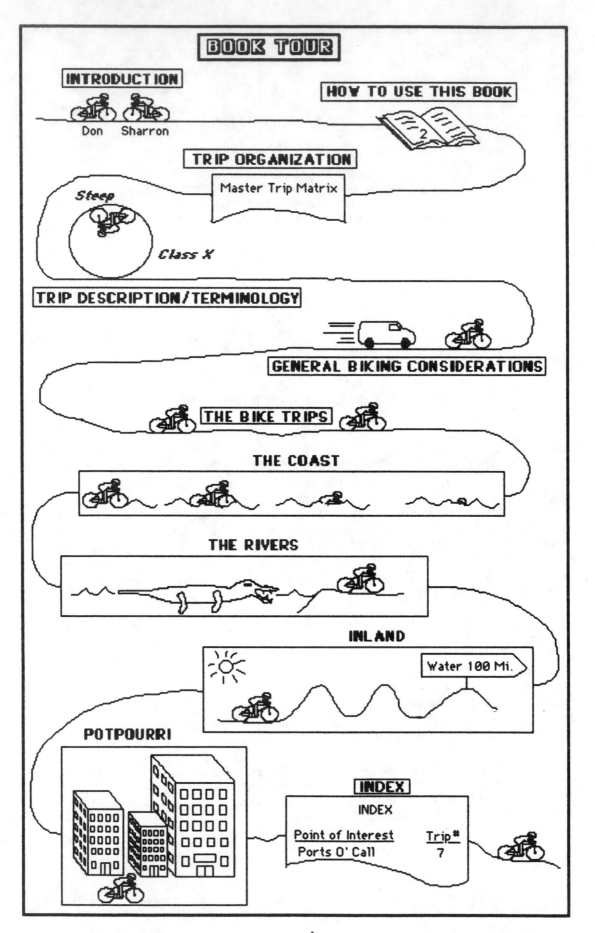

INTRODUCTION

We have divided out the Orange County section of our well received book, *BICYCLE RIDES LOS ANGELES AND ORANGE COUNTIES*. This book contains an update of those trips plus fourteen new tours: "Santa Monica Mountains Workout," "Santa Monica to Port Hueneme" coastal route, several inner-city Los Angeles tours including the 72 mile "Tour de Los Angeles," "Avalon, Santa Catalina Island Tour," and six new inland routes. The latter include "Diamond Bar Tour," "San Jose Hills," "Puente Hills Loop," "Baseline Road" foothills ride, and "Bonelli Regional Park" in the San Gabriel Valley area and two new city rides, "Torrance Tour" and "Gardena Bikeway/Dominguez Channel."

Again, we wanted to provide a trip guide that concentrates on trip navigation, contains a large number of well-documented trips, provides the necessary trip maps, and is reasonably priced. Hopefully we have succeeded!

This guide has been developed based on biking trips taken in 1987-1989. There are over 800 <u>one-way</u> bike miles described. The document identifies 50 biking trips in Los Angeles County. Trips of exceptional length are broken down into segments or "rides." There are a total of 62 individual bike rides described. Each ride is written to be as complete and self-standing as possible. The authors used eighteen-speed bicycles, although a vast majority of the trips can be easily ridden with ten-speeds.

A cross section of trips is provided. There are some short length family trips on separated bike paths, many longer exploratory and workout trips for more experienced bikers on various quality bike routes, and a few "gut-buster" trips on open roadway for the most physically fit and motivated bikers. The trip domains include parks, beaches, harbors, rivers, lakes, canyons, hills, basins and mountains. The trips vary from extremely scenic to somewhat monotonous (e.g., certain stretches of the concrete "wastelands" along the rivers). There's a little something for everybody!

The strong emphasis in this book is the "getting from here to there." This navigation is provided using detailed route descriptions in terms of landmarks, mileage, and a quality set of trip maps. Scenery, vistas, scenic or historic landmarks, and sightseeing attractions are regularly noted for each trip, although detailed information about these features must be sought out in other publications. Public restrooms and sources of water are identified on trips where these facilities are scarce. Pleasant rest spots are also pointed out. Finally, "wine and dine" spots are noted for two specific circumstances: 1) where places to eat along the trip are scarce; and 2) where the establishment is too unique or exceptional not to mention.

HOW TO USE THIS BOOK

There are two ways to use this book, one way for the person who wants to enjoy the research along with enjoying the bike ride and another way for the biker who is just anxious to get out there "amongst em" on a bike ride.

For the "anxious biker" , follow Steps 1 through 5 below and split!

1. Use the "Master Trip Map" in the "TRIP ORGANIZATION" section to select areas of interest for the bike ride.   Note the candidate trip numbers. (Another option is to select a trip based on landmarks and sightseeing attractions referenced in the "INDEX.")

2. Go to the "Master Trip Matrices" in the "TRIP ORGANIZATION" section and narrow down the number of candidate trips by reviewing their general features.

3. Read about the individual trips and select one.

4. Read and understand the safety rules described in the "GENERAL BIKING CONSIDERATIONS" section.

5. See you later. Enjoy the ride!

For the more methodical folks, continue reading the next chapter.   By the time you're through, you'll understand the trip description and maps much better than the "anxious biker."

TRIP ORGANIZATION

This bike book is organized by trip number. Extended length trips are broken down into trip segments by ride number, which is the trip number plus a letter. Thus, Trip #6 is the "Palos Verdes Peninsula Loop," while Ride #6A is the "Palos Verdes Drive North" segment of the trip. Trip numbers are in a general sequence governed by whether the tours are coastal, river, or inland. Refer back to the "TABLE OF CONTENTS" for the entire trip list.

The "Master Trip Map" shows the general location of trips and rides by a circled reference number (i.e., ⑦ refers to Trip #7). Extended length trips are identified by circled numbers at both beginning and terminal points.

The "Master Trip Matrices" provide a quick reference for selecting candidate trips for more detailed reading evaluation. The matrices are organized by trip/ride number. The key trip descriptors provided in those matrices are briefly explained in the footnotes at the bottom of the last matrix (page 11). A more detailed explanation of those descriptors is provided in the "TRIP DESCRIPTION/TERMINOLOGY" section which follows.

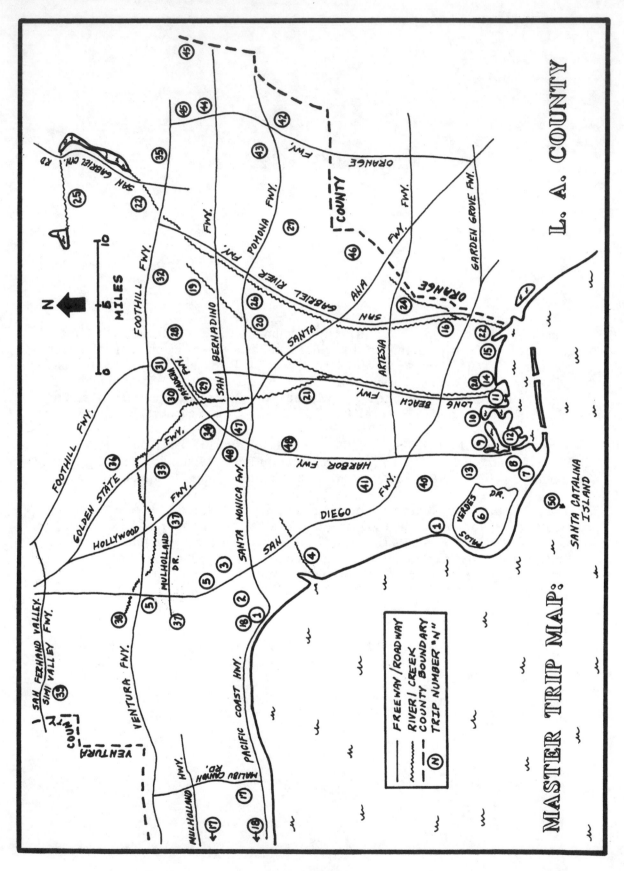

MASTER TRIP MAP:

L. A. COUNTY

4

MASTER TRIP MATRIX

TRIP NO.	GENERAL LOCATION	LEVEL OF DIFFICULTY			ROUTE QUALITY			TRIP CHARACT.[2]	COMMENTS
		L.O.D.[1]	MILES	ELEV.	BIKE TRAIL (%)	BIKE LANE (%)	OTHER (%)		
1	Redondo Beach-Santa Monica	M (1-w) M-S(r/t)	22.0 (1-w)	Flat	90	10	-	S, L,S/A,M	South Bay Bike Trail
1A	Redondo Beach-Manhattan Beach	E (r/t)	5.4 (1-w)	Flat	80	20	-	S, L,S/A	Southern Segment
1B	Manhattan Beach-Marina Del Rey	E(r/t)	7.3 (1-w)	Flat	100	-	-	S, L, S/A	Middle Segment
1C	Marina Del Rey-Santa Monica	E (r/t)	9.3 (1-w)	Flat	80	20	-	S, L, S/A	Northern Segment
2	Santa Monica	E(1-loop) M(2-loops)	6.4-11.9	Flat	10	90	-	S, L, S/A	Santa Monica Loops
3	Westwood	M	6.7-7.5	Flat-Mod.	10	70	20	S, L	Westwood Loop (2 options)
4	Marina Del Rey-Culver City	E(1-w) M(r/t)	6.6 (1-w)	Flat	100	-	-	M	Ballona Creek Bikeway
5	Westwood - Encino	S (1-w) VS (r/t)	7.4 (1-w)	Steep	-	50	50	S, E	Old Sepulveda Blvd.
6	Palos Verdes Peninsula	VS	23.2	Steep	20	80	-	S, L, S/A, E, M	Palos Verdes Peninsula Loop
6A	Rolling Hills	M (1-w) M-S (r/t)	5.8 (1-w)	Mod	70	-	30	S	Palos Verdes Drive North

1,2 See footnotes on page 11

MASTER TRIP MATRIX

TRIP NO.	GENERAL LOCATION	LEVEL OF DIFFICULTY			ROUTE QUALITY			TRIP CHARACT.[2]	COMMENTS
		L.O.D.[1]	MILES	ELEV.	BIKE TRAIL (%)	BIKE LANE (%)	OTHER (%)		
6B	Palos Verdes Estates	M (1-w) M (r/t)	5.1 (1-w)	Mod	-	-	100	S, L	Palos Verdes Drive West
6C	Rancho Palos Verdes	M (1-w) M (r/t)	5.7 (1-w)	Mod.	-	-	100	S, L, S/A	Palos Verdes Drive South
6D	Miraleste	S (1-w) VS (r/t)	6.6 (1-w)	Steep	10	-	90	S, E	Palos Verdes Drive East
7	San Pedro	M (1-w) M (r/t)	6.2 (1-w)	Mod	30	60	10	S, L	Cabrillo Beach, Point Fermin
8	San Pedro	E(1-w) M(r/t)	6.2 (1-w)	Flat	10	-	90	S, L, S/A	Main Channel
9	Los Angeles Harbor	E (1-w) M (r/t)	8.7 (1-w)	Flat	10	-	90	S, L	East and West Basins
10	Long Beach Harbor	M (1-w) M (r/t)	13.6 (1-w)	Flat	-	-	100	S,L	Cerritos and Back Channels
11	Long Beach Harbor	E (1-w) M (r/t)	6.9 (1-w)	Flat	-	-	100	S, L, S/A	Southeast Basin
12	Terminal Island	E	11.0	Flat	-	-	100	S, L	Terminal Island Loop
13	Harbor City	E	5.9	Flat	-	-	100	S, N	Harbor Regional Park Loop

1,2 See footnotes on page 11

MASTER TRIP MATRIX

TRIP NO.	GENERAL LOCATION	LEVEL OF DIFFICULTY			ROUTE QUALITY			TRIP CHARACT.[2]	COMMENTS
		L.O.D.[1]	MILES	ELEV.	BIKE TRAIL (%)	BIKE LANE (%)	OTHER (%)		
14	Long Beach	E	6.6	Flat	90	-	10	S, L, S/A	Shoreline Park Loop
15	Long Beach, Naples	M	10.9	Flat	50	20	30	S	Belmont Shores, Naples Loop
16	Long Beach-	E	4.3	Flat	100	-	-	S, N, S/A	El Dorado Park
17	Santa Monica-Port Hueneme	S (l-w) VS (r/t)	44.7 (l-w)	Mod-Steep	-	80	20	S, N, L, S/A, E, M	Bicentennial Coastal Route
17A	Santa Monica-Malibu	M (l-w) M (r/t)	10.5 (l-w)	Mod	-	-	100	S, N, L, S/A	Southern Segment
17B	Malibu-Sycamore Grove	S(l-w) S (r/t)	20.1 (l-w)	Mod-Steep	-	100	-	S, N, L, S/A, E	Middle Segment
17C	Sycamore Grove-Port Hueneme	M (l-w) M (r/t)	13.7 (l-w)	Mod	-	100	-	S, N	Northern Segment
18	Santa Monica Mountains	VS	41.6	Steep-Sheer	-	30	70	S, N, L, E, M	PCH-Topanga Canyon-Mulholland Hwy. Loop
19-20	El Monte-Long Beach	M (l-w) S (r/t)	28.1 (l-w)	Flat	100	-	-	S, N, L, M	Rio Hondo - L.A. River Bike Trail
19	El Monte	E (l-w) M(r/t)	8.2 (l-w)	Flat	100	-	-	S, N, L, M	Upper Rio Hondo River Trail

1,2 See footnotes on page 11

MASTER TRIP MATRIX

TRIP NO.	GENERAL LOCATION	LEVEL OF DIFFICULTY L.O.D.[1]	LEVEL OF DIFFICULTY MILES	LEVEL OF DIFFICULTY ELEV.	ROUTE QUALITY BIKE TRAIL (%)	ROUTE QUALITY BIKE LANE (%)	ROUTE QUALITY OTHER (%)	TRIP CHARACT.[2]	COMMENTS
20A	Downey	E(1-w) M(r/t)	9.0	Flat	-	-	100	S, N, L, M	Upper Lario Trail (Rio Hondo-L.A. Rivers)
20B	Long Beach	E (1-w) M (r/t)	10.9 (1-w)	Flat	100	-	-	S, N, l, M	Lower Lario Trail (Los Angeles River)
21	Southgate-Bell	E (r/t)	5.6 (1-w)	Flat	-	100	-	M	L.A. River (northern segment)
22	Seal Beach-Azusa	S (1-w) VS (r/t)	38.0 (1-w)	Flat	100	-	-	S, N, L, M	San Gabriel River (shore to mountains)
22A	Seal Beach-Long Beach	E (r/t)	5.6 (1-w)	Flat	100	-	-	S, N, M	Ocean to El Dorado Park
22B	Long Beach-Downey	E (1-w) M (r/t)	9.7 (1-w)	Flat	100	-	-	S, N, M	El Dorado Park to Wilderness Park
22C	Downey-Pico Rivera	E (1-w) M (r/t)	7.7 (1-w)	Flat	100	-	-	S, N, L, M	Wilderness Park to Whittier Narrows Dam
22D	Pico Rivera-Irwindale	E (1-w) M (r/t)	11.4 (1-w)	Flat	100	-	-	S, N, L, M	Whittier Narrows Dam to Santa Fe Dam
22E	Irwindale-Azusa	E(1-w) M (r/t)	7.5 (1-w)	Flat	100	-	-	S, N, L, M	Santa Fe Dam to San Gabriel Canyon
23	Sea to Montains to Sea (loop)	VS	83.5 (1-w)	Flat	90	5	5	S, N, L, S/A, M	San Gabriel - Rio Hondo - L.A. River Loop

1,2 See footnotes on page 11

8

MASTER TRIP MATRIX

| TRIP NO. | GENERAL LOCATION | LEVEL OF DIFFICULTY | | | ROUTE QUALITY | | | TRIP CHARACT.[2] | COMMENTS |
		L.O.D.[1]	MILES	ELEV.	BIKE TRAIL (%)	BIKE LANE (%)	OTHER (%)		
24	Long Beach - Cerritos	E (1-w) M (r/t)	9.2 (1-w)	Flat	100	-	-	S, M	San Gabriel River - Coyote Creek
25	Angeles National Forest	M (river) S (dam)	13.4	Flat, Sheer	100	-	-	S, N, E	West Fork, San Gabriel River
26	Pico Rivera	E	11.2	Flat	99	-	1	S, N, L	Whittier Narrows, Legg Lake Loop
27	Hacienda Heights	M	5.6	Mod	-	100	-	S	Hacienda Heights Loop
28	San Marino	M	6.8	Mod	-	-	100	S	San Marino Tour (loop)
29	Montecito Heights	E	7.5	Flat	50	50	-	S, N, L	Arroyo Seco Bike Trail (loop)
30	Highland Park	E	7.6	Mod	10	80	10	S, N, L, S/A	Highland Park Loop
31	Pasadena	E-M(1-w) M (r/t)	6.8	Mod	20	80	-	S, N, L	Kenneth Newall Bikeway
32	Arcadia	M-S	29.4	Mod	-	100	-	S, L, M	Arcadia Loops
33	Griffith Park	M-S	8.8	Mod	-	100	-	S, L, S/A	Griffith Park Loop

1,2 See footnotes on page 11

9

MASTER TRIP MATRIX

TRIP NO.	GENERAL LOCATION	LEVEL OF DIFFICULTY			ROUTE QUALITY			TRIP CHARACT.[2]	COMMENTS
		L.O.D.[1]	MILES	ELEV.	BIKE TRAIL (%)	BIKE LANE (%)	OTHER (%)		
34	Elysian Park	S	6.4	Steep	-	-	100	S, E	Elysian Park Loop
35	Glendora	M	8.3	Mod	-	100	-	S	Glendora Bikeway (loop)
36	Burbank	M-S (1-loop)	14.8	Steep	-	100	-	S, E	Burbank Bikeway (1 loop of several)
37	Encino - Universal City	VS (1-w)	13.0 (1-w)	Steep	20	80	-	S, L, E, M	Mulholland Drive
38	Encino	E	9.1	Flat	95	5	-	S, L	Sepulveda Dam Bikeway (loop)
39	Chatsworth	E	6.3	Flat	20	-	80	S, L	Chatsworth Tour, Brown's Creek (loop)
40	Torrance	M	14.3	Flat	5	55	40	S	Torrance Tour (loop)
41	Gardena	E	12.2	Flat	40	-	60	S, N	Gardena Tour, Dominguez Channel
42	Diamond Bar	M	10.4	Mod	60	-	40	S	Diamond Bar Loop
43	Walnut, City of Industry	M	12.9	M-S	-	20	80	S, E	San Jose Hills (loop)

1,2 See footnotes on page 11

MASTER TRIP MATRIX

TRIP NO.	GENERAL LOCATION	LEVEL OF DIFFICULTY			ROUTE QUALITY			TRIP CHARACT.[2]	COMMENTS
		L.O.D.[1]	MILES	ELEV.	BIKE TRAIL (%)	BIKE LANE (%)	OTHER (%)		
44	Pomona, San Dimas	M	8.9	Mod	30	20	50	S, N, L, S/A	Bonelli Park, Puddingstone Resevoir (loop)
45	San Dimas, La Verne, Claremont	M	22.3	Mod	-	-	100	S, L, S/A	Baseline Rd., San Gabriel Mtn. Foothills (loop)
46	La Mirada	E	10.0	Flat-Mod	30	55	5	S, N	La Mirada City Loop
47	Los Angeles Civic Center	M	9.8	Mod	-	35	65	S, L, S/A	Skyscraper Tour (Downtown Los Angeles)
48	Central Los Angeles	E	3.8	Flat	100	-	-	S, L, S/A	Los Angeles Bikeway System, Exposition Park, USC Campus
49	South Bay-Central L.A.-L.A. River-Long Beach-Palos Verdes	S	71.7	M-S	50	10	40	S, L, S/A,M	Tour de Los Angeles (loop)
50	Avalon, Santa Catalina Island	S	9.7	M-S	-	-	100	S, L, S/A, E	Avalon Tour

1 L.O.D. - Overall trip level of difficulty: VS-very strenuous; S-strenuous; M-Moderate; E-easy; 1-w -one way; r/t-round trip

2 TRIP CHARACTERISTICS - General trip features and highlights: S-scenic; N-nature trail; L-landmarks; S/A-sight-seeing attractions; E-elevation workout; M-mileage workout

11

TRIP DESCRIPTION/TERMINOLOGY

The trip descriptors in the "Master Trip Matrices" are described below in further detail. Several of these same descriptors are also used in the individual trip writeups.

GENERAL LOCATION: The general location of the bike trail is provided in terms of a city, landmark, or general area description, as applicable. The "Master Trip Map" may be useful in conjunction with this general locator.

LEVEL OF DIFFICULTY: The rides are rated on an overall basis as *very strenuous*, *strenuous*, *moderate*, and *easy*, based on elevation gain, trip distance, and condition of the bike route.

A *very strenuous* trip can be of any length, has very steep grades, and is generally designed for bikers in excellent physical condition. It should be noted that even on the most strenuous trip, the bike can be walked uphill for bikers in reasonably good condition. However, rather than suffer this fate, it is recommended that bikers start with the easier trips and work up. Alternately, trips are well enough described such that the biker might plan to ride the easier part of a stressing trip and link up with other easier trips.

A *strenuous* trip has some steep grades and/or relatively long mileage (on the order of 50 miles total). The trip is of sufficiently long duration to require trip planning and strong consideration of weather, water, food, and bike spare parts. Some portions of the trip may be on surfaces in poor condition or on shared roadway.

A *moderate* trip may have mild grades and moderate mileage, on the order of 15-20 miles. The trip is typically of a couple of hours duration and is generally on well maintained bike route.

An *easy* trip is on the order of 10 miles or less, is relatively flat, and is generally on well maintained bike trails or bike paths.

TRIP MILEAGE: Trip mileage is computed for the one-way trip length for *up and back* trips and full-trip length for *loop* trips. *Up and back* is specifically used for trips that share a common route in both outgoing and return directions. *Loop* specifically means that the outgoing and return trip segments are on predominantly different routes. *Round trip* is used without distinction as to whether the trip is an *up and back* or *loop* trip. In the trip writeups, the mileage from the starting point or "trailhead" is noted in parentheses to the nearest tenth mile, for example, (6.3).

Obviously, the one-way trips listed can be exercised with a planned car shuttle, ridden as an *up and back* trip, or biked in connection with another bicycle trip listed in this book. For convenience, connections with other trips are noted in the trip writeups or in a separate subsection for that trip titled, "Connecting Trips."

12

TRIP ELEVATION GAIN: The overall trip elevation gain is described in a qualitative fashion. *Flat* indicates that there are no grades of any consequence. Steepness of upgrades is loosely defined as follows: 1) *light* indicates limited slope and very little elevation gain; 2) *moderate* means more significant slope requiring use of low gears and may be ten's of feet of upgrade; 3) *steep* indicates workout-type grades that require low gears and high physical exertion; 4) *sheer* indicates gut-buster grades that require extreme physical exertion (and a strong will to live!).

The frequency of upgrades is divided into the following categories: 1) *single* for flat rides with a single significant upgrade; 2) *periodic* for flat rides where uphill segments are widely spaced; 3) *frequent* where narrowly spaced upgrades are encountered (e.g. rolling hills).

BIKE ROUTE QUALITY: The trip is summarized with respect to route quality in the "Master Trip Matrices" and a more detailed description is given in the individual trip writeups. The following route terminology (which is similar to that used by CALTRANS) is used:

. *Class I* - off-roadway bike paths or bike trails

. *Class II* - on-roadway, separated (striped) bike lanes

. *Class III* - on-roadway, signed (but not separated) bike lanes

If the route is on-roadway and not signed (i.e., not specifically marked as a bike route), it is arbitrarily referred to as *Class X*.

TRIP CHARACTERISTICS: The overall highlights of the bike trip are provided in the "Master Trip Matrices" to assist in general trip selection. The trip may be scenic (*S*), with sweeping vistas, exciting overlooks, or generally provide views of natural or man-made attractions such as cities. Alternatively, the trip may be a nature trail (*N*) or a path through areas which have an abundance of trees, flowers, and other flora. The nature trips or portions thereof are generally on Class I bike routes. The trip may highlight historical or well-known landmarks (*L*) or may have one or more sightseeing attractions (*S/A*). Examples of the former are the Whittier Narrows Dam on the San Gabriel River (Ride #22C), while the latter might be the Los Angeles Zoo in Griffith Park (Trip #33). Finally, some trips are potentially good workout trips in that there is significant elevation change (*E*) or lengthy mileage (*M*) if the entire trip is taken. Some trips may provide a mix of these characteristics and are so noted. Trips along well-lit Class I routes are so noted in the trip writeups.

Several descriptors are unique to the individual trip writeups. Those descriptors are defined below.

TRAILHEAD: The general location of the start of the bike path is provided for a single starting point. Driving directions to that trailhead are included. Nearby parking is also described in most cases. Always check to ensure that parking is consistent with current laws.

Note that for most trails, there are multiple points of entry beyond the primary point listed. For some of the trips in this book (particularly the river routes), alternate bicycle entry points are noted on maps by arrows (↗) along the bike route. Other alternate trailheads may be found using information obtained from other bikers, or from state or local publications for more popular routes.

WATER: In the "Trailhead" description, some general statements are provided about water availability. In the actual trip description, available water along the route is noted where water is scarce, although the trip should be planned to assume that water stops may not be operational. Particular emphasis is placed on public facilities for water and use of restrooms. Stores, shopping centers, and gas stations also are noted in many instances in the trip writeups, although the availability of water or other facilities in these instances is subject to the policies of those establishments.

CONNECTING TRIPS: Where bike trips can be linked to other trips in the book, they are so noted. *Continuation* trips are those where there is direct linkage at the beginning or end of the trip being described. *Connection* trips are either not directly linked (i.e., a Class X connector is required) or the linkage occurs at the interior of the trip being described. A brief "connector" route description is provided for the *Connection* trips.

BIKE TRIP MAPS: Each ride in the book has an accompanying detailed bike map. A summary of symbols and map features which are used in those maps is provided on the next page.

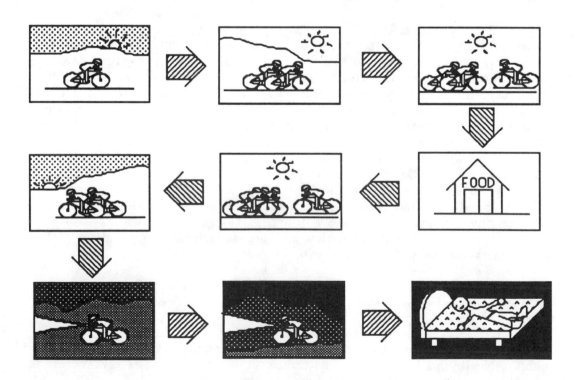

— — — —	Bike trail in trip description (unless otherwise noted).
• • • • • • •	Alternate bike route (unless otherwise noted).
LOS ANGELES RIVER ～～～～ or **COYOTE CREEK** • • • • •	River or creek when it is a major part of the trip description. The river or creek name is highlighted.
SAN JOSE CREEK	River or creek when it is a point of interest.
MAIN ST.	Roadway.
1-FISH HARBOR 2-DRY DOCKS	Key trip features. Numbers in key correspond to numbers marked along the mapped route.

VENICE	Nearby City	(park symbol)	Park	☐ 5 / ▨ 5	Landmark #5
W	Public Water Source	P	Parking	→	Entry Point to Trail
•—•	Locked Gate/ Limited Entry	++++++	Railroad Crossing or Overcrossing	(school symbol)	School(as a trip point of interest)
(mission symbol)	Mission	⋈	Gravel Pit	-	-

MAP SYMBOLS AND FEATURES

GENERAL BIKING CONSIDERATIONS

These are a collection of the thoughts that we've had in the hundreds of miles of biking that we have done:

SAFETY: Use common sense when you are biking. Common sense when combined with courtesy should cover most of the safety-related issues. But just to be on the safe side, write to CALTRANS (see the chapter on "OTHER BICYCLING INFORMATION SOURCES") for any of their publications and you get some excellent safety information along with it. The four safety "biggies" are: 1) understand bike riding laws; 2) keep your bicycle in safe operating order; 3) wear personal safety equipment as required (helmet is a must, bright or reflective clothes, sunglasses); 4) ride defensively--always assume that moving and parked car inhabitants are not aware that you are there.

Common courtesy is to offer assistance to bikers stopped because of breakdowns. Point out ruts, obstructions, and glass to bikers behind you.

EQUIPMENT: Necessary biking equipment includes a water bottle or two, tire pump, tool kit (typically tire irons, wrench(s), screwdriver), patch kit, and (sorry to say) bike lock. For longer trips add a spare tube and bike repair manual. We recommend a bike light even if there are no plans for night biking.

Necessary biking equipment includes a helmet, sunglasses, and clothes which will fit pessimistic weather conditions (particularly for longer trips). On all-day, cool or wet winter outings, we carry a layered set of clothes (this includes long pants, undershirt, long-sleeve shirt, sweater, and a two-piece nylon rain suit). Padded cycling pants and biking gloves are a must for long trips. Lycra clothes are light and extremely functional. For cool and dry days, we may drop the rain suit for a windbreaker (look for a windbreaker that folds up into a fanny pack). For other conditions, our outfits are normally shorts, undershirt, long-sleeve shirt and windbreaker. Laugh if you must, but wait until you find yourself biking home at night, in mid-winter, along a beach with a healthy sea breeze after you spent the day biking in the warm sun (an example of poor trip planning, we admit).

If you are going to get your money out of this book, get an automobile bike rack! The cost of bike racks is cheap compared to most bikes. Besides, it just doesn't make sense to bike fifty miles to take the planned twenty-mile bike trip.

GENERAL INFORMATION: A collection of seemingly random, unconnected, and useless comments are provided which we actually think are "gems of wisdom" based on hard experience:

o Develop and follow a checkoff list for a pre-trip bike examination (tires, brakes, cables, etc.) and equipment (water, food, clothing, tools, spare parts, etc.). It's embarassing to start a trip and realize that you've forgotten your bicycle!

o Check the weather (including smog conditions in urban areas) before going on an extended trip. Select trips and plan clothing accordingly.

o Plan the trip timing to ensure that there is a "pad" of daylight. Night biking just isn't as fun when it wasn't in the original plans. Night biking without the proper equipment is dangerous!

o Trip timing should include allowance for finding parking, trailheads, or connector routes. You never can fully trust authors of bike books!

o Trip conditions and routing are subject to change as a result of weather damage, building and highway construction, bike rerouting, etc. Especially for long trips, research these key elements before departing.

o Plan for afternoon headwinds when heading toward the beach (particularly west-facing beaches). "Pain" is what you feel when the last several miles of your fifty miler is spent bucking the sea breeze.

o Stay out of riverbeds, even concrete ones, unless it is marked part of the route. It may be a very long way to the next exit and it may also rain.

o Some river and creek trails flood out during heavy rains, particularly at river crossings and underpasses. Don't take these trips after heavy rains unless you are willing to plan on many route detours.

o Always take some water, no matter how short the trip. Having water available provides a feeling of security. Being thirsty creates a bad attitude.

o Bring enough water to provide for the contingency that "guaranteed" water spots may be dry.

o The best time of day for most trips on busy thoroughfares is before the rush-hour morning traffic. Morning is also best for rides on narrow country roads. With few exceptions, the best time of the week is the weekend, particularly Sunday.

o The best season for some trips depends on the person. If you want comradery, ride the more popular routes in the summer. If your pleasure is free-wheeling and wide-open spaces, save these routes for other seasons.

o Bring snacks for longer trips. Snacks provide needed energy and attitude improvement when the going gets tough. Having snacks available also allows more flexibility in selecting a "dining out" stop.

o Walk your bike through heavy glass-strewn areas. Lift your bike onto and off of curbs. Trips are more fun when you can ride your bike!

o Bring a map for trips that are not on well-marked bike routes. Once off the prescribed route, it is amazingly easy to lose the sense of direction.

o Maintain a steady pace when taking a long bike ride. For pleasure trips, the pace is too fast if you cannot carry on conversation while biking.

THE COAST

Book review crew, minus Jill, at Long Beach Shoreline Park

TRIPS #1A-#1C - SOUTH BAY BIKE TRAIL

It is appropriate that the book should start with the most popular bike route in Los Angeles County. The moderate-to-strenuous level South Bay Bike Trail (44 miles round trip) travels the beach front from Torrance Beach to Will Rogers State Beach. This trail is a segment of the Pacific Coast Bicentennial Bike Route.

Trip #1A starts at Torrance State Beach, explores King Harbor, Hermosa and Manhattan Beaches, and ends at the Manhattan Beach Pier. Trip #1B leaves that pier and continues north through Manhattan and Dockweiler Beaches, Playa Del Rey and the Del Rey Lagoon, terminating at Marina Del Rey. Trip #1C cruises the periphery of Marina Del Rey, visits Venice Beach and the Venice Pavilion, passes the Santa Monica Pier, and ends at Will Rogers State Beach.

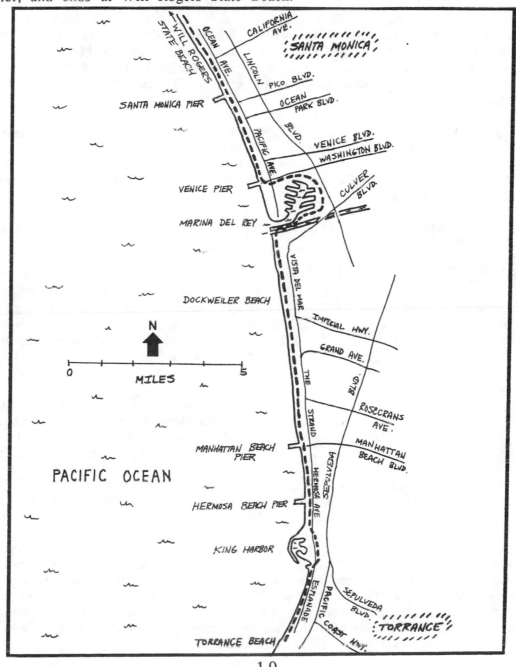

TRIP #1A - SOUTH BAY BIKE TRAIL:
REDONDO BEACH TO MANHATTAN BEACH

GENERAL LOCATION: Redondo Beach - Manhattan Beach

LEVEL OF DIFFICULTY: Up and back - easy
Distance - 5.4 miles (one-way)
Elevation gain - essentially flat

GENERAL DESCRIPTION: The southern segment of the Class I South Bay Bike Trail cruises Torrance, Redondo and Hermosa Beaches. This segment includes the Redondo Beach Pier and the King Harbor area, where there is plenty of sightseeing, as well as shopping spots and eateries. The path also visits Hermosa Beach Pier and passes near several small parks. The views south to the Palos Verdes Cliffs and north along the L.A. County beaches are spectacular. Water is plentiful and there are several bike parking racks placed strategically along the route.

TRAILHEAD: From Pacific Coast Highway in Torrance/South Redondo Beach, turn south toward the ocean at Palos Verdes Blvd. Continue about 1/2-mile and turn right at Calle Miramar. In a few hundred feet, veer left on Via Riviera and continue 0.1 mile to the terminus at Paseo De La Playa. Find free parking on this street, subject to local parking regulations.

Bring a light water supply. This path segment is well blessed with water and restrooms.

TRIP DESCRIPTION: **Redondo Beach.** Near Via Riviera and Paseo De La Playa, follow the asphalt path down the small bluff to the South Bay Bike Trail origin on the beach. There is a grand view of the Palos Verdes Cliffs to the south and Santa Monica and intervening beaches to the north. Bike north past the walkers, skaters, bathers, model airplane flyers, metal detector searchers, and other bikers along one of several lovely beaches on this trip segment. In about a mile, the trail passes a half-mile stretch of condominiums built up along the beach path.

At the end of condomania is a small grassy rest area which is a part of Veteran's Park (1.8). Just beyond is Monstad Pier and the backside of El Torrito Restaurant. There is a walking entry (i.e., no biking) into this area which leads left to the pier and straight ahead into a parking structure. Our route heads into the parking structure where bikers can remount and ride through, exiting the garage at Fisherman's Wharf. This scenic structure was partially distroyed by the high seas of the Winter of 1987 and a disastrous fire in the Spring of the following year. There is shopping, sightseeing, and munching nearby for the easily side-tracked.

The path continues alongside Redondo Beach Village, Basin No. 3 with its fishing boat moorings, and then the Redondo Beach Marina (2.1). In 0.2 mile at Beryl St., the route crosses Harbor Dr. and continues north on a Class II path. There is a diversion trip west on Beryl St. which becomes Portifino Way and leads to inner King Harbor and a swimming lagoon. However, we continue north past a series of beachfront restaurants/watering holes which includes the Cheesecake Factory. Continue past Marina Way and the steam powerplant to Herondo St. (2.9).

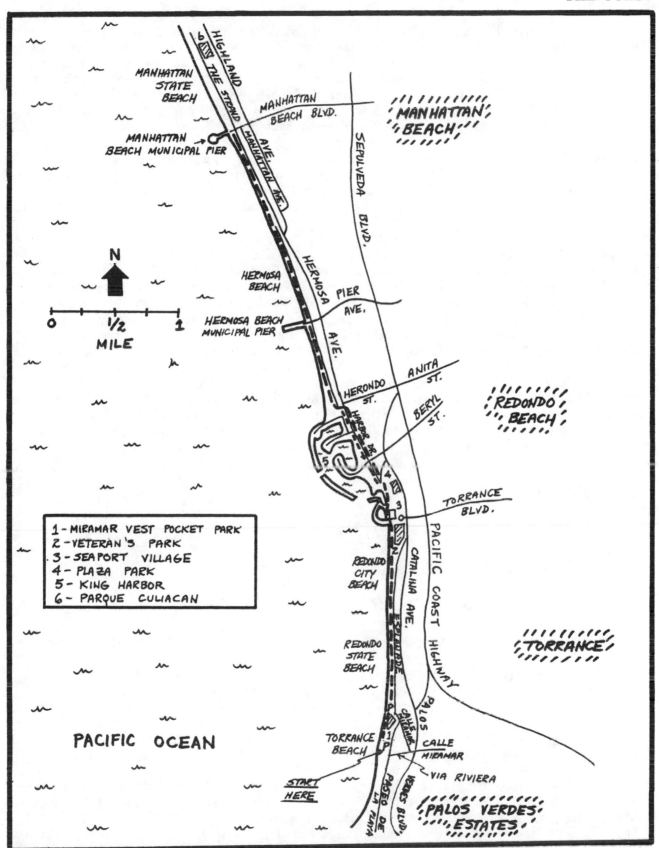

THE COAST

MANHATTAN STATE BEACH

MANHATTAN BEACH MUNICIPAL PIER

HIGHLAND

THE STRAND

MANHATTAN AVE.

MANHATTAN BEACH BLVD.

MANHATTAN BEACH

SEPULVEDA BLVD.

N

0   1/2   1
MILE

HERMOSA BEACH

HERMOSA AVE.

PIER AVE.

HERMOSA BEACH MUNICIPAL PIER

HERONDO ST.

ANITA ST.

BERYL ST.

REDONDO BEACH

HARBOR DR.

5

4

3

TORRANCE BLVD.

1 - MIRAMAR VEST POCKET PARK
2 - VETERAN'S PARK
3 - SEAPORT VILLAGE
4 - PLAZA PARK
5 - KING HARBOR
6 - PARQUE CULIACAN

REDONDO CITY BEACH

2

CATALINA AVE.

PACIFIC COAST HIGHWAY

TORRANCE

REDONDO STATE BEACH

ESPLANADE

PACIFIC OCEAN

TORRANCE BEACH

CALLE MAYOR

CALLE MIRAMAR

VIA RIVIERA

PALOS VERDES BLVD.

PASEO DE LA PLAYA

START HERE

PALOS VERDES ESTATES

TRIP #1A-SOUTH BAY BIKE TRAIL: REDONDO BEACH TO MANHATTAN BEACH

Hermosa Beach. Cross Herondo St. and follow the bikepath to the Hermosa Beach Strand. This is a designated shared pedestrian/biker path which passes local residences built next to the path--this stretch can be busy! The bikeway passes more great beach, volleyball courts, and one-after-another residences until it reaches the Hermosa Beach Municipal Pier and the Tim Kelly Memorial (3.7). Just beyond are a series of rental shops (surfboards, bikes) and several beachfront eateries. A favorite stop is La Playita, which dishes up some mean Mexican and Gringo dishes.

The path returns to a residential beachfront and continues another 0.9 mile before jogging away from the beach. The bike trail temporarily ends at 35th St. at a small series of steps where bikes must be carried a short distance. An option is to return about three short blocks to Longfellow Ave., turn left, left again at The Strand, and follow the marked bike route.

Manhattan Beach. The route continues on Class I bikeway along Manhattan State Beach passing more fine beach and volleyball country. Though still crowded together, the beachfront homes in this area are more stately and architecturally varied. There is a fine view back to the Palos Verdes Peninsula from this area. Continue 0.6 mile from 35th Street to reach the Manhattan Beach Municipal Pier (5.4). There is some interesting sightseeing at the pier and some local rest stops just up the hill on Manhattan Beach Blvd. Take a break before starting the return trip.

CONNECTING TRIPS; 1) Continuation with the South Bay Bike Trail to Marina Del Rey (Trip #1B) - continue north from the Manhattan Beach Pier; 2) connection with the bike routes along Palos Verdes Drive North (Trip #6A), and Palos Verdes Drive West (Trip #6B) - from the trip origin, return to Palos Verdes Blvd. and turn right (south) continuing another 0.8 mile to the three-way junction in Malaga Cove.

TRIP #1B - SOUTH BAY BIKE TRAIL:

MANHATTAN BEACH TO MARINA DEL REY

GENERAL LOCATION: Manhattan Beach , El Segundo, Playa Del Rey, Marina Del Rey

LEVEL OF DIFFICULTY: Up and back - easy
Distance - 7.3 miles (one-way)
Elevation gain - essentially flat

GENERAL DESCRIPTION: The middle segment of the Class I South Bay Bike Trail, this route tours Manhattan and Dockweiler Beaches. The segment starts from the Manhattan Municipal Pier, includes a pass below the L.A. Airport runway, and visits the Del Rey Lagoon of Playa Del Rey, Ballona Creek, and Fisherman's Village in Marina Del Rey. There are excellent views into Santa Monica Bay, the Santa Monica Mountains, and a fine boat watching vista along the Marina Del Rey entrance channel. Water is available at strategic spots along the way.

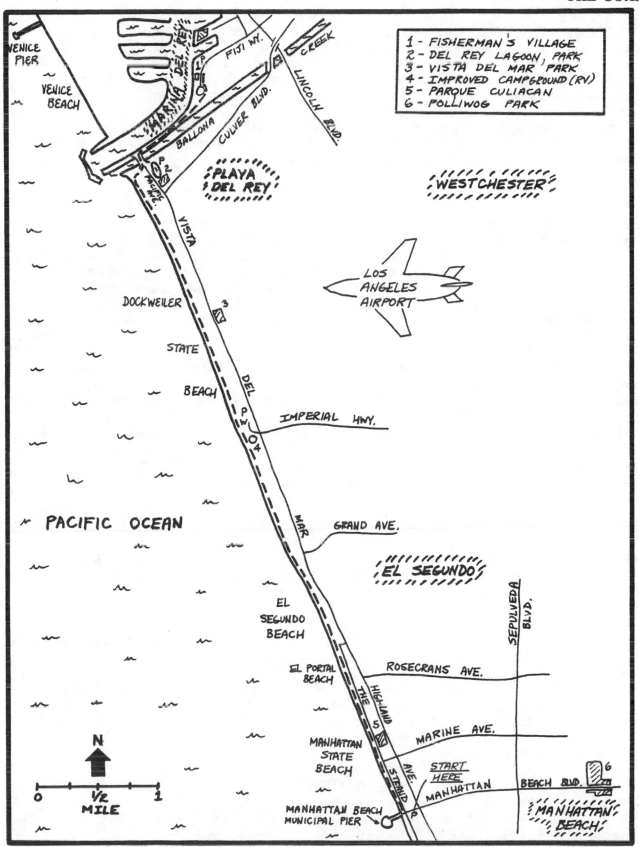

1 - FISHERMAN'S VILLAGE
2 - DEL REY LAGOON, PARK
3 - VISTA DEL MAR PARK
4 - IMPROVED CAMPGROUND (RV)
5 - PARQUE CULIACAN
6 - POLLIWOG PARK

TRIP#1B-SOUTH BAY BIKE TRAIL:MANHATTAN BEACH TO MARINA DEL REY

23

TRAILHEAD: From Sepulveda Blvd. in Manhattan Beach, turn west at Manhattan Beach Blvd. and continue about one mile. Find parking, subject to local parking laws, on Highland Ave., Manhattan Ave. or The Strand, most likely south of Manhattan Beach Blvd. From the San Diego Fwy., exit west on Manhattan Beach Blvd, and proceed about 2-1/2 miles to the parking area discussed above.

Another option is to park at pleasant Polliwog Park near Peck Ave. and Manhattan Beach Blvd., then bike about 1-3/4 pleasant extra miles through Manhattan Beach to the pier. This is a fine picnic base of operations.

Bring a light water supply. This is a well-stocked water route.

TRIP DESCRIPTION: **Manhattan Beach.** From the Manhattan Beach Pier at the foot of Manhattan Beach Blvd., follow the curved, marked bikepath to the right as it separates from the pedestrian walkway. There is a fine view across Santa Monica Bay in this area. Continue north past the tournament volleyball courts, playgrounds, and the expensive residences above the pedestrian walkway. A half mile from the pier, there is a great view of the city of Santa Monica. The houses come in all shapes, styles, and sizes up to the point where the path reaches the foot of Rosecrans Ave. at "Volleyball City" (1.2).

El Segundo. The path cruises El Porto Beach, then swings west and passes alongside the fenced-off power generating station (1.6). There is a narrow, exposed bike strip for the next 0.3 mile. There are large rocks on the seaward side and the signs warn of sand on the path, testifying that this strip can be very exciting and possibly dangerous in rough weather. Next is a small breakwater and probably the most secluded section of beach along the bikepath (2.0). In 0.2 mile, the route passes the Grand Ave. automobile entry to the beach and 0.4 mile further passes the northern end of the fenced-in plant (2.6).

The beach widens and the bikepath twists and winds past some bluffs which are one of the favorite local hang-glider training spots (3.0). Next is the Imperial Blvd. beach entry and a water stop in the middle of the only dry stretch of the trip. In another 0.4 mile is a small rise with a nice view down the beach to Santa Monica (3.6). For the next 0.3 mile, the path winds under the busy L.A. Airport flight path. Stop and watch the air traffic from an unusual vantage point.

Playa Del Rey. The route passes an automobile access road (4.0) and a large playground area with several sculptures (4.5). With the small bluffs to the landward side, the path reaches a pleasant palm-treed rest and watering area near the viewable residential edge of Playa Del Rey (5.2). In another 0.4 mile, the bike route passes residences built near the bikepath. The bikeway transitions from beach to strand and passes near Del Rey Lagoon Park and the Del Rey Lagoon. The trail then swings north along Ballona Creek (6.2) and continues to a small bridge across the creek in 0.1 mile. There are fine views of the creek and of the exit channel and marina for the next half mile.

Marina Del Rey. Once across the bridge, the bikepath follows a levee between Ballona Creek and the exit channel. Because of the winds, this is a "bear" of a bike segment when heading west in the late afternoon! There is a unique view of the Westwood and Century City skyscrapers from the levee (northeast direction), as well as a look into the Ballona Wetlands to the south.

The trail passes the U.C.L.A. boathouse (6.9) and reaches a junction point with the Ballona Creek Bikeway just beyond the end of a single apartment complex (7.0). Turn left at the junction, passing through a fence and biking 0.1 mile to the Fiji Way cul-de-sac. In 0.2 mile north on Fiji Way is Fisherman's Village (7.3). This is a fine place to stop and take a munchie break or to do some sightseeing before returning.

CONNECTING TRIPS: 1) Continuation with the South Bay Bike Trail to Redondo Beach (Trip #1A) - at the trip origin, head south; 2) continuation with the South Bay Bike Trail to Santa Monica (Trip #1C) - at the trip terminus, continue north; 3) connection with the Ballona Creek Bikeway (Trip #4) - at the junction discussed above at (7.0), take the right hand junction along Ballona Creek.

TRIP #1C - SOUTH BAY BIKE TRAIL:
MARINA DEL REY TO SANTA MONICA

GENERAL LOCATION: Marina Del Rey, Venice, Santa Monica, Pacific Palisades

LEVEL OF DIFFICULTY: Up and back - easy
Distance - 9.3 miles (one way)
Elevation gain - essentially flat

GENERAL DESCRIPTION: The northern segment of the Class I South Bay Bike Trail starts from scenic Marina Del Rey and visits exceptional Venice Municipal-, Santa Monica State-, and Will Rogers State-Beaches. This segment includes Venice Pier, Venice Pavilion, the Venice Beach Carnival, and Santa Monica Pier. The tour through Marina Del Rey includes scenic views of the marina and pleasure boats of all types, a passage along Admiralty Park, and a bird's eye view of the Duck Pond (yuk-yuk!). The passage through Venice Pavilion includes a visit to individualism at it's finest, or the other side of Mars, depending on your outlook. Be prepared for unusual flea markets, a guitar playing swami on skates, mimes, sidewalk preachers, and other surprises.

TRAILHEAD: Follow the Marina Fwy. to its terminus and continue west to Lincoln Blvd. Turn left (south) on Lincoln Blvd. and continue about 1/2 mile to Fiji Way. Take Fiji Way to the parking area at Fisherman's Village or use the overflow parking lot between the village and Lincoln Blvd.

Bring a light water supply. There are plentiful sources along the route.

TRIP DESCRIPTION: **Marina Del Rey**. Pedal north past Shanghai Red's in Fisherman's Village and pass a yacht dealership. In 0.5 mile just before reaching Admiralty Way, follow the signed path left into the boat storage and repair area. The route parallels Admiralty Way and passes Mindinao Way (0.8); to the left, a short spur path leads to Burton Chase Park, where there is an elevated platform for harbor viewing. Our route crosses Bali Way (1.0) and passes behind the Marina Library, then turns sharply right and follows the library parking lot to Admiralty Way.

25

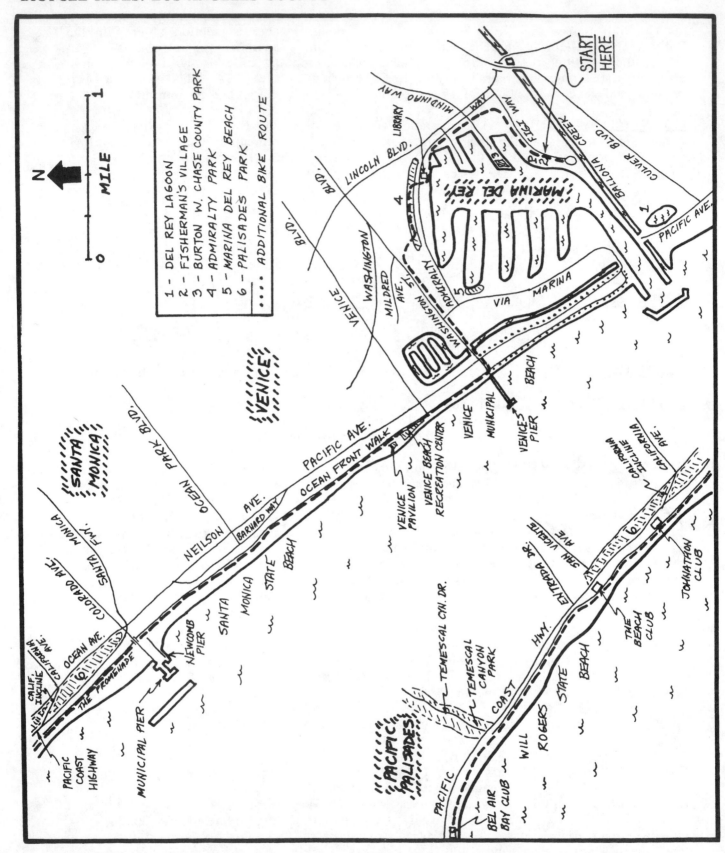

TRIP #1C - SOUTH BAY BIKE TRAIL: MARINA DEL REY TO SANTA MONICA

Cross the street and follow the bike route along Admiralty Park. There is an interesting Class X spur trip along Admiralty Way and south on Via Marina, however, our route continues along the park past the Marina Towers and Duck Pond (1.7). This pond is one of the last remnants of the Ballona Wetlands in this area and does have a fair number of friendly inhabitants. The route crosses Washington St. and follows that street toward the ocean on a Class II bikepath. The path crosses a small Venice Canal (2.6) and in another 0.1 mile passes 26 Beach Cafe, a fine outdoor bistro.

Venice Beach

Venice. At the foot of Washington St is the Venice Pier (2.7). Just before entering onto the pier, follow the signs right (north) to the Class I bikeway along the beach. There are residences along the beach and a small strip of grass for resting nearby. In 0.5 mile the path weaves past the Venice Beach Recreation Center, which has paddleboard and other courts, as well as gymnastics and weight lifting areas.

The twisting bikeway later passes the Venice Pavilion, where there are several structures with some very interesting murals and even more interesting people (3.5). In addition to the sidewalk entertainers and preachers, this is also the home of the Kamikaze skater! In another 0.1 mile is a palm-tree lined area and several outdoor cafes at the sand's edge, then a quarter mile of flea markets and mobile salesrooms in the form of hawkers on foot. In a short distance, the path crosses a more traditional set of store fronts (4.1-4.3), then cruises by a series of enclosed picnic shelters.

Santa Monica. The path bends toward the ocean and cruises a large parking area in what is now Santa Monica Beach (4.7). There is a great view of Santa Monica Bay and the Santa Monica Mountains from this area. The route passes a large volleyball area and continues to a series of beachfront commercial stores (5.4).

27

Next there is a biker/pedestrian trail split with the bikeway nearer the beach. The route passes a gymnastics and general workout area (5.6), then reaches and passes beneath the Santa Monica Pier (5.8). The pier itself can be reached by turning off the bikepath just north of the pier on a small boardwalk. However, our route continues north past another fine beach area with the palisades of the city of Santa Monica in the background. The path crosses under a walkway which passes over Pacific Coast Highway (PCH) (6.1) and cruises by a group of isolated homes/rentals. In another half mile of beach cruising, the bikepath passes a restroom just south of the California Incline on PCH (6.6) and continues on a section of path opened in Spring 1989. Bike past the Johnathan Club below the palisades until reaching the Beach Club and the Will Rogers State Beach boundary (7.5).

Pacific Palisades. Pedal past the Entrada Dr. entry, cross on a bridge over a small wash, and cruise past the area lifeguard headquarters. Continue alongside a narrower beach before reaching Temescal Canyon Rd. and the end of the separated bikeway(8.9). In another 0.4 mile on this narrow, shared path, this grand tour comes to an abrupt halt at the Bel Air Bay Club.

CONNECTING TRIPS: Continuation with the South Bay Bike Trail to Manhattan Beach (Trip #1B) - bike south from the trip origin; 2) connection with the Santa Monica Loop (Trip #2) - from the Johnathan Club area, follow an asphalt path to Pacific Coast Highway. Pedal up fast-moving, busy California Incline to Ocean Blvd.

TRIP #2 - SANTA MONICA LOOP

GENERAL LOCATION: Santa Monica

LEVEL OF DIFFICULTY: Loop - moderate (double loop)
Distance - 6.4 miles (single loop)
- 11.9 miles (double loop)
Elevation gain - single short, steep grade (double loop)

GENERAL DESCRIPTION: This is a very pleasant and scenic trip which takes in the pretty residential neighborhood along San Vincente Blvd., Palisades Park on the bluffs above Santa Monica State Beach, Santa Monica Pier, and the beach itself. This is one of the premier trips within the "big city." The trip can be divided into two loops, the 6.4 mile up and back along San Vicente Blvd. and the 5.5 mile Palisades Park-Santa Monica State Beach loop. Take one or both loops and take advantage of the well laid out Class I and Class II bike trails that exist for almost the entire trip.

TRAILHEAD: There is free public parking on San Vicente Blvd. or any paralleling street above Ocean Ave. Observe the signs before parking to ensure concurrence with the law. Another option is to "feed the meter" at Palisades Park where there is a five-hour limit. Take the Santa Monica Fwy. exit at Fourth St., drive north about 1-1/4 miles to San Vicente Blvd. and turn left (toward the beach).

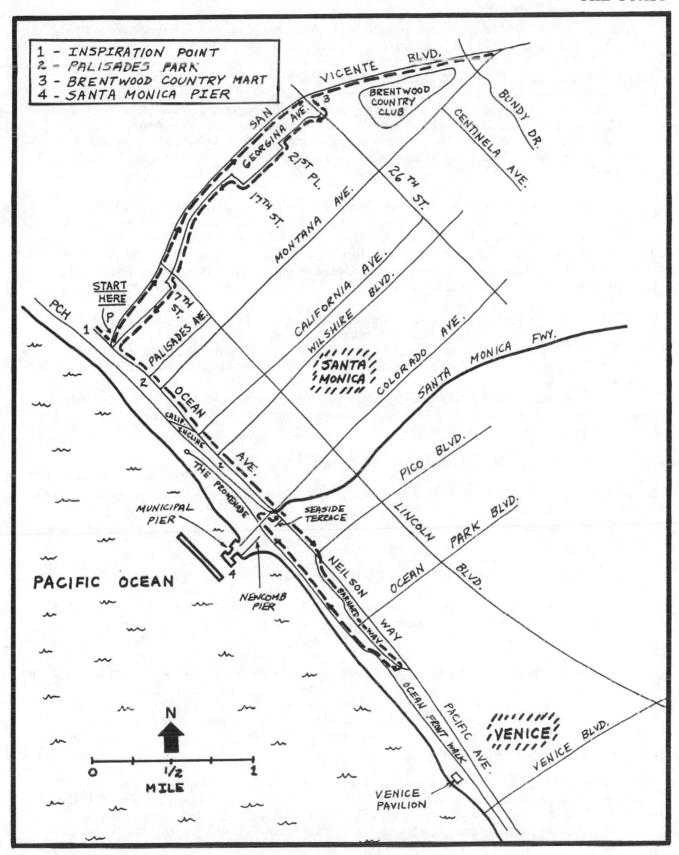

1 - INSPIRATION POINT
2 - PALISADES PARK
3 - BRENTWOOD COUNTRY MART
4 - SANTA MONICA PIER

TRIP #2 - SANTA MONICA LOOP

Continue about a 1/4 mile and park on San Vicente Blvd. just above Ocean Blvd. There are public facilities at Palisades Park and on Santa Monica Pier.

TRIP DESCRIPTION: **San Vicente Blvd. Loop.** Start northeast along the tree-lined, divided San Vicente Blvd. The entire route is a well marked Class II bikeway. The broad, grassy center strip is normally filled with joggers. Continue through this beautiful, elegant, and well-kept residential area and pass the Brentwood Country Mart (a great place to stop for exotic snacks or interesting meals) (2,0). A short distance later, the route travels alongside the exclusive Brentwood Country Club (2.7) and continues past Bundy Dr. to its terminus at Montana Ave. (3.2).

Turn around and return to 26th St. (4.4). The biker can return via San Vicente Blvd. from this junction or take one of many lovely residential alternate, paralleling routes to the left (southeast). The entire area is lightly travelled with good roadway. The recommended alternate is to take Georgina Ave. (one block from San Vicente on 26th) and follow its zig-zag route back to Ocean Blvd. (6.4). The upper portion of Georgina Ave. is excellent Class X which turns into Class III near 17th St.

Palisades Park-Beach Loop: Ocean Avenue. Turn right (northwest) on Ocean Ave., proceed up one block and take in the view from Inspiration Point. Turn around and head southeast on Ocean Ave. along lovely palm-treed Palisades Park. There are many scenic views along the 1-1/2 mile park stretch, particularly impressive because the park is high on the bluffs overlooking Santa Monica Bay. Bikers should walk their bikes into the park at some point and look "over the edge" from the restraining wall. One of the most beautiful sections of the park is 0.3 miles from the start at Palisades Ave.(6.8).

At 0.9 mile from Inspiration Point (7.4), the route passes the California Ave./California Incline turn-off to the beach. Our route follows Ocean Ave. past Santa Monica Blvd. (7.7) and Colorado Blvd. and the auto entrance to Newcomb Pier (8.0). The Palisades Park ends here. The route continues under the Santa Monica Fwy. to Pico Blvd. (8.4). At Pico Blvd., the trail turns to the right and diagonally onto Barnard Way.

Palisades Park-Beach Loop: The Promenade. Barnard Way descends to the beach and parallels the South Bay Bike Trail (Trip #1C). Just at the curve where Barnard Way turns towards Neilson Way and ends (9.2), turn toward the beach and link with the South Bay Bike Trail. Continue northward along the strand and pass under the Santa Monica Pier.

To visit the pier, turn right on the road which skirts the parking lot, then walk up the concrete steps which lead to the pier. After visiting the pier, return via the steps. Turn right (south) along Appian Way and continue two blocks to Seaside Terrace (10.4). A short, testy climb up Seaside Terrace returns the biker to Ocean Ave. Continue across Ocean Ave. to the northbound Class II bike route and return to the parking area at San Vicente Ave. (11.9).

Another option when leaving the pier is to continue north on the South Bay Bike Trail to the Johnathan Club, follow the asphalt path to Pacific Coast Highway (PCH), cross PCH, and bike up California Ave./California Incline to Ocean Blvd. There are exposed stretches along both PCH and California Incline which make this a much less preferred route.

CONNECTING TRIPS: 1) Connection with the South Bay Bike Trail (Trip #1C) as described in the trip text above; 2) connection with the Westwood Tour (Trip #3) - from the San Vicente Blvd./Montana Ave. intersection, follow Montana Ave. 1/2 mile southwest to Centinela Ave. Turn right (southeast) and continue about 1/2 mile to the trailhead at Texas Ave.

TRIP #3 - WESTWOOD TOUR

GENERAL LOCATION: Westwood

LEVEL OF DIFFICULTY: Loop Option 1 or 2 - moderate
Distance - 6.7 miles (Option 1); 7.5 miles (Option 2)
Elevation gain - periodic moderate grades

GENERAL DESCRIPTION: This trip through Westwood and surrounding areas visits some pleasant residential territory and skirts the edge of Westwood Village and the U.C.L.A. campus.   The best part of the tour might be a free-wheeling ride through the U.C.L.A. campus and surrounding residential areas, which is left as an exercise for the student.   Although this is a trip through exceptionally scenic surroundings, there are many roadway intersections, much traffic, and an abundance of borderline Class III bike routes.   A portion of the route is on a busy Class X roadway.

TRAILHEAD: The trip starts in the Sawtelle area of the City of Los Angeles at the beginning of the bike trail at Centinela Ave. and Texas Ave.   There are Class III bikepaths throughout the area.   This starting point was selected because it leads directly into the Westwood area.

Exit the San Diego Fwy. at Santa Monica Blvd., turn west and proceed about 1-1/4 miles to Centinela Ave.   Turn right (north) and travel 1/4 mile to Texas Ave.   Park in the residential area nearby; observe the parking signs, and do not block driveways.

TRIP DESCRIPTION: **Trip Origin to U.C.L.A.**   Head northwest on the Class III bike route past Bundy Ave. (0.3) and turn right (south) at Westgate Ave. at University High School (0.6).   Head downhill and continue another 0.2 mile to Ohio Ave.   Turn left on Ohio Ave. and continue on a moderate upgrade through pleasant residential areas.   At Sawtelle Ave. (1.4) the route turns into a Class II bikepath.   In another 0.1 mile, the route passes under the San Diego Fwy., then continues to Sepulveda Blvd. (1.7).   Stay on the west side of Sepulveda Blvd. and ride alongside the baseball field.   In about 100-200 yards, cross the street and follow the signed Class I bikeway along the Department of Water and Power Building.   Follow the path on the west side of Veteran Ave. (2.0) and continue north to Wilshire Blvd. (2.4).

Cross to the northeast corner of the intersection and continue on the U.C.L.A. bike route through the parking area.   The path parallels Gayley Ave. and fuses with a small road behind the buildings along Gayley Ave.   This is the exotic "backside" of Westwood Village!

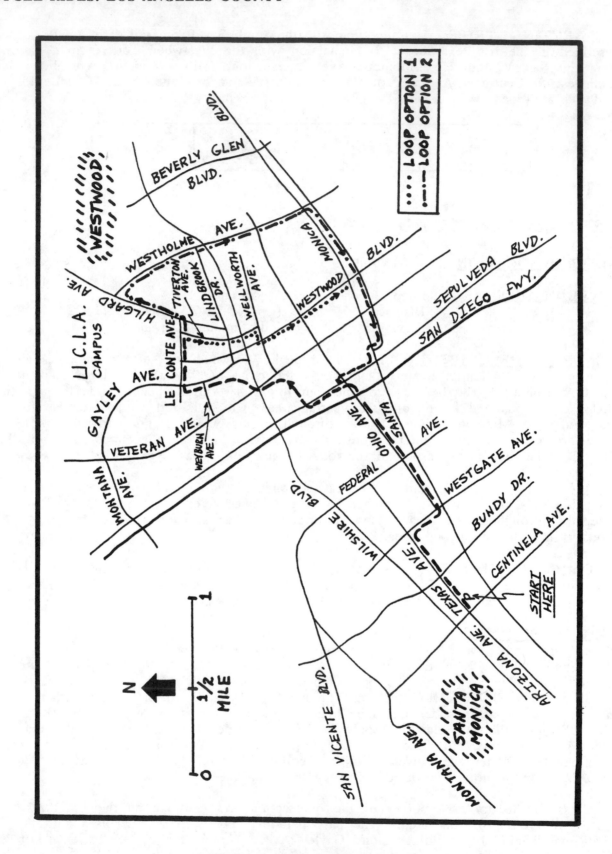

TRIP #3 -WESTWOOD TOUR

Turn right at Weyburn Ave. and in 100-200 feet, turn left onto Gayley Ave. (2.6).
Continue on a mild grade to Le Conte Ave. (2.8). One option is to continue up Gayley
Ave. and explore Fraternity Row and the pleasant (but hilly) residential areas.
However for this reference tour, turn right on Le Conte Ave. and continue 0.1 mile
on a Class X roadway to Westwood Blvd. A left turn here (north) would take the biker
into the U.C.L.A. campus and many riding areas. However, this trip continues on to
Tiverton Ave. (3.1) and a choice of two continuation options.

The Bruin Bear, UCLA Campus

Loop Option 1 - Westwood Blvd. If your desire is to see a part of the city of
Westwood, this is your tour. Continue downhill on the Class III bike route on Tiverton
Ave. past an automobile roadblock and follow the zig-zag crossing across Lindbrook
Ave. (3.3). The street is now named Glendon Ave. Cross Wilshire Blvd. onto a short
Class II stretch and continue another 0.1 mile to Wellworth Ave. Turn right (west)
and continue a short distance to make a left turn onto Westwood Blvd. (3.5). Take this
Class III route across Santa Monica Blvd. to "little" Santa Monica Blvd. just beyond the
intersection (this less travelled Class X roadway parallels the main boulevard). Turn
right (west) on "little" Santa Monica Blvd. and continue another 0.5 mile to Sepulveda
Blvd. (4.7). Turn right (north) on Sepulveda Blvd. and continue 0.2 mile to Ohio Ave.
From this intersection, retrace the original route back to Texas Ave. and Centinela
Ave (6.7).

Loop Option 2 - Westholme Ave. This option provides a Class X route along
Sorority Row and a pleasant Class III ride through some lovely outlying residential
areas. Continue on Le Conte past Tiverton Ave. and turn left in another 0.1 mile at
Hilgard Ave. (3.2). This route heads up a testy grade along Sorority Row, then flattens
out and meets Westholme Ave. (3.6).

33

Turn right (south) and continue downhill along a pleasant tree-lined residential street which continues across Wilshire Blvd. (4.3) and meets Santa Monica Blvd. in another 0.5 mile. Cross Santa Monica Blvd. and turn right just after the intersection onto "little" Santa Monica Blvd. Continue another 0.5 mile on the Class X route to Westwood Blvd. and continue on the route as described for "Loop Option 1" above. The total trip length is 7.5 miles.

CONNECTING TRIPS: Connection with the Santa Monica Loop (Trip #2) - continue 1/2 mile northwest on Centinela Ave. and turn right (northeast) on Montana Ave. Follow Montana Ave. 1/2 mile to its intersection with San Vicente Ave.

TRIP #4 - BALLONA CREEK BIKEWAY

GENERAL LOCATION: Marina Del Rey

LEVEL OF DIFFICULT: One Way - easy; round trip - moderate
Distance - 6.6 miles (one way)
Elevation gain - essentially flat

GENERAL DESCRIPTION: This is one of many 100 percent Class I river and creek trails. The route starts from Marina Del Rey along a segment of the South Bay Bike Trail (Trip #1B) and continues northeast along Ballona Creek to its termination at National Blvd. and nearby McManus Park. The route is lightly used, generally by folks who are adding extra miles to the South Bay Bike Trail and who enjoy the rapid-fire ups and downs at the street underpasses (or who are lost!). There is little scenery along the route and there are long stretches of wall-to-wall cement landscape. Perhaps the highlights of the route may be the side trips to three very pleasant parks, including Culver City Park with its excellent scenic vista.

TRAILHEAD: Follow the Marina Fwy. to its terminus and continue west to Lincoln Blvd. Turn left (south) on Lincoln Blvd. and continue about 1/2 mile to Fiji Way. Take Fiji Way to the parking area at Fisherman's Village or use the overflow parking lot between the village and Lincoln Blvd. McManus Park is difficult to reach by car. To start this trip from McManus Park, turn southeast from Washington Blvd. onto McManus Ave. and continue to the parking lot near that street's end.

Bring a filled water bottle. There are no sources on the route; however, water is available with a short diversion to Lindberg Park or at the McManus Park terminus.

TRIP DESCRIPTION: **Ballona Creek and Trip Diversions.** Head south to the turnaround loop at the end of Fiji Way (0.3). Cross the street and travel alongside the condominiums, passing through a gate at Ballona Creek (0.4). Take a hard left and head north along the cemented Ballona Creek Channel. The route passes under Culver Blvd. (1.2), Lincoln Blvd. (1.3), and at (1.7) passes a small channel split. There are more ups and downs at the Marina Expressway (1.8), Centinella Ave. (2.5), and Inglewood Blvd. (2.8).

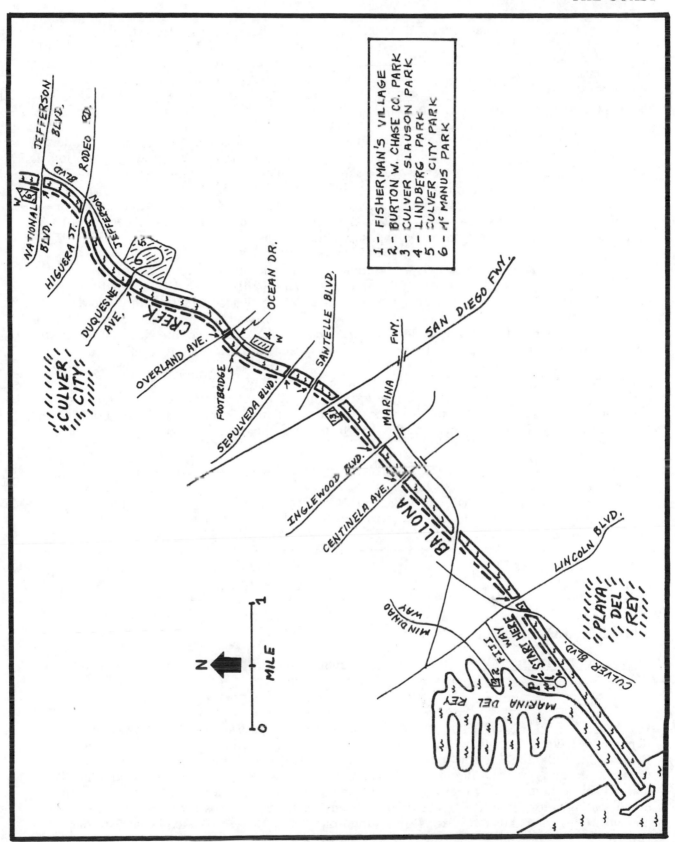

1 – FISHERMAN'S VILLAGE
2 – BURTON W. CHASE CO. PARK
3 – CULVER SLAUSON PARK
4 – LINDBERG PARK
5 – CULVER CITY PARK
6 – Mc MANUS PARK

TRIP #4 - BALLONA CREEK BIKEWAY

After passing another small channel split, the route passes alongside pleasant little Culver/Slauson Park (3.3). Beyond this point are the roller coaster rides below the San Diego Fwy. (3.4), Sawtelle Blvd. (3.6), Sepulveda Blvd. (3.8), and Overland Ave. (4.4). An option is to cross Ballona Creek using the small footbridge at the Culver City Junior/Senior High School, just before Overland Ave. After crossing the creek, turn right (south) and cruise one block to shady Lindberg Park for water and a rest break.

However, the reference route continues along Ballona Creek and passes under Duquesne Ave. 0.9 mile further up the path. Another highly recommended option is to take Duquesne Ave. east across Jefferson Blvd. and proceed uphill to Culver City Park about 1.0 mile from the creek exit point. At the top of the route, stop and enjoy one of the most spectacular, unobstructed views of the greater Los Angeles Basin available in the South Bay area. Note that this "diversion" has some steep uphill along an unshaded route and adds two miles to the overall trip.

McManus Park. Again, the reference route continues northward to Higuera St. (6.1) and ends at National Blvd. (6.5) where a chain partially blocks the path. Follow the switchback up to the opening in the fence which leads directly into McManus Park. There are water, restroom, and picnic facilities in this pleasant, grassy, shaded park. If the gate to the park is locked, ride west a short distance on National Blvd. to a short stairway entry (a short bike carry is required to enter from this direction).

CONNECTING TRIPS: Connection with the South Bay Bike Trail (Trip #1) - return to the gate at (0.4) in the trip description; continuing on the route back toward Fisherman's Village follows the northern segment of the South Bay Bike Trail (Trip #1C); following Ballona Creek to the beach follows the middle segment (Trip #1B).

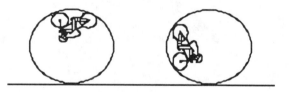

TRIP #5 - OLD SEPULVEDA HILL CLIMB

GENERAL LOCATION: Westwood, Encino

LEVEL OF DIFFICULTY: One way - strenuous; up and back - very strenuous
Distance - 7.4 miles (one way)
Elevation gain - long, steep grades

GENERAL DESCRIPTION: This week-end or non-rush-hour trip follows the old Sepulveda Blvd. route from the L.A. basin to the San Fernando Valley via Sepulveda Pass. The hill climb to the pass is a gut-buster on what varies between a Class II and Class X bikeway, depending on road width. In a few places, there is essentially no marked bike lane. There are excellent views into both valleys, although the uphill is tough enough to force the biker into a head-down, tail-up posture, and some of the downhill will demand the biker's full attention. This trip is basically a workout! Don't take the downhill over the other side of the pass until you have thought it over carefully; the return trip is rugged.

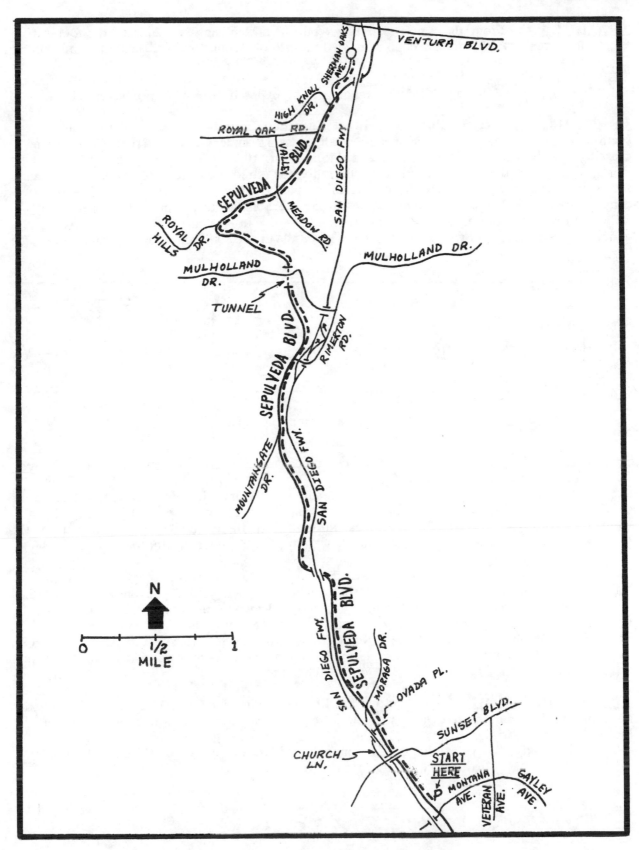

TRIP #5 - OLD SEPULVEDA HILL CLIMB

TRAILHEAD: From the San Diego Fwy., take the Montana Ave. exit in the Bel-Air/ Westwood area. Park along Sepulveda Blvd. north of Montana Ave. just east of the San Diego Fwy.

Bring plenty of water. This is a hot, tiring, exposed trip with no water stops.

TRIP DESCRIPTION: **The Upgrade.** The route starts along a residence-lined section of Sepulveda Blvd. and heads north, passing under Sunset Blvd. (0.4), then crossing Ovada Pl./Church Pl. (0.6), and Moraga Dr. (0.7). There is a beautiful, live floral display in the center section of that divided street, the last of such lush beauty for a long while. The route heads steadily uphill and views into the scrub-lined canyon open up almost immediately. At (1.5) there is a steep uphill for about 1/4 mile, followed by the Chalon Rd. intersection (1.9). In 0.2 mile, the route crosses under the San Diego Fwy. and continues parallel to that thoroughfare on its west side.

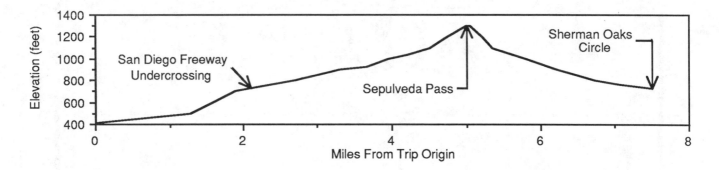

For about the next mile, the route continues up a grade interspersed with limited flats. There are some sections of this part of the route where the bike lane all but disappears. Beyond about (3.2) the path heads steeply uphill; this is a good chance to stop and admire the view back into the L.A. basin (that's what _we_ call "research stops"). The rugged upgrade continues through Mountaingate Dr. (3.5), Rimerton Dr. (4.1) and finally levels off at the tunnel which passes under Mulholland Dr. (4.4).

The Downgrade. At the tunnel exit is a really fine view of the San Fernando Valley. (This exit is also a possible trip turnaround point.) Just beyond this exit, the road begins to twist and wind through a steep downgrade and continues almost all the way into the valley. On the way down, this residentially-surrounded route passes Royal Hills Dr. (5.1), Valley Meadow Rd. (5.8), Royal Oak Rd. (6.3), High Knoll Dr. (6.8), and Sherman Oaks Ave. (6.9). Turn left at Sherman Oaks Ave. and take a break at the traffic circle about 1/2 mile further down the road (7.4).

CONNECTING TRIPS: 1) Connection with the Mulholland Dr. route (Trip #37) - exit at Rimerton Rd. and pass over the freeway to the east side. Continue north to the Mulholland Dr. bridge back across the freeway (west segment) or continue north beyond the bridge (east segment); 2) connection with the Westwood Tour (Trip #3) - at the trip origin, follow Montana Ave. east to Gayley Ave.

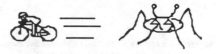

TRIP #6A-#6D - PALOS VERDES PENINSULA LOOP

The very strenuous Palos Verdes Peninsula Loop Trip (23.2 miles, frequent steep grades) is broken up into the individual Palos Verdes (P.V.) Dr. segments. The general area map is provided below. Also shown is a very strenuous Hawthorne Blvd. option as well as a strenuous option that replaces the P.V. Dr. East segment with Western Ave. Most of the routes are Class X with the exception of a major segment of P.V. Dr. North and some portions of P.V. Dr. West:

o Trip #6A explores a beautiful residential stretch through rolling hills which starts near the P.V. Reservoir and ends at pleasant Malaga Cove Plaza.

o Trip #6B follows the western Peninsula shoreline above the bluffs, starting at Malaga Cove Plaza and ending at scenic San Vicente County Park.

o Trip #6C leaves San Vicente County Park, traverses the bluffs above the southern beaches, wiggles its way through the Portuguese Bend landslide area, and terminates near the P.V. Dr. East junction.

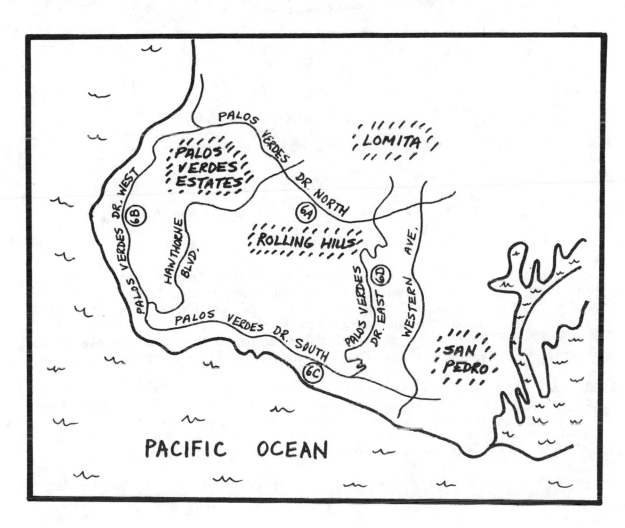

o Trip #6D starts at the junction of P.V. Dr. East, winds its way up a steep set of switchbacks and traverses the scenic peninsula "high country," letting out at the P.V. Reservoir.

The Hawthorne Blvd. segment is almost as difficult as P.V. Dr. East, although less steep. That route is provided for variety; use of this segment also provides the option for a shorter Peninsula trip (11 miles). This route features potential rest stops at Golden Cove Shopping Center, Rancho Palos Verdes Park and Peninsula Center (south to north).

The Western Ave. route provides the option to circumvent the steep, winding P.V. Dr. East trip segment. The total route mileage is increased slightly to 23 miles. The route is through rolling hills on a busy thoroughfare. Potential rest stops are the 25th. Ave. Shopping Center, Peck Park, and the Park Western Plaza (shopping center).

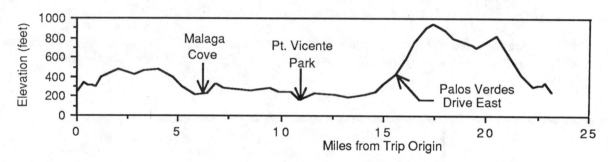

TRIP #6A - PALOS VERDES PENINSULA: PALOS VERDES DRIVE NORTH

GENERAL LOCATION: Rolling Hills Estates, Rolling Hills, Palos Verdes

LEVEL OF DIFFICULTY: One way - moderate; up and back - moderate
Distance - 5.8 miles (one way)
Elevation gain - frequent moderate grades

GENERAL DESCRIPTION: This is a pleasant but hard-working trip through the rolling hills along the tree-lined northern segment of Palos Verdes Dr. The trip starts at Western Ave., passes the Palos Verdes Reservoir, continues on rolling hills through several rural, wooded peninsula communities, and ends on a long downhill run to Malaga Cove Plaza. More than two-thirds of the trip is on a Class I bikeway and the remainder is on a wide Class X roadway with plenty of room for bikers.

TRAILHEAD: Free parking is available along Palos Verdes (P.V.) Dr. North, west of Western Ave. Read the parking signs carefully for current laws. An alternate option is to do the trip in reverse and use the parking in Malaga Cove Plaza or on nearby streets. Another option is to start this trip from Harbor Regional Park (see Trip #13), although this additional segment adds significant elevation to the trip.

Bring a moderate water supply. There is water along the way at the Rolling Hills Road Plaza and the Malaga Cove Plaza.

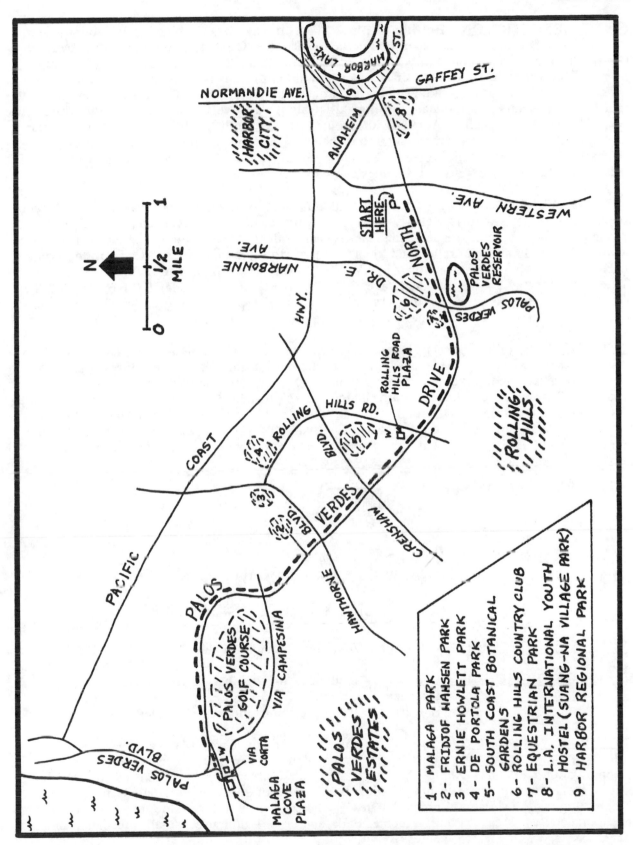

TRIP #6A - PALOS VERDES PENINSULA: PALOS VERDES DRIVE NORTH

TRIP DESCRIPTION: Rolling Hills. The two-way Class I bike trail is on the north side of P.V. Dr. North. Another option is to ride the Class II path along the roadway. The path immediately starts up a moderate grade and then reaches a small shopping plaza at the summit (0.3). After another 0.6 mile of mostly downhill, the route crosses P.V. Dr. East and passes the Dapplegray Equestrian Park. For the next three miles, the path roller-coasters over small rolling hills along a lovely tree-lined path which has a paralleling horse path. At (2.0) the route crosses Rolling Hills Rd., where bikers may use a pleasant rest area which has benches and an available water faucet. In succession, the path then crosses Crenshaw Blvd. (2.8), Hawthorne Blvd. (3.3), and the end of the Class I path at Via Campesina (4.0).

Palos Verdes Estates. The biking in this area is Class X, but has plenty of room for bikers. The street is heavily tree-lined with a lovely center strip which is frequented by walkers, joggers, and horseback riders. The route begins a moderate downgrade of about one mile, and then a sharp downgrade (5.0). At (5.2), the route reaches a three-point intersection of P.V. Dr. North, P.V. Blvd, and P.V. Dr. West. Bikers should stay to the left and take P.V. Dr. West into the Malaga Cove Plaza (5.8). There is a water fountain in the grassy square in the plaza - a great place for a break. The plaza also has a small market and delightful outdoor cafe.

CONNECTING TRIPS: 1) Continuation with the bike route along P.V. Dr. West (Trip #6B) - bike west from the plaza; 2) connection with the Harbor Regional Park bike ride (Trip #13) - continue this trip east on P.V. Dr. North across Western Ave. to Anaheim St. and take the bikepath under the highway; 3) connection with the South Bay Bike Trail (Trip #1) - return to the three-point intersection just above Malaga Cove Plaza and turn left (north) onto P.V. Blvd. Turn left toward the beach on Calle Miramar, veer left on Via Riviera, continue about 0.1 mile to the beach parking lot.

TRIP #6B - PALOS VERDES PENINSULA:
PALOS VERDES DRIVE WEST

GENERAL LOCATION: Palos Verdes Estates, Rancho Palos Verdes

LEVEL OF DIFFICULTY: One way - moderate; up and back - moderate
Distance - 5.1 miles (one way)
Elevation gain - periodic moderate grades

GENERAL DESCRIPTION: This highly scenic route leaves Malaga Cove Plaza and follows a moderately hilly route along Palos Verdes (P.V.) Dr. West, ending at Point Vicente County Park. Along the way, the route passes a spectacular scenic overlook of the local coastline and Santa Monica Bay. Part of the trip is along a pleasant divided highway in Palos Verdes Estates. There is also a nice side trip which explores the Lunada Bay area. Point Vicente Park sports a lighthouse, small museum, and serves as a whale watch center.

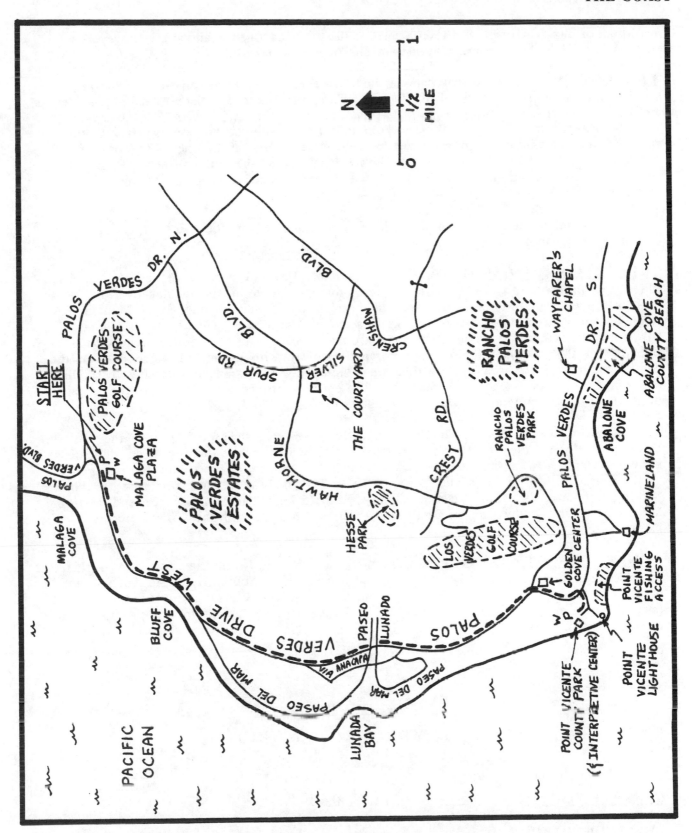

TRIP #6B - PALOS VERDES PENINSULA: PALOS VERDES DRIVE WEST

Most of the trip is on a Class X bike route (i.e., on open roadway). However, after the initial 1/2 mile, the roadway has a lot of room (hopefully) for bikers.

TRAILHEAD: There is free parking in the Malaga Cove Plaza on Sunday or on nearby streets on other days of the week. From the South Bay area, take Palos Verdes Blvd. south and stay to the right after passing the intersection with P.V. Dr. North. This road fuses into P.V. Dr. West. Turn left in a couple of hundred yards into the plaza. Another option is to do the trip in reverse. Park at the periphery of the Golden Cove Shopping Center on Hawthorne Blvd. or at the Point Vicente Park. To reach this area, continue 4.7 miles and 5.1 miles, respectively, from Malaga Cove Plaza on P.V. Dr. West.

Bring a moderate water supply. There are public water fountains at the trip origin and terminus.

TRIP DESCRIPTION: Malaga Cove - Lunada Bay. The route leaves Malaga Cove Plaza and proceeds about 1.0 mile on a steady upgrade to a spectacular overlook of Malaga Cove, Santa Monica Bay, and the beaches up to and beyond Santa Monica. A little further is a turnoff to the right at Paseo Del Mar (1.1). This leads to a nice side trip into the charming residential area around Lunada Bay. The reference trip remains on P.V. Dr. West along a separated roadway with a foot or horse path in the center section of the road. Continue on a relatively flat roadway, passing a small shopping center at Yarmouth Rd.(2.7). There are scattered views out to the ocean until the view completely opens up at about (3.5).

Golden Cove - Point Vicente. Shortly afterward, the route passes the Golden Cove Shopping Center at Hawthorne Blvd. (4.7) which has a homey little delicatessan hidden within. In another 0.4 miles of moderate downhill, the route intersects a small sharp turnoff towards the ocean. Take this roadway a short distance to the parking/rest area at Point Vicente County Park (5.1). There are water and restrooms here. Stop and enjoy an excellent ocean view, museum, and the Point Vicente Lighthouse.

CONNECTING TRIPS: 1) Continuation of the P.V. Dr. North trip (Trip #6A) - ride east from Malaga Cove Plaza; 2) continuation of the P.V. Dr. South trip (Trip #6C) - ride east from the Point Vicente Park; 3) connection with the Hawthorne Blvd. (strenuous) alternate route over the Palos Verdes Hills ridge (Trip #6D) - turn north at Hawthorne Blvd.

TRIP #6C - PALOS VERDES PENINSULA: PALOS VERDES DRIVE SOUTH

GENERAL LOCATION: Rancho Palos Verdes

LEVEL OF DIFFICULTY: One way - moderate; up and back - moderate
Distance - 5.7 miles (one way)
Elevation gain - periodic moderate grades

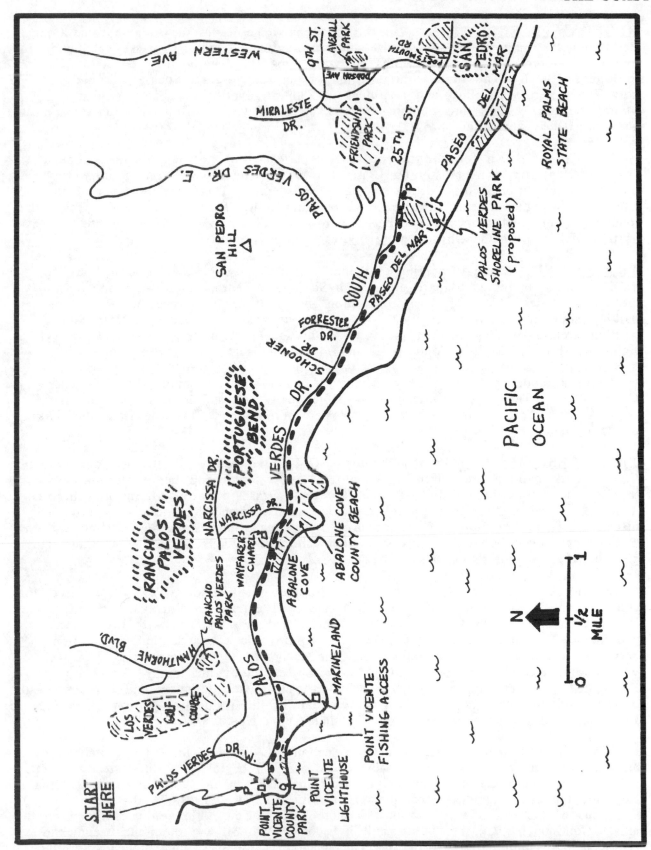

TRIP #6C - PALOS VERDES PENINSULA: PALOS VERDES DRIVE SOUTH

45

BICYCLE RIDES: LOS ANGELES COUNTY

GENERAL DESCRIPTION: This highly scenic route leaves the Point Vicente County Park, travels along rolling hills past the old Marineland turnoff, passes alongside the lovely Wayfarer's Chapel, and winds its way along the bumpy road through Portuguese Bend. The route continues up a long scenic grade, passes the junction with Palos Verdes Dr. East and continues to 25th St. overlooking Palos Verdes Shoreline Park. There are numerous grand views of the coastline, Pacific Ocean, and Catalina Island along the way.

This is not a trip for children or for inexperienced or nervous bikers. Though a very excellent trip, it is mostly on Class X roadway with a very narrow, hilly, and bumpy stretch through the Portuguese Bend slide area. There are portions of the 0.5-1.0 mile Portuguese Bend slide area where automobiles and bikers literally share the roadway. (Note that the road has been improved significantly as of late 1988; the test of time will tell whether this is a _permanent_ improvement.)

TRAILHEAD: There is parking at Point Vicente County Park, as described in Trip #6B. Another option is to park along 25th St. in San Pedro, roughly 0.5 mile east of the Palos Verdes (P.V.) Dr. East intersection and do the trip in reverse. Read the parking signs to ensure compliance with the latest laws. To reach the 25th St. parking area, take Western Ave. south to within about 1/2 mile of the ocean and turn right (west) on 25th St. Continue about 3/4 mile to reach the parking area.

Bring a moderate water supply. There are water and restrooms at San Vicente County Park. The next facilities are available on a "beg and borrow" basis in the small shopping area near 25th St. and Western Ave., about 3/4 mile from the parking on 25th St.

TRIP DESCRIPTION: **Point Vicente - Old Marineland.** From the Point Vicente County Park parking area, turn right onto P.V. Dr. South and begin the journey through the rolling hills. In 0.8 mile, the route passes the old Marineland turnoff. .(Thanks to some very unpopular corporate manipulations, Marineland is now history.) There are views of the ocean and Catalina Island along this stretch and the scenery gets even better later on. Another mile down the road is the stunning glass church, the Wayfarer's Chapel.

Portuguese Bend. (Note that the pre-improvement road description is used for conservatism.) In another 0.5 mile (2.3), the road enters the Portuguese Bend landslide area. The road is chewed up, bumpy, and very narrow, with little or no shoulder. The ride is also very hilly and requires the biker's complete attention between avoiding the largest bumps and the accompanying automobiles. You ask why we included this section of the ride? Stop and enjoy the lovely views into Portuguese Bend and the surrounding hills, as well as of the cliffs and beaches on the opposite side of the road. A short bicycle tour of the residential portion of Portuguese Bend is, in itself, a real experience. The route is on Narcissa Dr.

P.V. Drive South - 25th Street. Once out of the slide area, the route returns to an improved and roomy Class X roadway and at (3.7) begins a gradual, steady ascent. In this area, there are more sweeping vistas that take in the coastline and Catalina. Near the top of the grade is the intersection with P.V. Dr. East (4.7), the most strenuous of the four P.V. Dr. routes. There is a glorious unbroken ocean view in this area. Continue on P.V. Dr. South until it becomes 25th St. and the route becomes Class II (5.2). A continuation on the bikepath leads past (above) undeveloped Shoreline Park (5.7) and through pleasant residential areas to 25th St. and Western Ave. (6.4).

46

CONTINUING TRIPS: 1) Continuation of the P.V. Dr. West Trip (Trip #6B) and P.V. Dr. East Trip (Trip #6D) - from the trip origin or terminus, respectively, continue on the P.V. Drive loop; 2) connection with the San Pedro Beaches Tour (Trip #7) - continue east on 25th St. about one mile past the P.V. Dr. North intersection. Turn right (south) on Anchovy Ave. and free-wheel downhill about 0.5 mile to Pasco Del Mar.

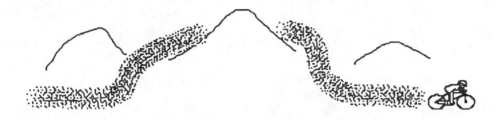

TRIP #6D - PALOS VERDES PENINSULA: PALOS VERDES DRIVE EAST

GENERAL LOCATION: Rancho Palos Verdes, Miraleste, Rolling Hills Estates

LEVEL OF DIFFICULTY: One way - strenuous; up and back - very strenuous
Distance - 6.6 miles (one way)
Elevation gain - periodic steep grades

GENERAL DESCRIPTION: This segment of the Palos Verdes (P.V.) Drive loop is a gut-buster! The uphill ride to the crest of the roadway is steep and the downhill is winding and fast. Yet for those in shape to bike this segment, it offers the finest views of the Los Angeles Harbor and the surrounding basin that can be found. On the early leg of the trip, there are clear Catalina Island views and near the terminus, there are excellent views into the city of Los Angeles and of the surrounding mountains. The route is highly scenic in itself, passing through some of the most beautiful residential areas in the county.

The entire route is Class X. Sections of the roadway are narrow and, when combined with the high-speed downhill stretches, are dangerous. It should be noted that in spite of these conditions, this roadway is well used by experienced bikers.

TRAILHEAD: Park on 25th St. in San Pedro roughly 1/2 mile east of the intersection of P.V. Dr. South and P.V. Dr. East (see description in Trip #6C). Another option is to park along P.V. Dr. North (as described in Trip #6A) and do the trip in reverse.

There are no public facilities along this route. Bring a filled water bottle or two.

TRIP DESCRIPTION: **The Switchbacks.** From the parking area on 25th St., continue west 0.5 mile and make a sharp right turn up P.V. Dr. East. The road starts steeply upward immediately and proceeds through a series of three murderous switchbacks to the crest near Marymount College. In this stretch, the biker pumps through an elevation gain of 600 feet in 1.8 miles! There are great views of Catalina Island, San Pedro South Shores, and old Marineland along this stretch of the roadway (and an excuse for a rest break along one of the turnouts).

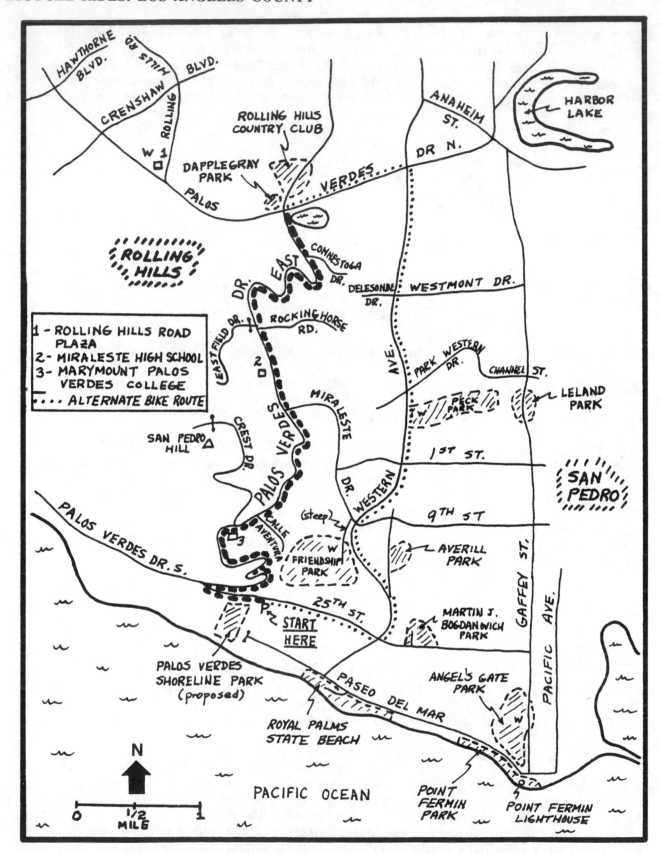

HAWTHORNE BLVD.
CRENSHAW BLVD.
ROLLING HILLS RD
ANAHEIM ST.
HARBOR LAKE
ROLLING HILLS COUNTRY CLUB
DAPPLEGRAY PARK
DR N.
VERDES
PALOS
W 1
ROLLING HILLS
EAST
CONNESTOGA DR.
DELESONDE DR.
WESTMONT DR.
DR.
EAST FIELD DR.
ROCKING HORSE RD.
AVE.
PARK WESTERN DR.
CHANNEL ST.
1 – ROLLING HILLS ROAD PLAZA
2 – MIRALESTE HIGH SCHOOL
3 – MARYMOUNT PALOS VERDES COLLEGE
••• – ALTERNATE BIKE ROUTE
2
PECK PARK
LELAND PARK
SAN PEDRO HILL
CREST DR.
PALOS VERDES
MIRALESTE
1ST ST.
SAN PEDRO
DR.
WESTERN
9TH ST
(steep)
CALLE AVENTURA
3
FRIENDSHIP PARK
AVERILL PARK
PALOS VERDES DR. S.
25TH ST.
GAFFEY ST.
MARTIN J. BOGDANOVICH PARK
PACIFIC AVE.
START HERE
PALOS VERDES SHORELINE PARK (proposed)
PASEO DEL MAR
ANGEL'S GATE PARK
ROYAL PALMS STATE BEACH
N
PACIFIC OCEAN
POINT FERMIN PARK
POINT FERMIN LIGHTHOUSE
0   1/2   1
MILE

TRIP #6D - PALOS VERDES PENINSULA: PALOS VERDES DRIVE EAST

The Second Crest. The route continues through roughly a mile of moderate downhill and then becomes a fast, winding, free-wheeling descent leading to the intersection with Miraleste Dr. (3.9). There are fantastic views of the harbor area in this stretch of the route. Near this intersection, there is a gas station and the small stategically-placed Miraleste Delicatessan. The road winds uphill again through some extremely pleasant, wooded residential areas, and crests at Rockinghorse Rd. (4.9).

Palos Verdes Drive Switchbacks

The Mad Downhill. Now begins a narrow, winding downhill section. Hug the shoulder and watch for automobiles. This dangerous route segment lasts for about 1-1/2 miles. At Connestoga Dr. (6.1), the route diverts over to a Class I bikepath (a little late!) and continues on the downgrade past the Palos Verdes Reservoir to P.V. Dr. North (6.6). Note that just above Connestoga Dr. is a premier view across the L.A. basin into the City of Los Angeles and into both the San Gabriel and San Bernadino Mountains. Cross P.V. Dr. North and turn right (east) or left onto Class I bikeway. Otherwise stand by for a rugged return trip.

CONNECTING TRIPS: 1) Continuation of the P.V. Dr. North Trip (Trip #6A) and the P.V. Dr. South tour (Trip #6C) - from the trip terminus or the trip origin, respectively, continue on the P.V. Drive loop; 2) connection with the Harbor Regional Park Trip (Trip #13) - see directions from Trip #6A; 3) connection with the San Pedro Beaches Tour (Trip #7) - see directions from Trip #6C.

SPEED MERCHANT

TRIP #7 - SAN PEDRO BEACHES TOUR

GENERAL LOCATION: San Pedro

LEVEL OF DIFFICULTY: One way - moderate; round trip - moderate
Distance - 6.2 miles (one way)
Elevation gain - periodic moderate grades;
two short, steep grades

GENERAL DESCRIPTION: This trip starts from the 22nd St. Landing at the terminus of Trip #8.   The biker visits the new Cabrillo Marina, Cabrillo Beach, Point Fermin Park, Angel's Gate Park, and Royal Palms State Beach.   This is one of the most scenic trips in the county, particularly the views of the rugged bluffs and coastline along Paseo Del Mar.   This trip is primarily Class I or Class II, with a small stretch of Class X roadway on the lightly-travelled stretch of Paseo Del Mar west of Western Ave.   There is a slightly different route provided for the return leg of this trip.

TRAILHEAD: Free parking is available along 22nd St. or along the periphery of the Cabrillo Marina parking lot.   To reach 22nd St., travel south on Pacific Ave. and follow the numbered streets (numbers increase in the southbound direction).   Turn left (east) and find a parking spot within the next mile or so along 22nd St.; check parking signs to ensure compliance with current laws.   Another option is to park along the west section of Paseo Del Mar and do the trip in reverse.

There are water and restroom facilities at each of the beaches and parks mentioned, except for Angel's Gate Park, which has only a water fountain.

TRIP DESCRIPTION: **Cabrillo Marina and Cabrillo Beach.**   About 1/4 mile east of Pacific Ave. on 22nd St., turn south onto Via Cabrillo Marina.   Travel about 0.2 mile and turn into a large parking loop with water and private restrooms.   From this area, there is a nice view of the new marina and a view across the bay to the Cabrillo Beach area.   Return to the main road and check out the benches up on the bluff-- there is a steep bikeway/walkway up to that overlook for the adventurous.

Continue down Via Cabrillo Marina a few hundred feet, veer right, and use the walkway around the roadway gate which separates the marina from Cabrillo Beach. The roadway is now named Shoshonean Rd.   Pass around a second gate and enter a boat launch area a few hundred yards further and enter the bikepath along the beach at (0.4) mile.   In the background is the Cabrillo Beach Marina Museum.   In another 0.3 mile, follow the path and roadway out towards the Cabrillo Beach jetty. Along this jetty, there are nice views of Cabrillo Beach to the left and the open ocean and Catalina Island to the right.   In 0.3 mile, there is a large fence with an ever-reopened hole in it.   Through these portals pass the "crazies" who (illegally) fish directly on top of the breakwater.   Don't follow - just look!

The path jogs to the left and enters Cabrillo Pier.   Continue another 0.2 mile to the end of the pier.   (This may mean walking your bike if the pier is heavily crowded with fisherman.)   There is a fine view of the ships in the harbor and the opening in the harbor breakwater known as Angel's Gate.

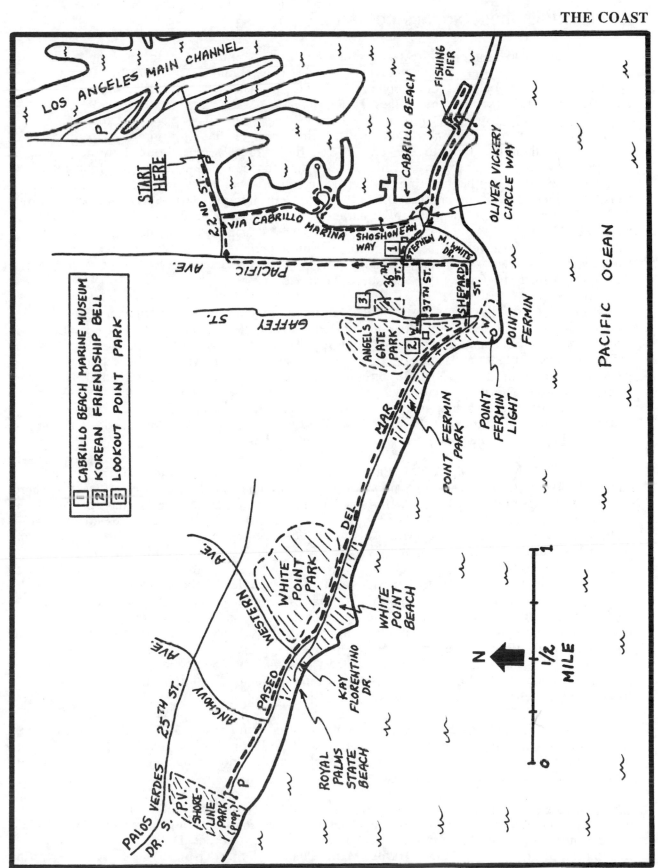

TRIP #7 - SAN PEDRO BEACHES TOUR

There are also water and restrooms on the pier. Return back to the end of the jetty, turn left, and take Oliver Vickery Circle Way through the Cabrillo Beach entrance (1.8). Turn right on Stephen M. White Dr. and in about 0.1 mile of testy upgrade, turn left (south) onto Class II Pacific Ave.

Point Fermin. Continue another 0.1 mile up a challenging upgrade to the top of the hill and then 0.2 mile to the end of Pacific Ave. at scenic Point Fermin parking area and overlook. There is a fine Catalina Island view from here and frequently a nice view of one of the entering or departing ships. Follow Shepard St. west on the Class II bikepath and in another 0.5 mile (2.6) turn left on Gaffey St. to Point Fermin Park. There are park benches and barbecue areas. Ride through this lovely treed park which sits on a bluff overlooking the Pacific Ocean; one of the best routes is along the walled periphery of the park. If time permits, stop over at Walker's Burgers across from the park - this is one of the favorite biker stops (chopper bikers, that is). Return to Gaffey St. and head north across Shepard St.

Angel's Gate Park. Continue on Gaffey St. and head up a very steep hill; chances are that, unless you are in very excellent shape, this will be an opportunity to walk your bike about 0.1 mile to 37th St. Turn left (west) into Angel's Gate Park and enjoy a spectacular unobstructed view of the south-facing coastline. In addition, walk your bike up to the temple on the knoll to look over the Bicentennial Korean Friendship Bell. Exit the park and take in the fine view (down 37th St.) of Angel's Gate. For the hearty souls, one of the best L.A. harbor views is just a little further up Gaffey St. at small Lookout Point Park. Return downhill to the intersection of Gaffey St. and Shepard St. and turn left (3.4) on Shepard St.

Paseo Del Mar and Royal Palms State Park. Continue on Shepard St. on the Class II bikepath; in a short distance, the street becomes Paseo Del Mar (PDM). There are spectacular views of the bluffs and cliffs, the general southern coastline, and out to sea for the next 0.3 mile. At (3.9) there is a grassy rest area with a restroom and water on the ocean side of PDM. This is a nice tree-lined section of road. In another 0.6 mile, there is another impressive view/overlook of the general coastline.

At (5.0) is a turn-off to the seaside of PDM which leads about 0.2 mile very steeply downhill to Royal Palms State Beach. It is work walking your bike both down and back uphill just to see this area close up. There is a small beach area to the right (west) and some excellent tide pools and natural reefs to the left (don't go out into this area near high tide!). Return to Paseo Del Mar and enjoy another fine coastline view about 0.2 mile down the road. At Western Ave. the bikepath ends. Continue another 0.6 mile along PDM through a quiet and pretty residential section to a locked gate (6.2) near Anchovy Ave.

A convenient alternate method of return is to continue back on PDM/Shepard St. to Pacific Ave., turn left (north) and take this Class II route back to 22nd St. This is a mild return leg which passes along the west (entry) side of the lower reservation of Fort MacArthur Military Reservation.

CONNECTING TRIPS: 1) Connection with Palos Verdes Dr. South Trip (Trip #6C) - near the trip terminus turn north on Anchovy Ave. and bike up a very steep grade for 0.5 mile to 25th St., turn left and continue to Palos Verdes Dr. South; 2) continuation with the L.A. Harbor:Main Channel Trip (Trip #8) - from the starting point, head east on 22nd St. (toward the harbor).

TRIPS #8-#12 - LOS ANGELES AND LONG BEACH HARBORS

The five trips, #8, #9, #10, #11, and #12, are connecting trips which explore the L.A. and Long Beach Harbors. The general area map for these trips is provided below:

o Trip #8 explores the scenic Main Channel of L.A. Harbor and includes several sightseeing attractions, such as Ports O'Call Village.

o Trip #9 visits the East and West Basins of the L.A. Harbor, which have both loading docks and yacht basins.

o Trip #10 tours the Long Beach Harbor, Cerritos, and Back Channels. This is the "working man's" look at some of the most remote parts of the harbor area.

o Trip #11 explores the Southeast Basin of the Long Beach Harbor. The route has several scenic highlights and includes the Queen Mary and Spruce Goose.

o Trip #12 visits Terminal Island, which includes visits to the L.A. Yacht Club and aromatic Cannery Row.

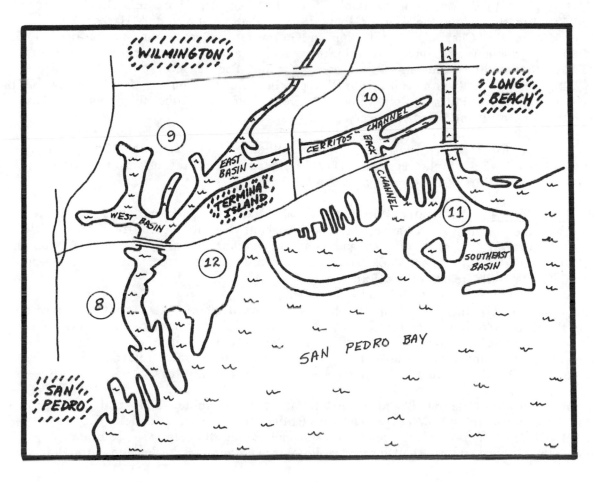

53

TRIP #8 - LOS ANGELES HARBOR: MAIN CHANNEL

GENERAL LOCATION: San Pedro

LEVEL OF DIFFICULTY: One way - easy; up and back - moderate
Distance - 6.2 miles (one way);
Elevation gain - essentially flat

GENERAL DESCRIPTION: This harbor trip is on the west side of the main channel of the Los Angeles Harbor.   The route passes the L.A. World Cruise Center, the large passenger ship terminal visited by such ships as the Queen Mary II and the "Love Boat." In addition, the trip includes the L.A. Maritime Museum, Ports O 'Call Village, and 22nd St. Landing.   There are several particularly scenic spots on the tour, including the point at the end of Admiral Higbee Way. This is probably the best view point along the L.A. Harbor Main Channel.

Most of the trip is on Class X roadway. However, much of the ride is through parking lots, along wide sidewalks, or in areas where motor vehicle traffic is very light.   This is an "any-day-of-the-week" trip; however, the best time to travel along Signal St. and Miner St. in the dock area is probably the weekend, when traffic is lightest.

TRAILHEAD: Free parking is available at the Los Angeles "Park and Ride" on Channel St. directly below the Harbor Fwy. in San Pedro. From the Harbor Fwy. southbound, take the Channel St. off-ramp to Gaffey St. Turn right and in one block turn right on Channel St., then left into the parking area. From central San Pedro, take Gaffey St. north to Channel St. as above. From Pacific Ave. northbound, take a left at Channel St. and turn right into the parking area. Another free parking option is at the periphery of Ports O'Call Village. In the latter case, the full round trip can be exercised with a modified itinerary.

Bring water for the first part of the trip, although there are water and restrooms at Ports O'Call in the middle section. There are also several restaurants to stop at should hunger or thirst strike along the way.

TRIP DESCRIPTION: **Upper Main Channel.** Exit the "Park and Ride" to the left (east toward the harbor) on Channel St. and in about 100 feet turn right on Pacific Ave.   At (0.2) turn left on Front St. and continue another 0.2 mile for a great side-on view of the current ship in drydock at Todd Shipyard. This street fuses into Harbor Blvd. and in 0.8 mile reaches Swinford St.

Turn left and continue on Swinford St. into a small parking area with a close-up view of the U.S. World Cruise Center and, most likely, a large cruise ship. Pass through the pay parking gate (don't pay) and pass by the Spirit of Los Angeles, a floating restaurant and scenic attraction. (This marvelous ship relaced the venerable S.S. Princess Louise -- where we were married no less!).

Continue to the Catalina Island boat terminal and helicopter pads and enjoy a neck-breaking view of the Vincent Thomas Bridge from its underside. Return to Harbor Blvd. (1.0) and turn left onto the sidewalk along the street. Continue alongside the harbor cranes and cargo containers another 0.9 mile and turn left at Sixth St.

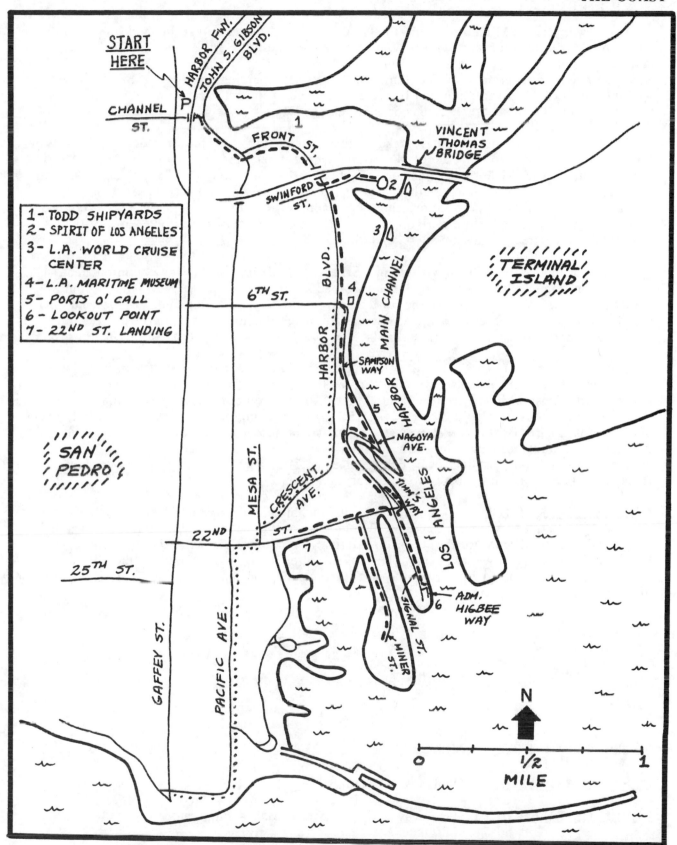

START HERE

CHANNEL ST.

HARBOR FWY.
JOHN S. GIBSON BLVD.

FRONT ST.

VINCENT THOMAS BRIDGE

1

SWINFORD ST.

2

3

HARBOR BLVD.

6TH ST.

4

MAIN CHANNEL

TERMINAL ISLAND

SAMPSON WAY

5

HARBOR

NAGOYA AVE.

MESA ST.

CRESCENT AVE.

ST.

SAN PEDRO

TIMM'S WAY

LOS ANGELES

22ND

25TH ST.

7

GAFFEY ST.

PACIFIC AVE.

SIGNAL ST.

MINER ST.

6

ADM. HIGBEE WAY

1- TODD SHIPYARDS
2- SPIRIT OF LOS ANGELES
3- L.A. WORLD CRUISE CENTER
4- L.A. MARITIME MUSEUM
5- PORTS O' CALL
6- LOOKOUT POINT
7- 22ND ST. LANDING

N

0   1/2   1
MILE

TRIP #8 - LOS ANGELES HARBOR; MAIN CHANNEL

L.A. Maritime Museum and Ports O' Call Village. Just beyond the turnoff is the L.A. Maritime Museum with a fine display of nautical artifacts, historical L.A. maritime goodies, and a great scale model of the Titanic. Turn right on Sampson Way and continue to the middle of the Ports O'Call Village parking lot (2.4). Stop and take a walking tour of this interesting village. Shop, have a bite to eat, or for "hard-core" bikers, forget the rest break and continue along Nagoya Ave.

In 0.1 mile at a locked gate, make a sharp right turn and return along Timm's Way. This is a great area to check out the local fishing fleet close-up. Continue another 0.1 mile to the Little Fisherman Restaurant (great fish) and make a hard left, returning to Sampson Way. Continue south on Sampson Way, staying on the marked scenic route. At (3.0) there is an interesting view across the channel into a Navy drydock. Shortly, the road turns to the right (west) and passes Canetti's Seafood Grotto (also fine food); the street name is now 22nd St.

The "Piers and Twenty-Second Street Landing. In a few hundred feet, turn left on Signal St. Continue down the road until it jogs to the left and becomes Admiral Higbee Way. At (3.6) the road ends at the tiny park-like area at the end of the landfill pier. There is a great view across the main channel into Reservation Point and to outer L.A. Harbor, and this is a pleasant place to stop for a breather.

Return to 22nd St. (4.2), make a left turn, and continue for about 0.1 mile. Turn left at Miner St. and head down another landfill pier. There is nearly continuous marina and pleasure boats to the right. At (4.7) the route passes a little market and bait store that sells ice cold drinks. At (5.1) at a parking lot near the pier's end, check out the San Pedro Boat Works or watch a bulldozer moving coal on a 50-foot high coal mountain. Return to 22nd St., turn left, and continue to the 22nd St. Landing for another close-up look at the local fishing fleet (6.2). This is a great place to buy fresh fish before heading back to the car and home.

CONNECTING TRIPS: 1) Connection with the bike route to San Pedro Beaches Tour (Trip #7) - continue west on 22nd St. 0.7 mile past the 22nd St. Landing and turn left on Via Cabrillo Marina to the Cabrillo Marina; 2) connection with the bike route to L.A. Harbor/East and West Basins (Trip #9) - after returning almost to the "Park and Ride" area on Pacific Ave., continue past Channel St. on Pacific Ave. as it transitions into John S. Gibson Blvd.

TRIP #9 - LOS ANGELES HARBOR: EAST AND WEST BASINS

GENERAL LOCATION: San Pedro, Wilmington, L.A. Harbor

LEVEL OF DIFFICULTY: One way - easy; up and back - moderate
Distance - 8.7 miles (one way)
Elevation gain - essentially flat

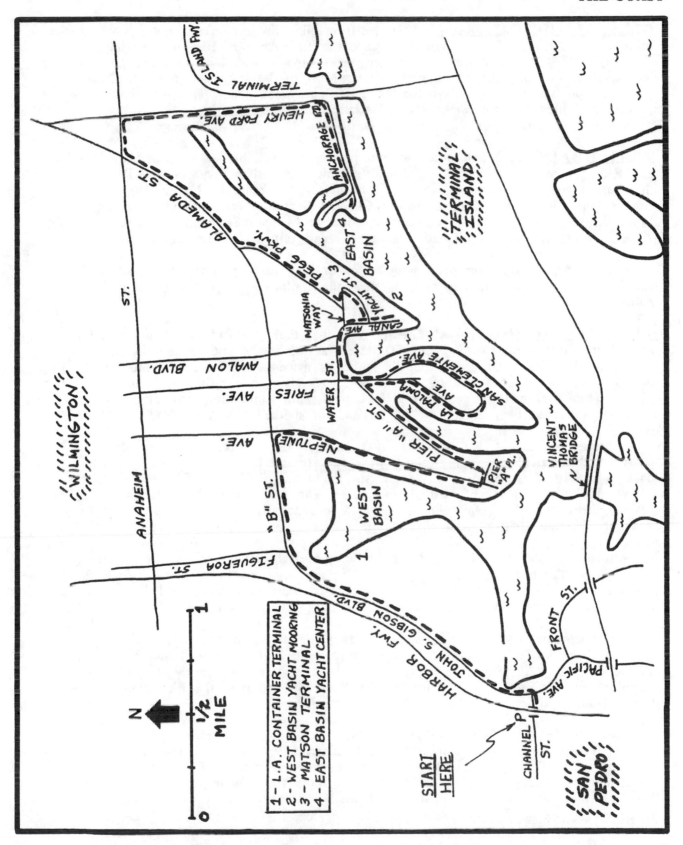

TRIP #9 - LOS ANGELES HARBOR: EAST AND WEST BASINS

GENERAL DESCRIPTION: This free-form bike trip has no set route; however, the reference route provides a chance to visit the Los Angeles Harbor first hand and close up. This is one of three trips (see also Trip #10 and Trip #11) that tour the harbor area west of the Los Angeles River. Most of the suggested route is Class X, but generally on small streets with limited traffic on weekends. The tour passes near several freighter loading docks, the classic old Matson Terminal, West Basin yacht moorings, and terminates at the East Basic Yacht Center (anchorage).

TRAILHEAD: Free public automobile parking is available at the Los Angeles "Park and Ride" located on Channel St. directly below the Harbor Fwy. in San Pedro. From the Harbor Fwy. southbound, take the Channel St. off-ramp to Gaffey St. Turn right and in one block turn right again on Channel St., then left into the parking area. From central San Pedro, take Gaffey St. north to Channel St. as above. From Pacific Ave. northbound, take a left at Channel St. and turn right into the parking area.

Bikers should come prepared with water or plan to stop along the way and "beg and borrow." There are gas stations near the trailhead and cafes along the bike route.

TRIP DESCRIPTION: **West Basin.** Exit the "Park and Ride" area and turn left toward the harbor on Channel St. Turn left at the road's end (a few hundred feet) onto John S. Gibson Dr. (note that the street is named Pacific Ave. to the right). Ride onto the Class I bikepath along the harbor. At about one mile, there are excellent views, from behind the restraining fence, of ships unloading containerized cargo. At (1.3), the road name becomes "B" St. and the marked bike route ends.

Continue on "B" St. and at (1.9) make a right turn on Neptune Ave. Neptune Ave. passes an electrical generating plant, new car storage lots, and a turnout with a view back across the East Basin and West Basin Yacht moorings. At (2.9) the route passes a cozy neighborhood port cafe called, of course, The Port Cafe. Neptune Ave. jogs just beyond the cafe and 0.2 mile later ends at a locked gate. There is a great view of the Vincent Thomas Bridge from this point.

Return towards the cafe and in 0.1 mile, turn right into Pier "A" St. Continue down Pier "A" St. about 0.7 mile and at (3.8) turn right on Fries Ave. Turn right on La Paloma Ave. at (4.1) and take the "loop" tour of Morman Island (La Paloma to Falcon St. to San Clemente Ave. to Anacapa St. and back to Fries Ave.).

San Clemente Ave. runs right alongside some active berths and provides ship viewing close up. Turn right from Fries Ave. onto Water St. (4.8) and bike past tiny Terminal Park. At (5.5) turn right on Canal St. and investigate the Liquid Bulk Terminal and loading docks. Turn left on Yacht St. and pass the Fire Station and U.S. Coast Guard Station and the nearby yacht moorings.

At (5.7) the route becomes Matsonia Way and passes alongside the classic old Matson Terminal. Stop and look at the architecture of the gates and buildings. Turn right on Pegg Pkwy./McFarland Ave. just beyond this point. In 0.1 mile, turn right on Alameda St. and continue until the route turns right again on Anaheim St. (7.1). Bike on this poor quality, well-travelled road and make a right turn (east) on Henry Ford Ave. (7.2).

East Basin. Continue on Henry Ford Ave. and pass over a small marina via a bridge (7.4). Stay on this road (do not turn onto the bridge route as bikers are not permitted) and continue down to the terminus at the "retired" Henry Ford Bridge (8.1). Turn right and travel on Anchorage Rd. along the Cerritos Channel--pick your own "dream" yacht or stop and watch some hard work being done on somebody elses.

Bike to a large free parking lot near the East Basin Yacht Center and turn toward the right. At (8.8) the route ends at a locked gate (walking access) at the edge of another part of the marina. Return 0.1 mile and take a break at the local coffee shop.

CONNECTING TRIPS: 1) Continuation with the bike route to Long Beach Harbor:Cerritos and Back Channels (Trip #10) - at the trip terminus, return to Henry Ford Ave. and continue to Anaheim St., then turn right; 2) connection with the bike route along the L.A. Harbor:Main Channel (Trip #8) - at the trip origin, leave the "Park and Ride," turn right on Pacific Ave. (street name John S. Gibson Ave. across the intersection); 3) connection with the bike route at Harbor Regional Park (Trip #13) - turn left from John S. Gibson Ave. onto the Figueroa St. bikepath (1.3), continue north on Figueroa St. and take the "L" St. tunnel below the Harbor Fwy. Continue on "L" St. to the park.

TRIP #10 - LONG BEACH HARBOR: CERRITOS AND BACK CHANNELS

GENERAL LOCATION: Long Beach Harbor, Long Beach

LEVEL OF DIFFICULTY: One way - moderate; up and back - moderate
Distance - 13.6 miles (one way)
Elevation gain - essentially flat

GENERAL DESCRIPTION: This free-form bike trip has no set route; however, the reference route provides a "working-man's tour" of Long Beach Harbor. This is one of three trips (see also Trips #9 and #11) that tour the harbor area west of the Los Angeles River. It can serve as the middle link between the other two trips for the truly hearty (over 30 miles one way for the suggested routes). Most of the reference route is Class X, but generally on small streets with limited traffic on weekends. This link of the three harbor trips is probably the least exciting in terms of scenery and landmarks, but has the true harbor flavor for harbor lovers. The tour passes near several freighter docks, the 7th St. Landing, Queen's Wharf, and does provide a spectacular view from below of the Gerald Desmond Bridge.

TRAILHEAD: Free parking is available at the East Basin Yacht Center at the terminus of Trip #9. Another option is to start from the large parking area near the Long Beach Pilot Station (Trip #11) and do this trip in reverse. Other less attractive options are to park along Anaheim St. near Santa Fe Ave. or along 9th St. between Santa Fe Ave. and Pico Ave. in Wilmington. The parking locations are described as part of the trip route. In all cases, read the parking signs for latest parking rules.

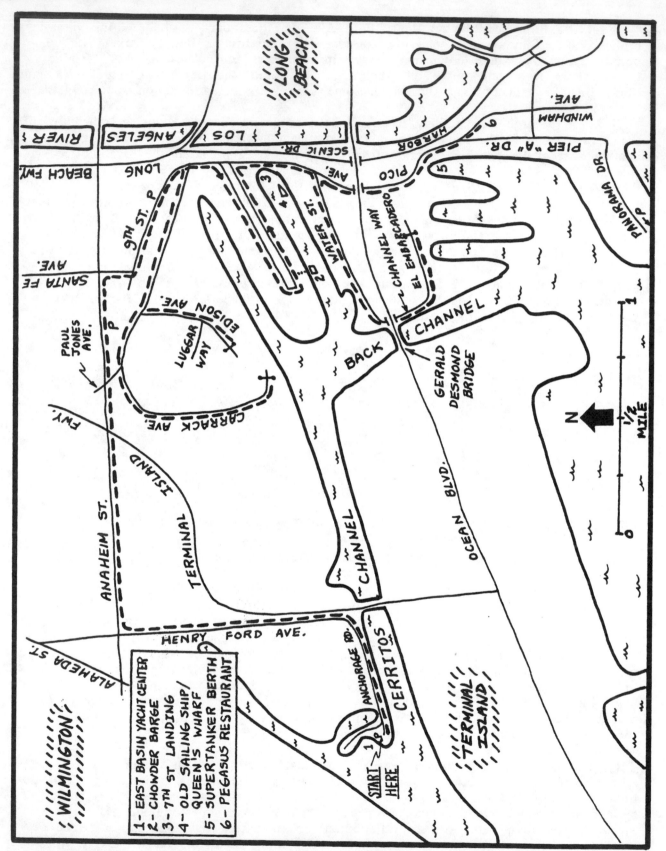

TRIP #10 - LONG BEACH HARBOR: CERRITOS AND BACK CHANNELS

Bikers should come prepared with a couple of filled water bottles or plan to "beg or borrow" along the way. There is a coffee shop at the East Basin Yacht Center and cafes along the way and at the terminus of this trip.

TRIP DESCRIPTION: Cerritos Channel Area. Start at the East Basin Yacht Center along Anchorage Road and turn left at the road terminus onto Henry Ford Ave. At (1.7) turn right on Anaheim St. and continue on a bridge over the Dominquez Channel (2.0). The route passes under the Terminal Island Fwy. (2.8) and in another 0.1 mile, there is an option to get off Anaheim St. at Paul Jones Ave. and continue on 8th St. For bikers willing to stay with a relatively unattractive but classic harbor route, continue on Anaheim St. to Santa Fe Ave. (3.3). Turn right (south) and continue 0.1 mile, then make a left turn on 9th St. The route soon passes Texas Loosey's Chili Parlor and Saloon (how could we not mention that!). At (3.9), the street becomes Pico Ave. and leaves the run-down industrial area.

Cerritos Channel

In a short distance, turn right on 8th St. This is biker's territory. At (4.8) the route meets Paul Jones Ave. and at (5.3) ends at a gate into private property. Turn left at this junction on Carrack Ave. At (6.0) stop and enjoy a great view of the Gerald Desmond Bridge. At (6.1) at the gated terminus, check out the ships along the Cerritos Channel from close up. This territory is deep into "Harbor Country" and rarely visited by "outsiders." Return about 0.9 mile and turn right onto 8th St. In 0.5 mile (7.5), turn right on Edison Ave. Cruise about 0.4 mile down Edison Ave. for another view of the channel and return to 8th St. Turn right and at (8.9) return to Pico Ave.

Turn right on Pico Ave. and at (9.1), take a right turn at 7th St. Continue down 7th St. (between Channels 2 and 3) and pass the large Proctor and Gamble Mfg. Co. plant (9.4). Continue to the terminus at a blocked gate. Turn around and return a short distance, then turn right (south) into a small parking area. Walk to the end of the lot, up the steps, and out along the jetty. Take in a great view of the local marina, surrounding harbor, Gerald Desmond Bridge, and then stop in at the rustic sea-going man's Chowder Barge Restaurant for a great snack and liquid refreshment. Return to Pico Ave. (10.5) and turn right.

Continue on Pico Ave. to Queen's Wharf (10.6). At the wharf are a coffee shop, restaurant, and well-stocked fresh fish market. Behind the market is the Sports Fishing Landing, the starting point for many "part-time" fisherman's trips. With good fortune, the private three-masted sailing ship "Bounty" may be tied up nearby. Admire from a distance as this is "entry by permission" only.

Back Channel Area. Continue 0.3 mile on Pico Ave. and turn right on Water St. Continue about 0.6 mile to the gate at the Fire Boat Station (11.7) and turn left on Channel Way. This route travels directly under the middle of the Gerald Desmond Bridge and along the Back Channel; the spectacular view of the bridge is a guaranteed "neck breaker." At (11.9) the road ends at a locked gate. Turn left at El Embarcadero and continue about 0.1 mile to a closed gate. This must be the end of the world! Return the same way and turn right at Pico Ave. (13.2).

Continue on Pico and pass under the Gerald Desmond Bridge entry at (13.3). Continue past Seaside Ave. and end this segment of the trip (13.6) at the junction of Pico Ave. and Windham Ave. With luck, there will be a supertanker in one of the nearby slips. These great ships are awesome close up! With or without the supertanker, there is an opportunity to take a break and fuel up at the nearby Pegasus Restaurant.

CONNECTING TRIPS: 1) Continuation of the L.A. Harbor:East and West Basin (Trip #9) - from the East Basin Yacht Center, return to Henry Ford Ave., turn left and continue to Anaheim St. and turn left; 2) continue south on Pico Ave. from the trip terminus at the Pegasus Restaurant. Pico Ave. turns into Pier "A" Ave.

TRIP #11 - LONG BEACH HARBOR: SOUTHEAST BASIN

GENERAL LOCATION: Long Beach Harbor, Long Beach

LEVEL OF DIFFICULTY: One way - easy; up and back - moderate
Distance - 6.9 miles (one way)
Elevation gain - essentially flat

GENERAL DESCRIPTION: This free-form trip has no set route; however, the reference route provides a chance to see the harbor area at its best. Of the three trips visiting the L.A. Harbor/Long Beach Harbor areas (Trips #9 and #10), this is definitely the most scenic and landmark-filled.

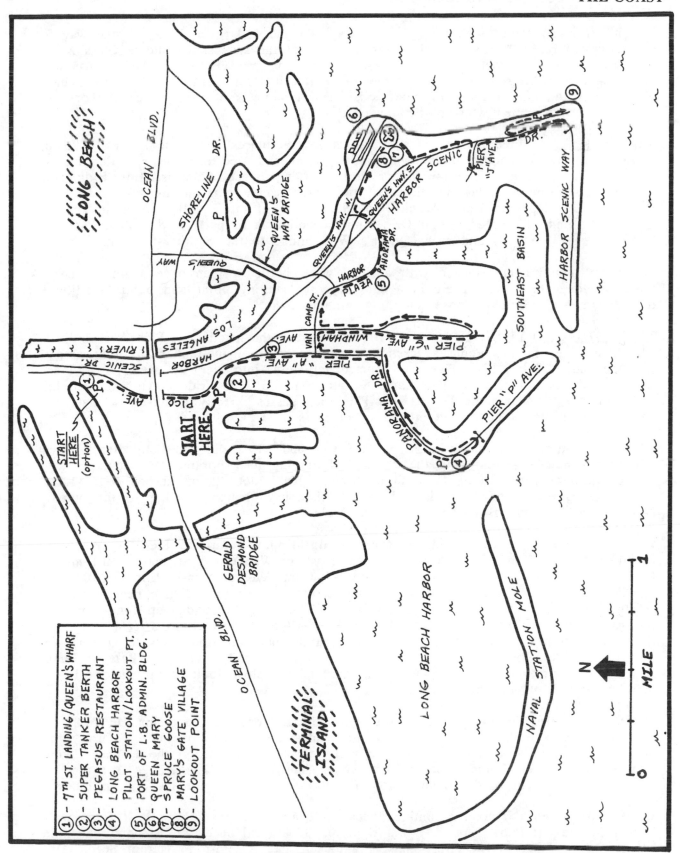

LONG BEACH

Legend:
1 - 7TH ST. LANDING/QUEEN'S WHARF
2 - SUPER TANKER BERTH
3 - PEGASUS RESTAURANT
4 - LONG BEACH HARBOR
5 - PILOT STATION/LOOKOUT PT.
6 - PORT OF L.B. ADMIN. BLDG.
7 - QUEEN MARY
8 - SPRUCE GOOSE
9 - MARY'S GATE VILLAGE
· - LOOKOUT POINT

TERMINAL ISLAND

LONG BEACH HARBOR

NAVAL STATION MOLE

N

MILE
0   1

TRIP #11 - LONG BEACH HARBOR: SOUTHEAST BASIN

This trip can serve as the end link of Trips #9 and #10 (over 30 miles one way for the suggested route) or can be taken alone. Most of the suggested route is Class X, but generally on small streets with very limited traffic on weekends. The trip starts in a super-tanker berthing area, includes the Long Beach Pilot Station and a great harbor view, visits the Queen Mary /Spruce Goose, and terminates at the end of Harbor Scenic Dr. with a great view of San Pedro Bay.

TRAILHEAD: Free parking is available at several places along the suggested route, allowing bikers to choose their own starting point and free-form route. Parking is available in the Pegusas Restaurant or Port of Long Beach Administration Bldg. parking lots (Sunday only), in either of two large scenic parking areas off of Panorama Dr. near the Long Beach Pilot Station, or at the equally scenic parking area at the end of Harbor Scenic Dr. Another option is to park at Shoreline Park in Long Beach (Trip #14) and cross Queen's Way bridge to the Southeast Basin.

Bikers should come stocked with a filled water bottle or plan once again to "beg or borrow" along the way. There is a cafe near the starting point and public facilities at the Queen Mary/Spruce Goose shopping village area.

TRIP DESCRIPTION: **Panorama Drive.** Start at the junction of Pico Ave. and Windham Ave. at the Pegasus Restaurant and near the supertanker berthing area (see the end of Trip #10). Pico Ave. immediately turns into Pier "A" Ave. Take Pier "A" Ave. south and pass the Van Camp St. junction (0.6). Joy ride down the small hill and turn right at Panorama Dr. (0.8). This road passes directly alongside a giant grain elevator and a motel-size mound of ocean salt (1.2).

At (1.4) turn right into a large parking area and check out the Long Beach Naval Station and the Navy ships in the harbor. Returning to Panorama Dr., continue to the end into a large parking lot with the Long Beach Pilot Station at one edge (1.5). From this excellent lookout point, check out the busy channel leading to the outer harbor and the Long Beach Naval Station Mole.

Port of Long Beach Administration Building. Return to Pier "A" Ave. and backtrack to Van Camp St. (2.6). Turn right (east) on Van Camp St. and, in 0.1 mile, turn right on Windham Ave. Continue on Windham Ave. and pass Panorama Dr. (3.9). Windham Ave. fuses into Pier "G" Ave. and continues to a locked gate near two large storage elevators (3.5). Return on the Pier "G" Ave. northbound loop (one-way traffic) and turn right at Van Camp St. (4.3). In 0.2 mile, Van Camp St. angles to the right and becomes Harbor Plaza. A left turn at the next junction leads to Queen's Way Bridge; however, this reference route stays to the right and passes the Port of Long Beach Administration Building (4.6). Stop and take a close look at the historical murals painted on the building face.

H.M.S. Queen Mary. Harbor Plaza bears left and ends at Panorama Dr. (4.8). Turn left, cross Harbor Scenic Dr. and ride under the freeway overpass. Turn right on Queen's Hwy. North and revel in the glory of the Queen Mary, the Hughes Flying Boat Exhibit Center (Spruce Goose), and Mary's Gate Village. The village is a nice place for a rest and replenishment stop and has sturdy racks for locking up bikes.

Harbor Scenic Drive. Continue back on Queen's Way south until it fuses with Harbor Scenic Dr. (5.5). At (5.7) turn right on "J" St. and check out some of the more "rustic" harbor areas. The street ends at a locked gate. Return to Harbor Scenic Dr. and turn right (6.1).

There are excellent views of the Long Beach Outer Harbor, Long Beach city skyline, cruising yachts, and with a little luck, maybe even a supertanker. The ride on the roadway ends at a private entry gate (6.6). Continue back north to the open gate and parking area. Ride south to the end of the parking area (6.9) and have a few laughs with the individuals and families who are fishing at land's end. There is a simply unique view of the outer harbor from this area.

CONNECTING TRIPS: 1) Continuation with the Long Beach Harbor:Cerritos and Back Channels route (Trip #10) - at the trip origin at the Pegasus Restaurant, continue north on Pico Ave.; 2) connection with the Long Beach Shoreline Park tour (Trip #14) - at (4.5) on Harbor Plaza, turn left (northeast) on Queen's Way and continue over Queen's Way Bridge. Exit right at the "Convention Center/Shoreline Area" turnoff and right again at Pine Ave. Parking is available around the Shoreline Park lagoons or in the Shoreline Marina Village parking lot.

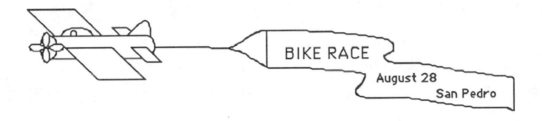

TRIP #12 - TERMINAL ISLAND TOUR

GENERAL LOCATION: Terminal Island

LEVEL OF DIFFICULTY: Loop - easy
Distance - 11.0 miles (loop)
Elevation gain - essentially flat

GENERAL DESCRIPTION: This is a touring trip around an island that is little known to most bikers (or anybody else for that matter). Among other goodies, the tour offers some great vistas across the Los Angeles Harbor Main Channel, a visit to the home of the local tuna fleet at Fish Harbor and a spectacular close up of drydocked ships. For the more vigorous bikers, there is a view from the Gerald Desmond Bridge of the current U.S. battleships under upkeep and refurbishment. This is one of those trips for bikers who have a special liking for the harbor environment or who just flat out like to explore out-of-the way territory. The entire route is Class X, but on wide roadways with very little traffic on weekends.

TRAILHEAD: Free parking is readily available throughout the island. This journey starts from Ferry St. across from the Federal Building where there is parking in the shade of a few eucalyptus trees. From San Pedro, cross the Vincent Thomas Bridge and exit to the right just beyond the toll gate ("free" direction). Follow the road through a hairpin turn and continue to the road's end at Ferry St. Cross Ferry St. and find parking.

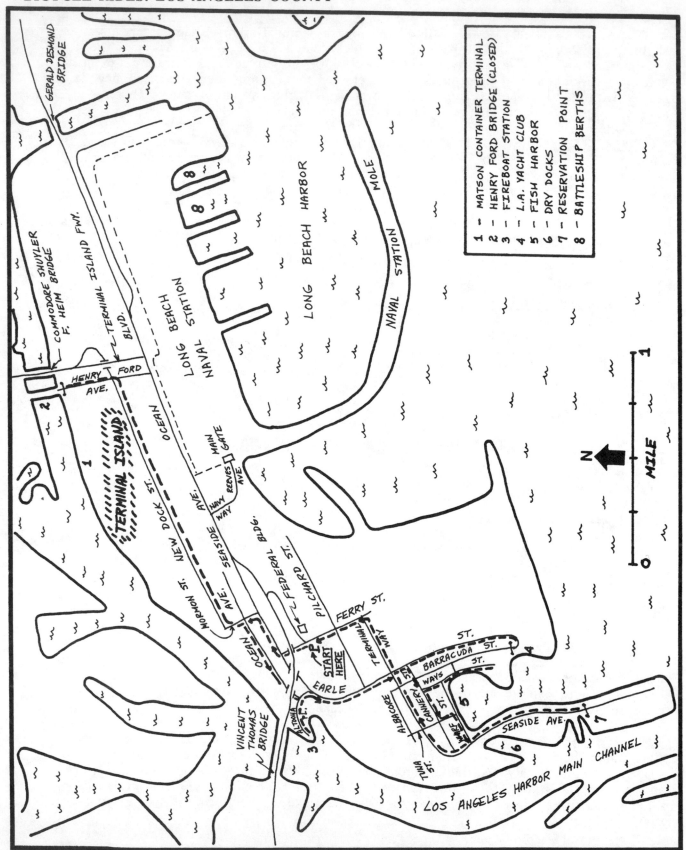

1 — MATSON CONTAINER TERMINAL
2 — HENRY FORD BRIDGE (CLOSED)
3 — FIREBOAT STATION
4 — L.A. YACHT CLUB
5 — FISH HARBOR
6 — DRY DOCKS
7 — RESERVATION POINT
8 — BATTLESHIP BERTHS

TRIP #12 - TERMINAL ISLAND TOUR

From the Long Beach area, cross the Gerald Desmond Bridge and continue on Ocean Blvd. which eventually changes its name to Seaside Ave. Just before passing under the Vincent Thomas Bridge, turn left on Ferry St. and proceed under the bridge to parking across from the Federal Building. From Wilmington, take the Terminal Island Fwy. across the Commodore Shuyler E. Heim Bridge to the road's terminus at Ocean Ave. Turn right and continue on Ocean Blvd./Seaside Ave. as just described.

The single walking/biking access to the island is over the Gerald Desmond Bridge. The views from the bridge are breath-taking! However the access is steep, on a small raised walkway, and right next to fast-moving traffic. Truck your bike over on a car bike rack unless you enjoy cheap thrills!

Bring water, munchies, and make a pit-stop before you start. We found one (closed) gas station and one restaurant on the entire island.

TRIP DESCRIPTION: **New Dock Street.** Head north on Ferry St. and pass under the Vincent Thomas Bridge. Continue across Seaside Ave. and turn right (east) on Ocean Ave. (0.1). The route passes along the fenced-in dock areas and meets Mormon St. (0.4). Turn left, continue to New Dock St. and then steer right. For the next 0.2 mile are a collection of large scrap metal works with the attendant "metal mountains" and large machinery. There is also a great view back to San Pedro Hill from this area.

The route passes the Matson Container Terminal where at times there are at least a half dozen mammoth container cargo cranes lined up together (1.6). New Dock St. ends in 0.3 mile at Henry Ford Ave. Turn left and continue to the end of the roadway for a close inspection of the "retired" Henry Ford (draw) Bridge (2.3).

Fireboat Station/L.A. Yacht Club. Return along the same route (unless you are willing to bike on the busy, fast-moving Ocean Blvd.) to the intersection of Seaside Ave. and Ferry St. (4.4). Pedal under the Vincent Thomas Bridge and turn right at Altoona Pl. (4.6). Continue on this street to its terminus at a fireboat station on the harbor channel (4.9). From this area, there is an excellent view across to the L.A. World Cruise Center, Spirit of Los Angeles floating restaurant, and a "neck breaker" view from below the Vincent Thomas Bridge.

Return to Seaside Ave. and continue south. The street name changes to Earle St. and continues another 0.8 mile past large lots of cargo containers and new cars to its terminus at the L.A. Yacht Club (private property) (6.4).

Fish Harbor. Backtrack along the same route and turn left (west) on Cannery St. (7.0). In a short distance, turn left and travel along the wharf on Ways St. and continue south to the terminus at the Starkist Tuna Processing Plant. At this pleasant point (pleasant view, unpleasant odor) is a view down the docks of some of the local tuna fleet. There are also several out-of-place shade trees here (7.5).

Return along Ways St. and turn left on Cannery St. The area here almost has the appearance and desolation to remind one of a long-deserted razed town (at least on weekends). Turn left (south) on Tuna St. (8.1) and pass the local Sushi Bar/Japanese Restaurant and Harbor Light Mini-Mart. The street terminates at Wharf St. at a classic Fish Harbor viewpoint. Turn right and continue to South Seaside Ave. (8.4).

Drydocks/Federal Prison. The tour continues and reaches a nice viewpoint in 0.2 mile that provides a view of outer Fish Harbor as well as the ships at anchor in outer Los Angeles Harbor. In a short distance, the trip passes two massive drydocks; if the drydocks are occupied, the close-up, bow-on look at these mammoth ships is nothing but impressive. The path terminates at the Federal Prison at the visitors parking area (don't venture in and take notes, as we found out!).

Terminal Way Return Route. Retrace the original route and continue on S. Seaside Ave. past Wharf St. S. Seaside Ave. turns right (east) and fuses into Terminal Way (9.9). In a short distance, the bike route meets Earle St. (10.2); here a biker can take a well deserved food and drink break at "salty" Joe Biff's Bar and Grill and shoot some pool, too. Continue on Terminal Way to Ferry St. and turn left (north). The route passes Prichard St. (10.8) and returns to the Federal Building at 11.0 miles from the trip start. (Note that there is an interesting spur trip along Prichard St. that passes alongside the massive Terminal Island "coal mountain" and ends at the Naval Station Main Gate. (Add 1.2 miles round trip if this spur is taken.)

<u>**CONNECTING TRIPS**</u>: 1) Connection with the Long Beach Shoreline Park route (Trip #14) - continue over the Gerald Desmond Bridge and the bridge over the Los Angeles River. Turn right on Shoreline Dr. and turn right again at Golden Shore Blvd.; 2) connection with the southern segment of the Lario Trail (Trip #32B) - continue as above except turn right into the first <u>public</u> parking area on Shoreline Dr.

TRIP #13 - HARBOR REGIONAL PARK

<u>**GENERAL LOCATION**</u>:   Harbor City

<u>**LEVEL OF DIFFICULTY**</u>: Loop - easy
Distance - 5.9 miles (loop)
Elevation gain - essentially flat

<u>**GENERAL DESCRIPTION**</u>: This is a short trip that explores Harbor Regional Park. More specifically, it visits Harbor Lake from its highly accessible west side, as well as its less visited east side. The trip provides a good look at the lake as well as the marshy wildlife preserve that surrounds it. In addition, there is a side excursion through the L.A. Harbor College campus. The west side lake tour is Class I. The route along Pacific Coast Highway (PCH) and Figueroa Pl. is on Class X roadway; however, there is plenty of room for bikers. The route through the campus mixes travel on roadways with light traffic and combination bikeways/walkways.

<u>**TRAILHEAD**</u>: Free public parking is available at the park. From the Harbor Fwy., exit at Anaheim St. and head west about one mile. Turn right into the park at the Harbor Regional Park sign. From Anaheim St., Palos Verdes Dr. North, or Gaffey Street (these streets intersect near the park), take Vermont St. north at the intersection. In about 0.3 mile, turn right into the park at the park sign. Note also that there is a separate bike/walk access to the park. Just east of Gaffey St. at the intersection, there is a path which travels under Anaheim St. and enters at an undeveloped area near the southwest end of the park.

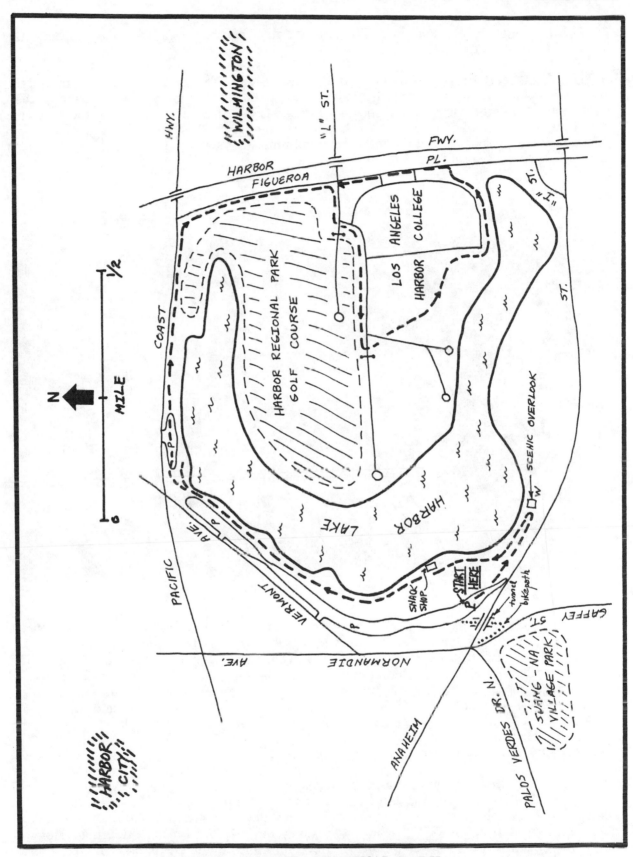

TRIP #13 - HARBOR REGIONAL PARK

Bring a light water supply.   There are water and restroom facilities at both the park and at the city college.

TRIP DESCRIPTION: **Harbor Lake, West Side.**   The bikepath follows the edge of the lake with spokes radiating out from this path to the individual parking areas. From the southernmost parking lot, head toward the lake and take a turnoff to the small roofed overlook above the south edge of the lake (0.1).   There is a water fountain here.   To the east is a gravel road into the marshy preserve area; it is not advised to take a thin-tired bike into this area.

Harbor Regional Park

Head back towards the parking lot and join the bike trail/walkway along the lake. At (0.3) cruise by a snack bar and at (0.5) pass a point which juts out into the lake; this is "duck city" with every type of duck you can imagine.   There are plenty of fishermen along the lake in harmony with the ducks.   At about (0.6) pass a second lake finger and a restroom just beyond.   Continue around to the north end of the lake to the end of the trail (1.1).   Head towards the northern parking lot and follow it parallel to PCH for about 0.1 mile.   At the end of the parking lot, join PCH and ride along the Harbor Lake drainage (1.3).   At (1.8) turn right (south) on Figueroa Pl. and continue 0.4 mile to "L" St.   Turn right on "L" St. onto the L.A. Harbor College Campus.

Harbor College Campus and East Side of Harbor Lake.   Continue 0.2 mile on "L" St. until it jogs to the left along a fence.   Continue on "L" St. until it ends in 0.3 mile (2.7 from the start).   It is a short walk to the lake and a small pier surrounded by high reeds.   Return on "L" St. and ride along the athletic fields.   Continue along the parking area and at (3.2) take in the view into the southeast corner of the preserve. The roadway continues along the marsh and in about 0.3 mile, returns to Figueroa Pl.

Return Route. Return north on Figueroa Pl. and once across "L" St., repeat the route in reverse for an additional 2.2 miles (5.9 total trip miles). Do not complete the loop by heading south on Figueroa Pl. unless you are willing to chance playing "bumper cars" along narrow and busy Anaheim St.

CONNECTING TRIPS: 1) Connection with the northern section of Palos Verdes Peninsula Loop (Trip #6A) - take the bike underpass to Gaffey St. Continue along the south side of Palos Verdes Dr. North for 0.8 mile. At Western Ave., cross the street to the north side; 2) connection with the L.A. Harbor:East and West Basins tour (Trip #9) - take "L" St. under the Harbor Fwy. and in 0.1 mile, turn right (south) on Figueroa St. Continue about one mile to link up with Trip #9 on "B" St.

TRIP #14 - LONG BEACH SHORELINE PARK

GENERAL LOCATION: Long Beach

LEVEL OF DIFFICULTY: Loop - easy
                         Distance - 6.6 miles (loop)
                         Elevation gain - essentially flat

GENERAL DESCRIPTION: This is one of the prime candidates for an easy-going family trip. Almost the entire trip is on an excellent Class I bike route and resides within the Shoreline Park/Long Beach Marina area away from heavy traffic. The scenery is great and there are plenty of recreation spots along the way, including playgrounds, barbecue and picnic facilities, and fishing platforms. The trip is of modest length, but provides a wide variety of interesting biking territory, including views of water skiers in L.A. Harbor, the Catalina Island cruise ships at Queen's Way Landing, two lagoons crossed by a bridge, the yacht-filled downown Long Beach Marina, and a terrific view of the Queen Mary. Bike traffic is light and the bike lane is large; however, the Shoreline Park area has heavy competing foot traffic on pleasant weather days, particularly weekends.

An option exists to add a small segment to this trip. This involves crossing Shoreline Dr. and traveling the bikepath along the Hyatt Regency fresh water lagoon and into the Long Beach Convention Center area.

TRAILHEAD: From Ocean Blvd. in Long Beach, turn south (toward the harbor) on Pine St. and continue to it's terminus. There is free public parking around the Shoreline Park lagoons. From the Long Beach Fwy., continue south and take the Downtown Long Beach exit. Take the turnoff to Convention Center/Catalina Island and continue along Shoreline Dr. past the Golden Shore exit. Turn right on Pine St.

For busy days, pay parking is available between Ocean Blvd. and Shoreline Dr. An option is to park for free along the north-south streets above Ocean Blvd., and then bike to the trailhead. Check parking signs carefully if the latter option is used.

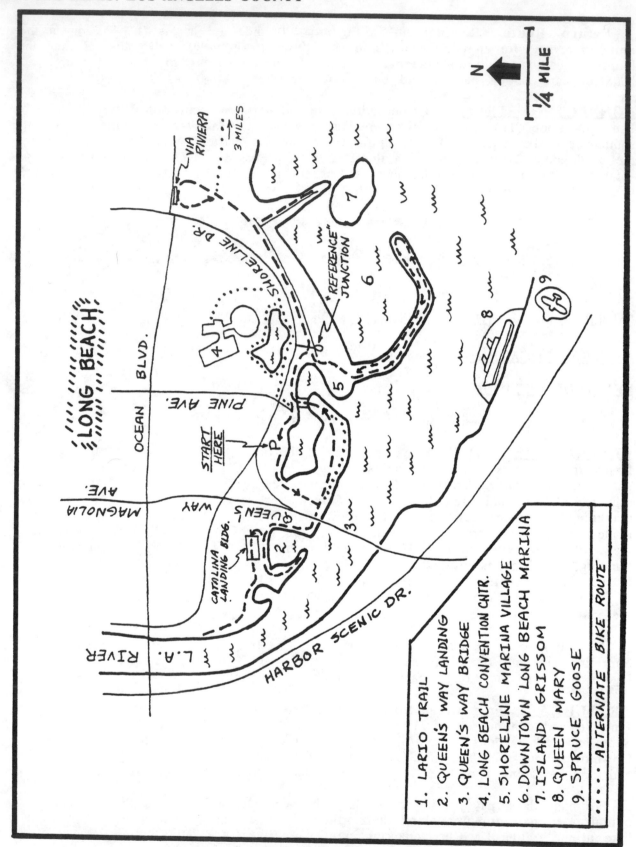

TRIP #14 - LONG BEACH SHORELINE PARK

There are plenty of water and public restroom facilities along the route. Shoreline Village also offers many options to "eat, drink, and be merry."

TRIP DESCRIPTION: **Lagoon and L.A. River Channel.** From the lagoon parking area, take the bikepath west (toward the Queen's Way Bridge). Near the west end of the lagoon, follow a junction to the right and pass a recreational vehicle parking area (0.2). Continue on this path to the L.A. River Channel. Take a hard right turn (north), continuing along the channel and pass under the Queen's Way Bridge (0.3). Follow the path around the entire Queen's Way Landing rim and admire both the small lighthouse and Catalina Cruisers (0.8).

Return from the rim to the main bikepath, turn right and backtrack about 100 yards. Bike up the east ramp of the Catalina Landing Building to the second-story walking plaza (1.1). Leave the building via the west ramp and pass the small boat launch area into a large pay parking lot (1.3). Cruise north and west on the well-marked trail to the parking lot edge to the marked entry to the Lario Trail (1.5). This is a great spot to watch water skiers and jet skiers.

Return on the path along the channel. Just before passing under the Queen's Way Bridge, note the steps to the left; this is one route up to the bridge. Continue along the channel to a three-way junction (2.3). A hard left returns the biker along the incoming route and the right (channel-hugging) route travels the periphery of the lagoon area. This reference trip takes the middle route and travels up to a playground/view area/restroom stop atop a grassy knoll.

From here, the trail heads down a moderate grade and continues along the lagoon edge. In 0.3 mile from the grassy knoll/playground, the route passes a pleasant palm-tree surrounded area with several park benches. Just beyond, the path leads to a small bridge across the lagoon (2.7).

Long Beach Marina. Follow the bridge across the lagoon and make a right turn (east). Continue on the bikepath which parallels the small parking access street for about 0.1 mile. Shortly afterward, the bikeway crosses under a concrete walkway. Stop and climb the overhead walkway, which provides a great view of the harbor, channel, marina and the convention center area.

Continue on past a set of wooden stairs to the right which leads to Shoreline Village. The trail crosses the access road to the village at this point (2.8) and continues along a black wrought iron fence along the perimeter of the parking lot. The trail then crosses a street which leads to marina parking. There is a flower-bedecked vehicle turning circle at this point. The bike route will explore both directions at this "reference junction" (3.0).

First take a right turn (west) at that junction and continue along the Shoreline Village perimeter about 0.1 mile to the road's end. To the right is Parker's Light-House. Turn left onto the outermost bike trail along the jetty. Ride along the jetty and enjoy the vista of the pleasurecraft and large commercial ships in the harbor, a spectacular view of the Queen Mary across the channel, and a good look at the yachts in the marina. Stop and observe from one of several observation/fishing platforms.

Continue to the end of the jetty at the Downtown Marina Administration Building. Return along the inner edge of the jetty for a better view of the marina craft. Follow the path back to the "reference junction" noted above.

Pass this "reference junction" (4.3) and continue east along the path through the parking area to the excellent city beach (4.8). There is a Class I path which junctions east in this area, continuing two miles along the beach to Belmont Shore. However the reference bikepath turns north at this point and terminates in the parking lot just beneath the historic Via Riviera Hotel (5.0). Return 0.2 mile and turn left (south) on a small asphalt road. This road follows the jetty which forms the east end of the marina. The road terminates at one of the more popular fishing spots just across from Island Grissom (5.6).

Return to the "reference junction" and turn right. Follow the route back to the Pine St. intersection, which is just above the trail to the bridge across the lagoon (6.5). Turn right and continue another 0.1 mile to the parking lot at the trip origin. An option at that intersection is to take the short side trip below.

Long Beach Convention Center. Continue north across Pine Ave. and take the bikepath to the right alongside the Hyatt Regency Hotel. In a short distance, the path travels along a lagoon. Take a short trip around the lagoon and enjoy the birds, water fountains, and the serene surroundings (do not bike across the footbridges over the lagoon, as they were not designed for bicycle travel). At (0.5) return to the lagoon loop starting point and continue on the path along Shoreline Dr. until it terminates at the Long Beach Convention Center (0.7). Options at this point are to cruise the convention center area and then the quaint Seaside Ave. area (Class X roadway) or to return directly to the parking area at the Shoreline Park lagoon.

CONNECTING TRIPS: 1) Connection with the Los Angeles River/Lario Trail (Trip #20B) - continue to the marked Lario Trail as described above; 2) connection with the Long Beach Harbor:Southeast Basin route (Trip #11) - bike just north of the Queen's Way Bridge to a set of steps leading up to the bridge (refer back to this trip writeup); carry your bike up the steps and walk your bike on the walkway across the bridge (steps only for strong bikers in good condition); 3) connection with the Belmont Shore/Naples Tour (Trip #15) - turn east at the junction at (4.8) above.

TRIP #15 - BELMONT SHORE/NAPLES TOUR

GENERAL LOCATION: Long Beach

LEVEL OF DIFFICULTY: One way - easy; round trip - moderate
Distance - 10.9 miles (one way)
Elevation gain - essentially flat

GENERAL DESCRIPTION: This is a very pleasant trip, particularly for sightseeing, which concentrates on the beach community setting. The trip starts at the Belmont Pier, transverses a jetty to the Alamitos Bay entrance, passes onto Naples Island and ends at Long Beach Marine Stadium. An alternate and more direct return route along the Alamitos Bay shore is also provided. The highlight of the trip is the Naples tour.

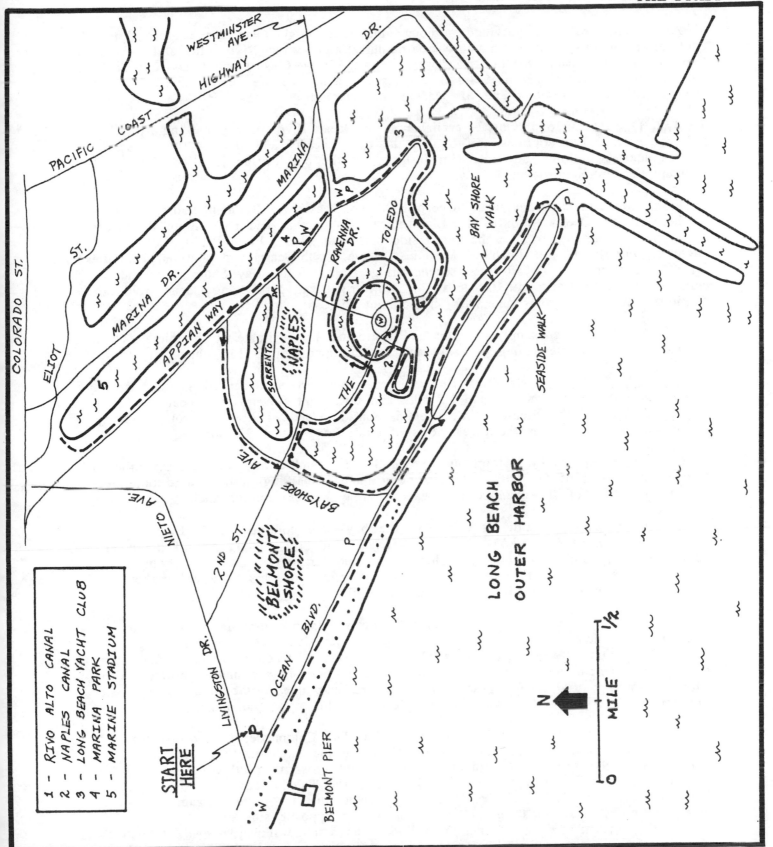

Legend:
1 – RIVO ALTO CANAL
2 – NAPLES CANAL
3 – LONG BEACH YACHT CLUB
4 – MARINA PARK
5 – MARINE STADIUM

START HERE

TRIP #15 - BELMONT SHORE/ NAPLES TOUR

A reference route is provided, although the biker might plan for a more thorough exploration of this island community, particularly around the Rivo Alto and Naples Canal areas. The route is a mix of Class I along the jetty, Class I and Class X throughout the Naples area, and a mix of Class II and Class X along the Marine Stadium. The only heavy traffic area is along 2nd St. leading into Naples.

TRAILHEAD: Free parking is available along Ocean Blvd. or pay parking near the Belmont Pier. Other options are to alter the trip itinerary and start at other free parking locations along the route (for instance, at the end of the jetty or along Appian Way in Naples).

From Long Beach proper, take Ocean Blvd. southeast into Belmont Shore. Continue to the right on Ocean Blvd. to the Livingstone Dr. junction and park along the street or in the pay parking area on the beach side of Ocean Blvd. From Pacific Coast Highway, turn west onto 2nd St. (Westminster Ave. to the east) and continue 1.2 miles across two bridges. Just after the second bridge, turn left on Bay Shore Ave. and continue to its terminus with Ocean Blvd. Turn right and park along Ocean Blvd., or continue one mile further and park at Belmont Pier.

Bring a light water supply. Water and restrooms are available at the pier. There is also plenty of water along the way and several opportunities for other "pit stops."

TRIP DESCRIPTION: **Belmont Shore.** Pedal southeast on Ocean Blvd. and pass Bay Shore Ave. (0.7). Continue about 0.1 mile and turn right (toward the ocean) on 55th Pl. At the end of this pleasant little street is Seaside Walk. Follow this route and enjoy the beach folk as well as the great views of outer Long Beach Harbor and the ocean.

Continue to the walkway terminus at 69th St. (1.7) and follow the path 0.1 mile further to the end of the jetty. At this point there is parking, a life guard building, and a nice view of the channel and Seaport Village across the channel.

For the return trip, turn right (toward the bay) and continue along Bay Shore Walk to Bay Shore Ave. (2.5). Turn north (right) and cruise along one of the nicer, better sheltered, and more populated beaches in the territory. Continue about 0.6 mile further and turn right (west) on 2nd St. Continue on this busy and rather narrow street over the bridge into beautiful Naples.

Naples. This small community consists of three islands, one large island, one small island which is nearly surrounded by the large island, and a second small island which nearly "seals off" the small central island. Once over the bridge, turn right at The Toledo and continue about 0.3 mile (3.4) to another smaller bridge. Cross onto the small central island, pass a small market, and bike to the lovely spray water fountain (and drinking fountain) in the pleasant outdoor central plaza (3.6).

Take a spin around the traffic circle and find The Colonnade; follow this little street to its terminus at the grassy mini-park along the bay and turn left (east). Follow the walkway/bikeway around the island and cross the following streets (bridge exits) in succession: Neopolitan Ln. East, The Toledo (east), Ravenna Dr., The Toledo (west), and Neopolitan Ln. West (4.9). (Note that the route ziz-zags and appears to end at every street crossing, but continues on the opposite side of the street.) Cross over the bridge at the latter junction and take the small walkway/bikeway (Corso De Napoli) around the smallest of the three islands. Return across the Neopolitan Ln. West bridge (5.4) and continue to The Toledo.

Turn right at the end of Garibaldi Ln. and follow a small walkway/bikeway along the Rivo Alto Canal. Continue along the small path and admire the tightly packed little community of gardens and varied architectures along the canal. There are small sailboats, power boats, even canoes in this 0.8 mile stretch of canal. The street crossings in order are at Ravenna Dr., The Toledo (east), and Neopolitan Ln. West.

Rivo Alto Canal, Naples

At (6.4) the bikepath takes a sharp change of direction and leaves the canal for a 0.7 mile open stretch along Alamitos Bay. At (6.9) the route passes a cozy little Overlook Park and at (7.1) ends near the Long Beach Yacht Club. This spot is at the southern terminus of Appian Way and is one of the better spots to watch the water traffic in Alamitos Bay. Continue 0.1 mile north on Appian Way past the yacht basin (parking, water fountain, <u>private</u> restrooms), pass under the 2nd St. bridge, and reach Marina Park at (7.3).

Marine Stadium. Marina Park has a grassy lawn for resting, parking, water and restrooms, a great beach, and a fine place to watch the sailboaters and windsurfers. Continue north along Appian Way (Class II bikepath), pass over the small bridge, and turn right about 100 yards before Nieto Ave. At (8.3) is the entrance to the Marine Stadium parking lot (free to bikers). The stadium is a great place to watch boat races and individual power boats performing time trials.

One option at this point is to head north to Nieto Ave., turn right on Eliot St., and bike down Marina Dr. on the other side of the stadium. This route terminates at a launch ramp/view point at the Pete Archer Rowing Center and adds 2.2 miles to the total trip mileage.

77

Return Route. Our reference route returns directly to Appian Way from Marine Stadium. Return south about 0.7 mile and turn right just before the bridge at Bay Shore Ave. (9.0). Continue 0.9 mile across 2nd St. to Ocean Blvd. and turn right. About 1.0 mile up the road is the Belmont Pier -- a total trip length of 10.9 miles.

CONNECTING TRIPS: Continuation with Long Beach Shoreline Park (Trip #14) - at the trip origin, bike toward the ocean to the Class I beachfront path and turn right (northwest); 2) connection with the trailheads for San Gabriel River Trail, and Coyote Creek (Trips #20A, #24, respectively) - from Marina Park, take Appian Way south of the 2nd St. bridge, turn onto the marked "on-ramp" to 2nd St., and turn right at the next traffic signal at Marina Dr. Take Marina Dr. to the parking area along the San Gabriel River (see Trip #20A instructions for further specifics).

TRIP #16 - EL DORADO PARK

GENERAL LOCATION: Long Beach

LEVEL OF DIFFICULTY: Loop - easy
Distance - 4.3 miles (loop)
Elevation gain - essentially flat

GENERAL DESCRIPTION: This is near the top of the list as a great family bike route and general outing. The entire route resides within East El Dorado Regional Park. There is something for everybody. The Class I bikepaths and routes along the park roadways are relatively uncrowded and in great condition. The biker can roam just the park boundaries in the two basic picnic areas (Area II north of Spring St. and Area III north of Wardlow Rd.) and travel 4.3 miles. The route is free form and the biker can travel the interior park paths as well, putting in whatever mileage is suitable. There are four small lakes to cruise around, lovely stands of trees, and a variety of beautiful birds, including ducks and geese in the lakes.

In addition to the biking paths, there is an archery range, model boat pier, model glider area, paddle boats, youth camping area, and plenty of nice picnic sites with barbecue facilities. There is a Nature Center in Area I across Spring St. (near the Area II entrance) with an excellent nature hike (for a small fee). Finally, one can leave the El Dorado East Regional Park and head across the San Gabriel River to the west portion of the park. This is a non-fee area with a tennis center and baseball diamond just south of Spring St., and an additional picnic area with a small lake south of Wardlow Rd. The entry to both areas is via Studebaker Rd.

TRAILHEAD: From the San Diego Fwy., turn north on Palo Verde Ave. and drive 0.9 mile to Spring St. Turn right (east) and continue about 0.8 mile to free parking along Spring St. just west of the bridge over the San Gabriel River. Other options are to continue over the bridge and park in the Nature Center parking area (turn south at the park entrance) or continue up Spring St., make a U-turn, and return to the Area II park entrance to the north (right). Both the latter options are pay parking.

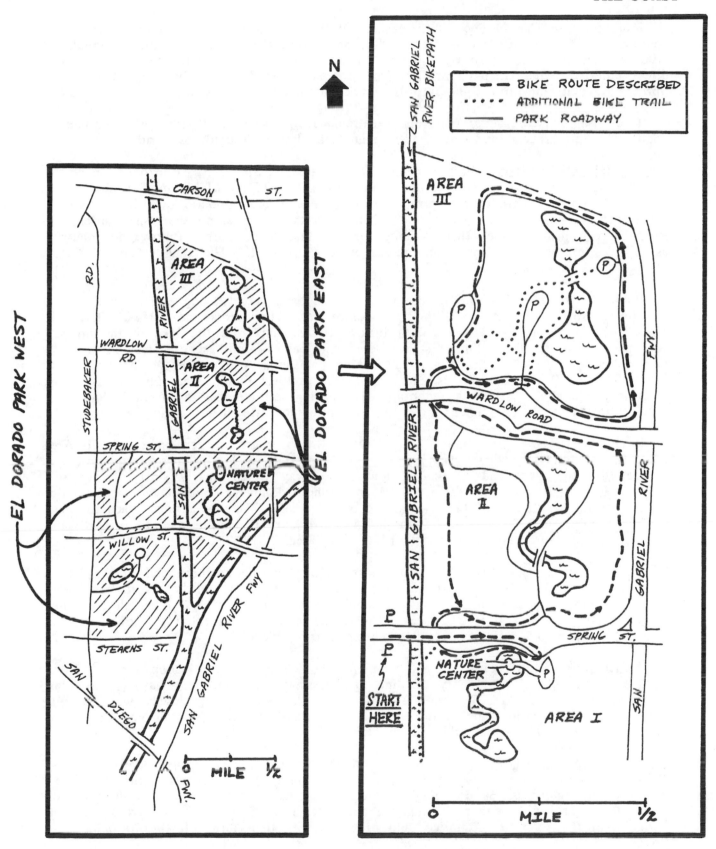

TRIP #16 - EL DORADO REGIONAL PARK

From the San Gabriel Fwy., turn west on Willow St. (Katella Ave. to the east), continue about one mile to Studebaker Rd. and turn right (north). Continue about 0.3 mile to Spring St. and turn right (east). Follow the parking instructions above. For direct entry at Area II (pay parking) from the southbound San Gabriel Fwy., take the Spring St. exit and turn right into the park entrance.

There is plenty of water and many restroom facilities in this park. Bring some good food to barbecue and enjoy great munchies after a "tough" bike ride.

TRIP DESCRIPTION: From the free parking area on Spring St., ride over the bridge and turn right (south) at the Nature Center entrance (0.3). Make another sharp right and continue parallel to Spring St. (but now in the opposite direction) along the Nature Center roadway. Continue 0.2 mile to the fence along the San Gabriel River bike route. Rather than passing through that fence entry, follow the roadway as it turns to the right (north) and passes under Spring St. The road enters Park Area II.

Park Area II. Continue to the right at (0.5) and travel along the bikepath paralleling Spring St. At (0.7) the trail passes the archery area and 0.1 mile later, crosses the park entry roadway and a little outlet stream from the lake to the north. The path turns north a short distance later and passes along several tree-covered grassy knolls. At (1.4) the now west-heading path crosses over the feeder stream between Areas II and III; this is near one of the prettiest picnic areas on the lake. At (1.8) the path again reaches a junction. By heading left (south), the Area II loop (2.3 miles total) can be completed; however, the reference trip heads right.

Park Area III. Cross under the Wardlow Rd. overpass and continue over to Area III. To the left is another access to the San Gabriel River Trail; however, this route proceeds to the right and continues along a roadway which nearly skirts the entire Area III. In 0.5 mile from the Area III entry, the road passes one of the nicer picnic areas near the south end of the lake at the outlet stream. This is a great place to see the birds up close. At 0.6 mile from the Area III entry (2.4), the road turns north and in another 0.1 mile passes the paddle boat rental area.

Next the road bends west (2.9) and passes alongside the northern end of the lake. At (3.2) the roadway passes a firing range (outside the park) and begins to head south along the model glider bluff. Continue south on both roadway and bikepath and close the Area III outside loop at 2.0 miles. Cross back under the Wardlow Rd. overpass and continue another 0.5 mile south to the Area II trip origin.

Additional Sightseeing. This completes the 2.3-mile Area II loop and the 2.0-Area III loop and allows plenty of time to investigate the inner bikeways. Particular points of interest in Area III are the bridge over the isthmus, the lovely wooded area near the Ranger Station, the Billie Boswell Bike Path Memorial marker and the little walkway/bikepath along the edge of the lake below the bridge.

CONNECTING TRIPS: 1) Connection with the San Gabriel River Bike Trail (Trips #20A and #20B) - use access points south of the Spring St. underpass or north of the Wardlow Rd. underpass as described in the trip above; 2) connection with the Coyote Creek Trail (Trip #24) - take the San Gabriel River Bike Trail south and cross the foot bridge over the river at 0.6 mile south of Spring St., then turn left (north) onto Coyote Creek.

Biking   Worldwide

TRIP #17 - SANTA MONICA MOUNTAINS WORKOUT

GENERAL LOCATION: Santa Monica Mountains

LEVEL OF DIFFICULTY: Loop - extremely strenuous
Distance - 41.6 miles (loop)
Elevation gain - 2500 feet total elevation gain;
continuous moderate-to-sheer grades

GENERAL DESCRIPTION: O.K.! SO YOU TRY IT! Sharron was too smart to try this trip. Don got through the Malibu Canyon Rd. segment, turned west onto Mulholland Hwy., and commenced to "puke out" on the initial set of gut-busting upgrades. So we drove the remainder of the trip and concluded that triathlete Sally Bond was right. This journey is an absolute scenic masterpiece! So we wrote up the initial segment and highlighted the remainder of the trip. The idea is to present an excellent trip for the limited group of bikers with the right physical and mental makeup and to identify easier, bikeable segments for the rest of us.

TRAILHEAD: The trailhead has been selected such that the final trip segment is an extended downhill. There are options to start the trip from points closer to Santa Monica, for instance, Malibu or Zuma County Beach.

From the Santa Monica Fwy. terminus at Pacific Coast Highway (Hwy. 1) in Santa Monica, drive west 28 miles and turn right at Mulholland Hwy. (If you pass Yerba Buena Rd., you've gone too far.) Turn right in a short distance into the Leo Carillo State Beach picnic/camping area (shade, water, restrooms, barbecues).

From the Ventura Fwy. in the San Fernando Valley, exit south at Westlake Blvd. Continue on what becomes Decker Rd. (Hwy. 23) to the coast. Turn right (west) and continue 2-1/2 miles to Mulholland Hwy.

For folks going the entire loop, bring at least two filled water bottles. In the mountains, we found water at Tapia County Park, the Rock Store just beyond the Peter Straus Ranch, and at Rocky Oaks Park just beyond Kanan Rd. on Mulholland Hwy. Perform a bicycle maintenance check, including brakes, before starting this mountain tour.

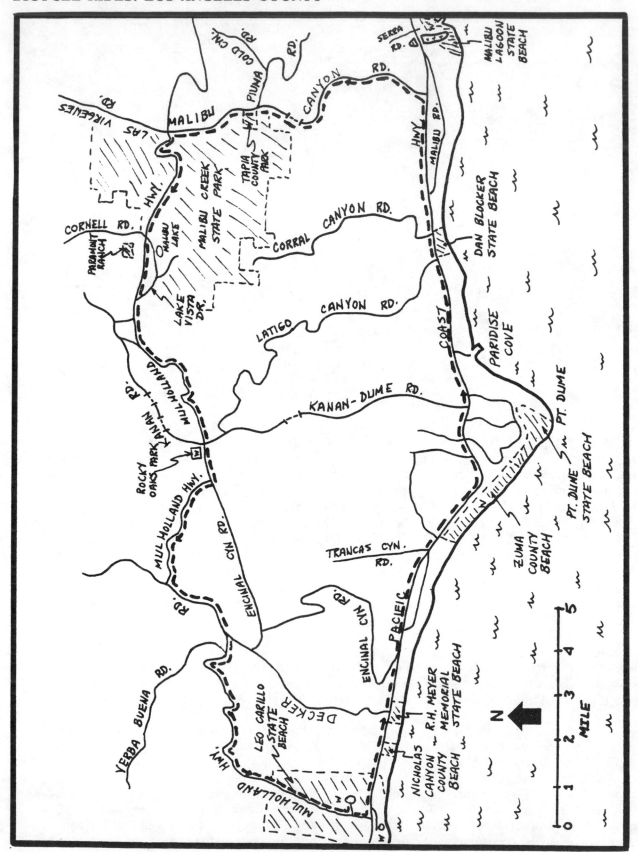

TRIP #17 - SANTA MONICA MOUNTAINS WORKOUT

TRIP DESCRIPTION: **Pacific Coast Highway (Leo Carillo State Beach to Malibu Canyon Rd.).** The trip starts on the Pacific Coast Bicentennial Bike Route. (Note that a more detailed discussion of this segment is found in Trip #18B) Most of this segment and that on Malibu Canyon Rd. is on a highway with a striped shoulder. The Malibu Canyon Rd. stripe disappears in some areas so caution is required. Bike east on Pacific Coast Hwy. (PCH) and follow a half-mile steep upgrade which levels and passes Nicholas Canyon County Beach (1.2). Ride a roller-coaster downgrade-upgrade, passing Decker Rd. at the low point. Pass La Piedre State Beach, Encinal Canyon Rd., El Matador State Beach (3.4) and follow another roller coaster to a flat near Trancas Canyon Rd. (gas station) (5.4).

Continue past the entrance to Zuma County Beach (water, restrooms) (7.0) and follow a long workout upgrade past the Corral Beach turnoff. This grade crests near Heathercliff Rd. (gas station) (7.8). Just beyond, the road heads back downhill past Kanan Dume Rd. (8.1) and stairsteps its way down to Paradise Cove Rd. (9.0). Next is a stairstep upgrade which leads to a flat near Geoffrey's Restaurant (9.9).

Follow the continued steep roller-coaster route past Latigo Canyon Rd. (11.1) and then pedal on the flat to Corral Canyon Rd. (gas station) (11.7). Just beyond is a long, steep upgrade; at the crest is an excellent coastal view back to the north (12.8). Continue past John Tyler Dr. and bike uphill to a crest at Malibu Canyon Rd. (13.9).

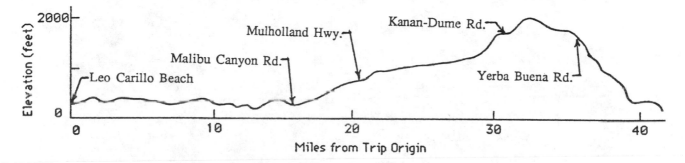

Malibu Canyon Rd. Turn left and follow a mild upgrade past the elegant, well-manicured Pepperdine University Campus. Bike on a flat past Seaver Dr.; there is a fine long-distance view west and south, as well as a nice look down into the Malibu Lagoon. Start a steeper upgrade and pass Harbor Vista Dr. (14.7); the coastal view is even more spectacular here. Follow the winding roadway and in another mile bike a steady, moderate-to-steep upgrade with the Santa Monica Mountains dead ahead.

In 2.6 miles from PCH, the roadway is clearly within the canyon. There is a turnout with a great canyon overlook in this area plus a peek back to the ocean (16.5). (Note: pull completely to the edge of the turnouts or take the chance of becoming a large automobile hood ornament!) Follow the winding downhill which hugs the mountainside; the deep canyon and surrounding mountain views in this area are nothing short of spectacular! At the canyon bottom is Malibu Creek. The road continues winding through the canyon between the towering peaks, then follows a workout upgrade. This grade becomes steep just before cresting near yet another turnout (Don used these turnouts for "research breaks"). Just beyond is the Malibu Canyon Rd. tunnel (17.7). The roadway roller-coasters northward in this area alongside the paralleling canyon. There is a nifty open area canyon view to the north and east at about a mile north of the tunnel.

83

The grade lessens as the route passes Piuma Rd. (18.7) and Tapia County Park (camping, shade, water). The road follows another roller-coaster section of more open canyon and reaches a little valley just beyond (20.0). In 0.3 mile and 6.4 miles from PCH is an entry to Malibu Creek State Park and just beyond is Mulholland Hwy.

Mulholland Hwy., Malibu Canyon Rd. to Cornell Rd. (3.3 miles). The little two-lane country road heads uphill almost immediately, becoming progressively steeper and eventually transitioning into a series of switchbacks. (Don calls this "Pukeout Hill" for obvious reasons.) There is an exceptional view from the summit down into Malibu Creek and Malibu Creek State Park (22.1). Next the road traverses a small valley on a moderate uphill and proceeds to Cornell Rd. (north)/Lake Vista Dr. (south) (23.6).

Cornell Rd. to Kanan Rd. (5.8 miles). The first mile is through rolling hills with a nice view across the paralleling canyon to the left (south). The roadway passes the west end of Lake Vista Dr. (24.7), crosses a small meadow, and reaches Peter Straus Ranch/Lake Enchanto (possible water, restrooms) and Troutdale Dr. (25.6). Next the road stairsteps upward past Sierra Creek Rd. and in a half mile reaches The Rock Store (water, refreshments, motorcyclist haven) (26.4).

Seminole Canyon Overlook

The road continues on mild rolling terrain for a short distance before heading up a murderous two-mile upgrade which crests near the Seminole Canyon Overlook. The panoramic view of the canyon and surrounding mountains is great! While parked along the roadway, Don commented to the biker in the accompanying photo that it must be a tough ride. His slow smile and accompanying response as he pedaled uphill was, "It's all part of the plan." A half mile downhill puts the biker at Kanan Rd. (29.4).

Kanan Rd. to Yerba Buena Rd. (6.2 miles). Continue on Mulholland Hwy. past Rocky Oaks Park (water, shade, restrooms) and follow a workout upgrade in an open and exposed hilly area. The road becomes progressively steeper, passes Encinal Canyon Rd. (30.6), and reaches a summit after about a total mile workout. There are periodic peeks at the Pacific Ocean and some Channel Islands on the upgrade, plus nice views into a valley to the northwest from this summit area.

The road rides the crest with continuous views into the canyons and valleys before reaching Decker Rd. (33.0). The route proceeds left (south) on an extremely windy roadway (5-10 mile-per-hour curves), then enters a light residential valley. In two miles from this intersection, turn sharply right off Hwy. 23 (Decker Rd.) onto the Mulholland Hwy. continuation. Bike a short distance to Yerba Buena Rd. (35.4).

Yerba Buena Rd. to PCH (6.4 miles). The earlier hard work pays off on the predominantly downhill final segment. The winding downhill provides an overlook of the GTE Satellite Tracking Station and in a mile reaches the valley where the station is sited. In two miles from the Yerba Buena Rd. junction, Mulholland Hwy. follows a steep, winding downgrade. The canyon outlet to the coast comes into view in the far distance. After about two miles of exciting downgrade, the road winds through a sparsely populated valley (39.5), passes Camp Bloomfield, and in 0.2 mile, enters the upper reaches of Leo Carillo State Beach (as noted by the roadsign). There is a 1/2-mile upgrade which graduates from moderate to very steep and reaches a crest with a refreshing ocean view (41.4). In another 0.2 mile, the route reaches the park and the end of a grueling and satisfying trip.

CONNECTING TRIPS: You've got to be kidding! 1) Continuation with the PCH ride (Trip #18B) - near the trip origin, turn either east or west on PCH.

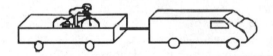

TRIPS #18A-18C - PACIFIC COAST HIGHWAY

The entire tour described follows the Pacific Coast Bicentennial Bike Route. The main part of the trip hugs the coastline, following Pacific Coast Highway (PCH) from Santa Monica to an outlet near Point Mugu. The remaining 4.9 miles follows Navalair Rd. inland, turns west on Hueneme Rd., and follows that road to Bubbling Springs Linear Park. The total 44.7 mile trip, which is mapped below, is a strenuous one-way shot, and very strenuous up and back trip. With an extention into Port Hueneme/Oxnard, the round trip could be turned easily into a "Century" ride.

Trip #18A is relatively flat, but on congested roadway with limited bike room over long stretches. There are, however, some fine coastal views on the route, plus the bonuses of tours through Santa Monica, Topanga Beach, and Malibu. Trip #18B is on roadway with a wide, striped shoulder (Class II bikeway but unmarked) and is the most naturally scenic; it is also one mean roller-coaster ride! This tour visits Malibu, Pt. Dume, and Leo Carillo Beach. Trip #18C, the easiest segment of the tour, is on a comparable roadway. On this trip portion, the biker visits Sycamore Cove, Pt. Mugu, and the agricultural Ventura County countryside.

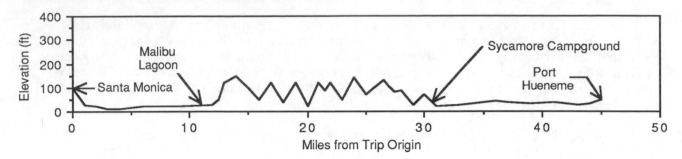

TRIP #18A - PCH: SANTA MONICA TO MALIBU LAGOON

GENERAL LOCATION: Santa Monica, Topanga State Beach, Malibu

LEVEL OF DIFFICULTY: One way - moderate; up and back - moderate
Distance - 10.5 miles (one-way)
Elevation gain - periodic moderate grades

GENERAL DESCRIPTION: An excellent scenic stretch of PCH, this well-trafficked portion of the Pacific Coast Bicentennial Bike Route is short on bike room, but long on outstanding views, landmarks and sight-seeing attractions. Don't bike this one if you are nervous about sharing roadways with high-speed traffic. The relatively flat roadway starts at cozy Palisades Park and, as part of its itinerary, passes near such points of interest as the J. Paul Getty Museum, Will Rogers State Beach, Topanga State Beach, Big Rock, Las Flores Beach, and Malibu Lagoon State Beach. There are also numerous exploratory adventures that can be taken off this 10.5 mile Class X tour.

TRAILHEAD: From the Santa Monica Fwy., exit at 4th St. (the last turnoff before the freeway fuses into PCH). Drive 1-1/4 miles to San Vicente Blvd. and turn left, following this street to its terminus at Ocean Ave. Park on San Vicente Blvd. near Ocean Ave. Do not use the pay parking at Palisades Park unless you plan to return within the five-hour meter limit.

From PCH southbound, turn left at Chautauqua Blvd., then immediately veer right onto Channel Rd. Drive 0.3 mile to its terminus, turn right and proceed across Entrada Dr. to Ocean Ave. Follow this winding uphill 0.3 mile to San Vicente Blvd.

Bring a filled water bottle. There are a couple of public water sources and scattered commercial sources along the way. Bring a second bottle if you want to squirt water at non-yielding car drivers (just kidding!).

TRIP DESCRIPTION: **Santa Monica to Topanga State Beach.** Bike northwest on Ocean Ave. and follow the steep 0.3 mile downgrade, then continue around the hairpin turn to Entrada Dr. Cross this road and turn left at Channel Rd., freewheeling another 0.3 mile to Chautauqua Blvd. Turn right in a short distance and follow beach-hugging PCH below the bluffs of northern Palisades Park (entry from Chautauqua Blvd. at Corona Del Mar). There are views of the jagged coastline to the west and the Palos Verdes Peninsula back to the southeast.

The winding highway continues to hug the Will Rogers State Beach coastline. The biker is forced to ride on varying width shoulder alongside high-speed traffic; this situation continues all the way into Malibu.

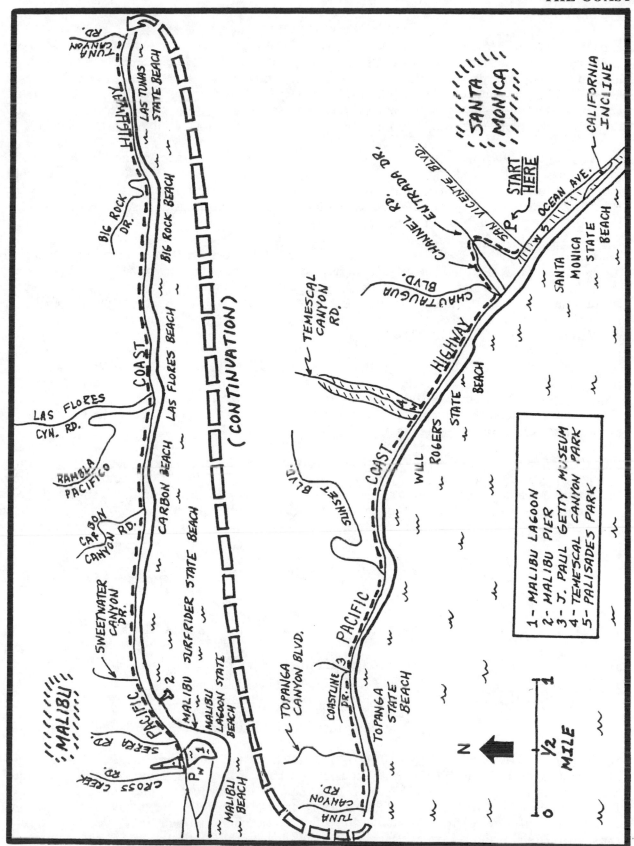

TRIP #18A - SANTA MONICA TO MALIBU LAGOON

The road passes Temescal Canyon Rd. (1.9) (Temescal Canyon Park with its shade and water is to the north), enters the Pacific Palisades area, passes along a mile-long slide area, then reaches Sunset Blvd. and a gas station (2.8). The road continues to hug the coast and passes Coastline Rd. and the entrance to the J. Paul Getty Museum (3.8). Bike through an area with a high density of residences in the nearby palisades and past the oceanside Chart House Restaurant (an old favorite of ours). In a short distance, the road reaches Topanga Canyon Rd. and Topanga Canyon State Beach (4.6).

Topanga Canyon State Beach to Malibu Lagoon State Beach. This coastal tour passes another slide area near Big Rock, crosses Big Rock Rd. (6.0), and reaches the waterfront Moonshadows Bar and Restaurant. Just beyond is Las Flores Canyon Rd. (6.7) and the entry into a light commercial area sporting shops with names like the Screaming Clam, Tini Bikini, and Malibu Divers.

Bike past Rambla Pacifico and a gas station (7.7), then visit a lovely and mixed hillside/seaside residential area just before reaching Carbon Canyon Rd. (8.5). Next is a high-density residential area with frequent stop signs. Inviting "pork-out" stops in this area are the Nantucket Light Restaurant (9.6), Malibu Beach Bar and Grill, and La Salsa Tacos El Carbon Restaurant (complete with a giant sombreroed Mexican caricature on the roof).

Continue through the well-trafficked section of town with limited bike shoulder past the Malibu Inn. In a short distance is Malibu Surfrider State Beach and the Malibu Lagoon Museum. Bike on the bridge over the ocean-side tide pools and land-side Malibu Lagoon. Stop and enjoy the cozy and picturesque lagoon before proceeding to Serra Rd. and Malibu Lagoon State Beach.

<u>**CONNECTING TRIPS**</u>: 1) Continuation of the PCH: Malibu Lagoon to Sycamore Grove tour (Trip #18B) - at the trip terminus, continue west on PCH.; 2) continuation with the Santa Monica Loop (Trip #2) - at the origin, bike northeast on San Vicente Blvd.; 3) connection with the South Bay Bike Trail (Trip #1C) - bike southeast on Ocean Ave. past Colorado Ave. to Seaside Terrace; turn right and follow the beach entry route.

TRIP #18B - PCH: MALIBU LAGOON TO SYCAMORE COVE

<u>**GENERAL LOCATION**</u>:   Malibu, Leo Carillo Beach, Pt. Dume, Sycamore Cove

<u>**LEVEL OF DIFFICULTY**</u>: One way - strenuous; up and back - strenuous
Distance - 20.1 miles (one way)
Elevation gain - continuous moderate-to-steep grades

<u>**GENERAL DESCRIPTION**</u>: This is the roller-coaster portion of the PCH route, rich in hills and also rich in breathtaking coastal scenary. The tour leaves Malibu Lagoon State Beach and visits Malibu, Point Dume, Zuma County Beach, and Leo Carillo State Beach, ending at the Sycamore Cove Campground. The hills are many and varied in challenge, with the entire workout trip being on a wide, striped bike shoulder. A round-trip tour provides what appears to the eye to be two distinctly different trips.

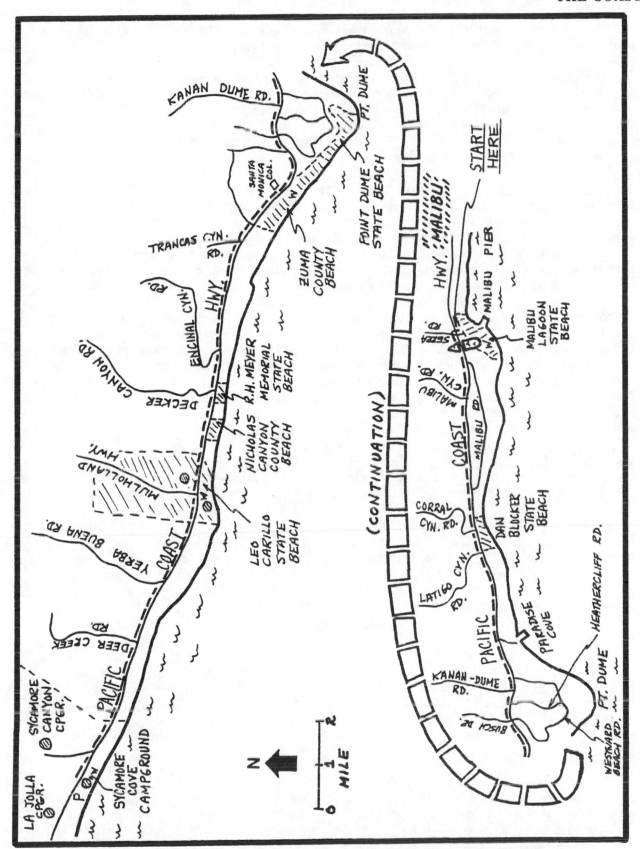

TRIP #18B - PCH: MALIBU LAGOON TO SYCAMORE COVE

Why did God made hills? More knowledgeable bikers than us explain: "so that bikers can stand up and pump, thereby awaking their backsides."

TRAILHEAD. From Santa Monica, drive on PCH about 12 miles from the Santa Monica Fwy. terminus. At Serra Rd., find pay parking at Malibu Lagoon State Beach or park for free on PCH itself per local parking laws.

Bring a filled water bottle. There are several scattered, but reliable, water stops on this challenging trip.

TRIP DESCRIPTION: **Malibu Lagoon to Paradise Cove.** Exit Malibu Lagoon State Beach and bike past Cross Creek Rd. and the Malibu Country Mart. The road moves away from the coast and continues through more open countryside with several beautiful structures built upon the hillside to the north. This refreshing scenery continues past Webb Way and a gas station (0.4), where the road divides and bikers are treated to a very nice and wide biking shoulder. This excellent bikeway continues nearly all the way to Port Hueneme.

Shortly after is a steep upgrade and the beginning of a series of rolling hills for about the next 15 miles. At the top of the grade to the north is lovely Pepperdine University campus and Malibu Canyon Rd. (1.2). The roller coaster route continues and sporadic views open up in about a mile. In another half mile is a particularly steep grade, followed by a nice downhill that returns the biker to near sea level at Dan Blocker State Beach (3.1). The road is next to a long line of steep palisades in this area.

After enjoying the beach scenery, "suck it in" and begin the long and relatively steep upgrade, passing Latigo Canyon Rd. (4.7), and reaching the crest in another 0.3 mile. The road moves inland and roller coasters through more hills, passes posh Geoffry's Restaurant (5.5), and follows a downgrade to the Paradise Cove area.

Paradise Cove to Trancas Beach. In another 1-1/2 miles of stair-step uphill is the first of three southern road accesses to the Point Dume area and just after this is Kanan Dume Rd. (7.6). Note that there are some very scenic coastal coves off these roads which can be reached with a modest hike. However, for the steady pedaler, continue on this hilly road to Heathercliff Rd. (gas station) and enjoy the scenic ocean views which open up in this area. Freewheel downhill past the Corral Beach turnoff (gas station) and return to sea level at Zuma County Beach (water and restrooms) (8.6).

The bike tour generally hugs the coastline from this point until reaching the Pt. Mugu area. The ocean views are constant and spectacular and the ocean breeze is refreshing any time of year. Pedal alongside scenic Zuma County Beach, then pass Trancas Creek and the local marina, which is the home of the Malibu Yacht Club. In a short distance is Trancas Canyon Rd. and the Trancas Beach turnoff (gas station) (9.7).

Trancas Beach to Leo Carillo State Beach. Follow a long overdue flat stretch before returning to the series of rolling hills. There are scattered residences in the area and more great coastal views. Follow the workout upgrade past the El Matador State Beach turnoff (11.7) and continue to Encinal Canyon Rd. In 0.2 mile is the La Piedra State Beach turnoff and a high-density pocket of expensive beach homes.

Follow the refreshing downhill past Decker Canyon Rd. and stare straight ahead at yet another challenging upgrade. Pedal past the Malibu Ride and Country Club, the Nicholas Canyon Country Beach turnoff (13.9), and follow a half-mile runout which returns the biker to sea level and Leo Carillo State Beach; there are water and restrooms at this beach.

Leo Carillo State Beach to Sycamore Cove Campground. The bikeway follows the steep uphill and passes Mulholland Dr. (15.1). At the end of the beach boundary, the route crosses the Los Angeles County/Ventura County Line. Bike on the long upgrade and enjoy the views directly ahead into the Santa Monica Mountains. The road returns quickly to sea level, passes a surfing area, and reaches Yerba Buena Rd. (16.8). Mercifully, the worst (or best?) is over as the path enters a section of lightly rolling hills.

The bike route continues through the hills with steep palisades just to the inland side. There are excellent views in both directions along the coastline in this area. The route passes the coastal access at Deer Creek Rd. (18.4), continues through the gentle hills and reaches the westernmost edge of the extensive Pt. Mugu State Park. In about one-quarter mile is the entry to the Sycamore Canyon Campground and, just beyond, is the access to Sycamore Cove Campground (20.1). There is water and a restroom here, a fine beach, and a ranger station. It is also a scenic rest point before returning west or continuing to Port Hueneme.

CONNECTING TRIPS: 1) Continuation with the PCH: Santa Monica to Malibu Lagoon ride (Trip #18A) - at the trip origin, bike south; 2) continuation with the PCH: Sycamore Cove to Port Hueneme tour (Trip #18C) - from the trip terminus, continue north; 3) connection with the Santa Monica Mountains Workout (Trip #17) - at Malibu Canyon Rd., turn north (inland).

TRIP #18C - PCH: SYCAMORE COVE TO PORT HUENEME

GENERAL LOCATION: Sycamore Cove, Point Mugu, Port Hueneme

LEVEL OF DIFFICULTY: One way - moderate; up and back - moderate
Distance - 13.7 miles (one way)
Elevation gain - periodic moderate grades

GENERAL DESCRIPTION: The northern segment of this tour along PCH starts at Sycamore Cove Campground and cruises the scenic coast with a visit to "picture postcard" Point Mugu. The route passes along the Pacific Missile Test Center, then tours the open farmland of eastern Port Hueneme before reaching the Bubbling Springs Linear Park terminus. The tour passes through varied scenic areas on a mix of roadway classes; the highlight area is certainly the scenic coastal portion from Sycamore Cove Campground to Pt. Mugu. The route is primarily Class II or on a marked roadway with a very wide shoulder.

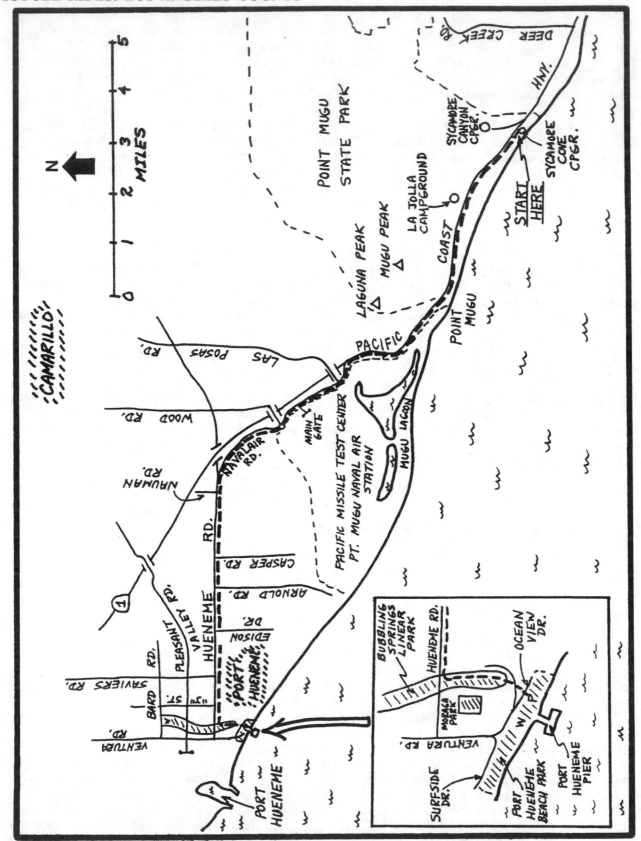

TRIP #18C - PCH: SYCAMORE COVE TO PORT HUENEME

TRAILHEAD: From Santa Monica, drive on PCH about 32 miles from the Santa Monica Fwy. terminus. About a mile beyond the Los Angeles County/Ventura County Line, turn into the Sycamore Cove Campground.

Bring a filled water bottle. For the up and back trip on a hot day, think about a couple of bottles.

TRIP DESCRIPTION: **Sycamore Cove Campground to Point Mugu.** Exit the campground and follow the flat which gives way to a modest steady upgrade. PCH passes a massive natural sand dune built up alongside the cliffs - an impressive sight! Next is a passby of the La Jolla Canyon Campground and a seemingly unending line of recreational vehicles, as well as rock-strewn La Jolla Canyon Beach (1.5).

Just beyond, the route meanders along the land-side cliffs about 20 feet above the ocean and passing several scenic locations. The road climbs a grade and returns to the beach near Point Mugu (3.1). The road has been blasted through the rock in this area; once up to and through the resultant portals, there are fine views in both directions. To the west are the first views into the Oxnard/Port Hueneme area and back to the east is the rugged coastline. Take advantage of the scenic turnouts near Point Mugu.

Point Mugu to Hueneme Road. Pass a rifle range, saltwater marshes of Mugu Lagoon, and pass under the "watchful eye" of the tower-bedecked Mugu Peak (5.1). Pass over Calleguas Creek and continue to the Las Posas Rd. off-ramp (7.0). Exit at this street since PCH becomes an automobile-only road just beyond, cross over PCH, and follow Navalair Rd. alongside the Pacific Missile Test Center/Point Mugu Naval Air Station. Follow the fenced-in road past the main entrance gate, the missile model display (7.5), and Wood Rd. In another mile is Hueneme Rd.

Port Hueneme. Turn left and take a country bike ride through a predominantly agricultural area. The Port Hueneme/Oxnard skyline is directly ahead. This is a Class X road with a wide bike shoulder and limited traffic. Pass Edison Dr. (11.9), Saviers Rd. (12.4) and bike through what becomes a mixed residential/light commercial area. Continue about 3/4 mile, passing "J" St. and turn left into pleasant and shaded Bubbling Springs Linear Park.

This is a fine place to end the trip as there are also water and restrooms at the park. Another option is to continue biking south another mile along the manicured canal to Port Hueneme Beach Park.

CONNECTING TRIPS: 1) Continuation with the PCH route (Trip #18B) - at the trip origin at Sycamore Grove Campground, bike south.

THE RIVERS

San Gabriel River Near the Ocean

TRIPS #19, #20A, #20B - UPPER RIO HONDO/LARIO TRAIL

The Upper Rio Hondo Trail (Trip #19) and Lario Trail (Trips #20A and #20B) can be ridden as a complete 28 mile one-way trip. The general area map is provided below. The entire route is a Class I bike trail. There are four street intersections where the biker may have to leave the bike trail in high water. They are in the southern (third) segment of the trip at Rosecrans Ave., Compton Blvd., Alondra Blvd, and Del Amo Blvd.

The Upper Rio Hondo Trail explores the segment of the Rio Hondo from its current "origin" at the Peck Road Water Conservation Park (reservoir) through a short stretch of some excellent river bottom land, and ends in the Whittier Narrows Recreation Area (Whittier Narrows Dam, Nature Center and Legg Lake). Trip #20A (Upper Lario Trail) starts near the Whittier Narrows Dam and follows the lower Rio Hondo River just beyond its conjunction with the Los Angeles River, ending at Hollydale Park. The lower segment of the Lario Trail (Trip #20B) starts at Hollydale Park and finds its way into Long Beach Harbor and San Pedro Bay.

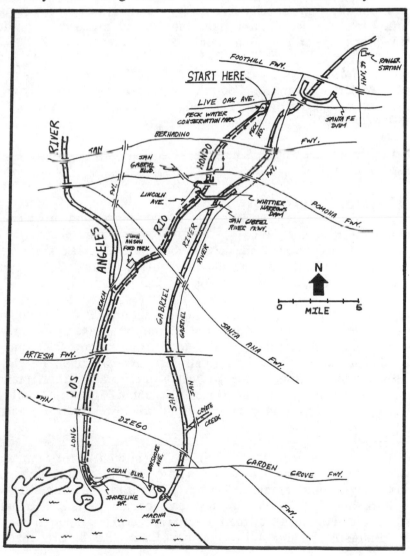

TRIP #19 - UPPER RIO HONDO BIKE TRAIL

GENERAL LOCATION: El Monte-Whittier Narrows

LEVEL OF DIFFICULTY: One way - easy; up and back - moderate
Distance - 8.2 miles (one way)
Elevation gain - 50 ft. (Whittier Narrows Dam)

GENERAL DESCRIPTION: This uppermost section of this river trail follows the Rio Hondo River from its origin to its confluence with the Los Angeles River and ultimately to Long Beach Harbor.   This little known and little used segment travels from the pleasant Peck Road Water Conservation Park (reservoir) through the Whittier Narrows Recreation Area to the top of the Whittier Narrows Dam.   There is fishing in the park at the trip origin.   The lower section of the trip is exceptionally pretty, traveling along natural, forested riverbeds.   The entire route is Class I and also qualifies as a nice, fast workout trip.

TRAILHEAD: From the San Gabriel River Fwy., exit at Lower Azusa Rd. and continue west about 1.2 miles to Peck Rd.   Turn right (north) and proceed 0.6 mile to Rio Hondo Pkwy.   Turn left into the parking area alongside the lake.

From the San Bernardino Fwy., exit north on Peck Rd., travel about 2.3 miles to Rio Hondo Pkwy. and turn left.   From the Foothill Fwy., exit south to Myrtle Ave.   Drive 2.3 miles on Myrtle Ave., which becomes Peck Rd., and turn right at Rio Hondo Pkwy. into a parking lot.

Bring a moderate water supply.   There is water at two strategically placed parks near the middle of the trip.

TRIP DESCRIPTION: **Upper River.**   Near the southern end of the parking area, follow a short direct trail through an opening in the fence and proceed on a Class I bike trail on the east side of the lake.   In 0.4 mile, the route passes the lake spillway where there is a raised diversion trail across the backside (lakeside) of the spillway.   Our route stays on the main trail on the east side of the lake.   Just beyond the spillway, the Upper Rio Hondo Trail actually begins.

The upper segment of the trip is along the concreted Rio Hondo riverbed through a commercial area.   Other then counting the shopping carts in the riverbed, the greatest excitement is the undercrossings at Santa Anita Ave. (0.9) and Lower Azusa Rd. (1.2).   In a short distance, there is a small rest area which sits right next to the El Monte Airport; this is an exciting place to watch the small aircraft takeoff and land (1.4).   The stretch along the airport continues for about 3/4 mile, followed by passage under a railroad tressel (2.2), alongside a raised railway structure, and under Valley Blvd. (2.5).

In a short distance is Pioneer Park (2.6) which stretches for another 0.3 mile along the bikeway.   At the park are water, restrooms, picnic areas, baseball diamonds, tennis courts, and playground areas.   The architecturally-striking El Monte Busway Station and RTD Park and Ride areas are just east of the park.   The path eventually passes under the raised concrete railroad overpass (2.7), a special bus-lane overpass (2.8), and passes alongside quaint little Fletcher Park just before reaching the San Diego Fwy. (3.0).

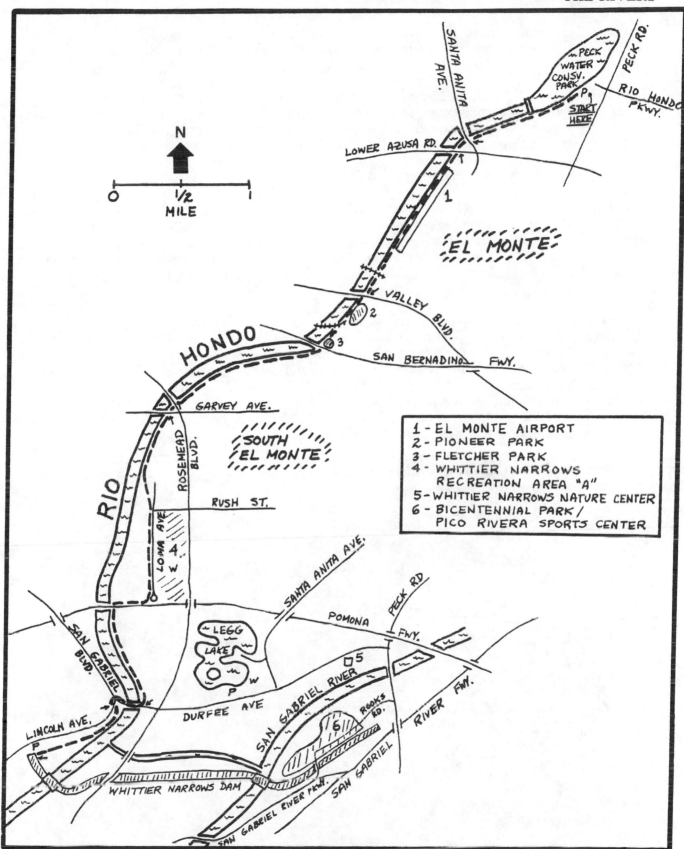

TRIP #19 - UPPER RIO HONDO TRAIL

The next mile passes through an area with some residences to the left and commercial areas across the river. The bikepath meets Rosemead Blvd. (4.1), Garvey Ave. (4.2), and later passes a "cablecar" river crossing apparatus (4.7).

After over four miles of concrete, there is a sudden transition to a natural riverbed just beyond this point (5.0). Near the juncture, there is a short spur to the right that provides a grand overlook of the river transition point. However, our reference trip follows the main trail which heads south and away from the river. In another 0.2 mile, the route reaches the northeast end of the Whittier Narrows Recreation Area "A" at Loma Ave. and Rush St.

Whittier Narrows Recreation Area. Recreation Area "A" is roughly 1/2 mile north-south and 1/4 mile east-west. There are numerous spur trails on bikepaths and on the slow, lightly travelled car roadways in the park. There are also restrooms, water, shade, picnic areas, recreational fields, playgrounds, model airplane flying area, and model car racing area. Our trip is on the west edge of the park on Loma Ave.

At the very south end of Loma Ave. (5.8), pass through the opening in the fence. Continue the route west, parallel to and on the same level as the Pomona Fwy. In another 0.6 mile, the path cuts under the freeway and rejoins the Rio Hondo River. This is natural river bottom with lush trees and other greenery. Further down-river, the growth thickens up and blocks the river from view (6.7). Another half mile or so of this lovely stretch of river gives way to an exit trail which takes the biker up to San Gabriel Blvd. (7.3). A spur trail just before that exit leads to a fine wading and rest area just below the San Gabriel Blvd. bridge.

Whittier Narrows Dam Near Four Corners Trail Intersection

Whittier Narrows Dam. To the east on San Gabriel Blvd. is Legg Lake and the Four Corners Trail Intersection (see Trip #26). Our trip heads west on San Gabriel Blvd. over the river to Lincoln Ave. (7.6). Turn left onto Lincoln Ave. and make an immediate left turn into an asphalt roadway which is blocked to automobiles. The trail follows above and at some distance from the west bank of the Rio Hondo. In this section, there is scrub brush, an oil well pump or two, and low, eroded hills to the west. The trail pulls away from the river at about 0.2 mile from the Lincoln Ave. entrance and comes within close view of that street. Just beyond, there are the first views of the backside of the Whittier Narrows Dam. In another 0.2 mile, the route follows a steep trail up the backside of the dam. In a short distance, the biker is atop the west levee of the Whittier Narrows Dam (8.2).

Stop and enjoy the sweeping views from the dam's crest, including the San Gabriel Mountains, surrounding hills, local communities, and the lush bottomland of the Narrows area back up river. There is a sign noting that this is the origin of the Lario Trail (see Trip #20A). Continue beyond the sign and ride out along the dam for some additional scenery.

CONNECTING TRIPS: 1) Continuation with the Lario Trail (Trip #20A) - continue south from the Whittier Narrows Dam at the terminus of the trip; 2) connection with the Whittier Narrows Recreation Area/Legg Lake Bike Trail (Trip #26) - head east on San Gabriel Blvd. from the bridge over the Rio Hondo and continue 0.9 mile on Durfee Ave. (same street, new name) to the Legg Lake parking lot; 3) connection with the San Gabriel River Trail (Trips #22C and #22D) - head east on San Gabriel Blvd. as above. Once across Rosemead Blvd., follow the Class I bikepath to the right into the Whittier Narrows Wildlife Refuge. Continue on this path past the Four Corners Trail Intersection to the San Gabriel River.

TRIP #20A - LARIO TRAIL: WHITTIER NARROWS DAM TO HOLLYDALE PARK

GENERAL LOCATION: Montebello, Downey, Bell Gardens, Hollydale

LEVEL OF DIFFICULTY: One way - easy; up and back - moderate
Distance - 9.0 miles (one way)
Elevation gain - essentially flat

GENERAL DESCRIPTION: This Class I trip starts from atop the Whittier Narrows Dam, travels southward along the Rio Hondo River past its confluence with the Los Angeles River, and ends at pleasant, little Hollydale Park. The river is not the attraction, but rather the running streams and holding basins alongside the river and the interesting trail diversions that visit this particular territory. This is a particularly interesting trip right after a heavy winter rain! There are several nice parks to visit along the way. Finally, this is a limited-use stretch; it is a good route for bikers looking for a speedy, unobstructed workout.

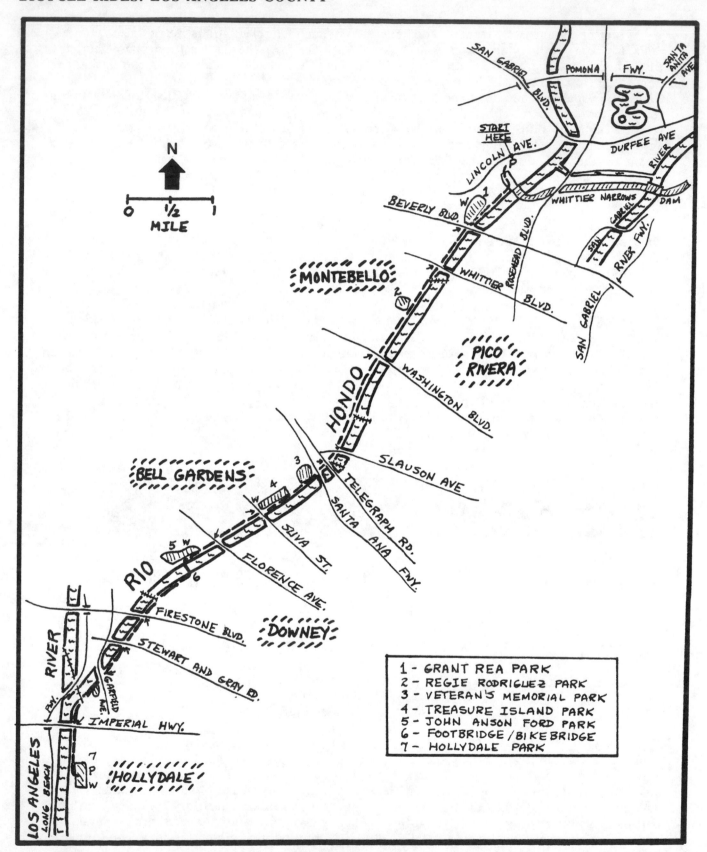

TRIP #20A - LARIO TRAIL: WHITTIER NARROWS DAM - HOLLYDALE PARK

TRAILHEAD: From the Pomona Fwy., exit south at San Gabriel Blvd., drive 0.8 mile to Lincoln Ave., and turn right (south). Proceed 0.8 mile to the parking area at the dam west levee/view site. From the San Gabriel River Fwy., exit west on Beverly Blvd. and continue 1.2 miles to Rosemead Blvd. Turn right (north) and proceed 1.5 mile to San Gabriel Blvd. Turn left and continue 0.3 mile to Lincoln Ave. Turn left again and proceed 0.8 mile to the parking area at the dam viewing site.

The route is exposed, with almost no shade other than underpasses and parks. Bring a moderate water supply and refill at the parks as noted.

TRIP DESCRIPTION: **Whittier Narrows Dam.** Leaving the parking area, lift your bike over the low barrier, and proceed across the Whittier Narrows Dam west levee. At 0.4 miles, follow the paved downhill route which exits the south face of the dam. The path winds downhill and rejoins the Rio Hondo River west levee just beyond the spillway (1.0). The riverbed is solid concrete, as it will remain for the rest of this trip. The more interesting scenery generally is to the right (west) where there are ravines, equestrian trails, and running streams.

Grant Rea Park. In 0.4 mile beyond the spillway, there is a footbridge over the equestrian trails which leads to Grant Rea Park. This small, delightful park has recreation fields, tree cover for shade, a small barnyard zoo (with the common farm animals and then some), and pony-cart rides. Our route continues past the bridge where bikers can see the red barn and barnyard animals from the path. Further south is a footbridge over a ravine which leads to Beverly Blvd. (1.7); the area beyond the ravine is marshy with much greenery.

The Middle Section. Further down the road, the bikeway passes Whittier Blvd. (2.2), a railroad tressel (2.4), and a stagnant marshy area. Just beyond are barnyard and horse stalls in a treed, rural setting. The route passes another footbridge, this one heading to Reggie Rodriguez Park (2.8). In another 0.8 mile, the bikepath crosses Washington Blvd. and passes a series of water holding basins interspersed with equestrian trails. Later the bike route leaves the river, and races downhill through a tunnel under a railroad bridge before returning to the levee (4.3).

Further south, the trail crosses Slauson Ave. (4.6) and then follows another diversion off the levee through a railroad tunnel underpass (5.1). Shortly afterward, the path crosses Telegraph Rd. and the Santa Ana Fwy. Immediately afterward, the bikepath leaves the levee and crosses a little bridge over the marshes, returning to the levee in a short distance (5.3).

In another 0.1 mile, the route passes a footbridge which leads to Veteran's Memorial Park. Next the river route passes alongside long and narrow Treasure Island Park (5.8). There are shade and water with direct access through an open section of fence near the park center or from the formal southern entry (Foster Bridge Rd. to Bluff Rd. north to the park).

John Anson Ford Park and the River Crossing. The route passes Suva St. (5.9) and Florence Ave. (6.2) before reaching John Anson Ford Park (6.4). This park is an excellent rest stop or alternate turnaround point. There is plenty of shade, a small lake, and even a swimming pool! More important, there are restrooms and water.

Just south of the park is a small wooded pedestrian bridge that leads the Lario Trail across the river to the east levee; it is important not to miss this crossing as the west levee path deadends 3/4 mile down the path.

Rio Hondo River to the L. A. River Confluence. On the east levee, the route passes the Rio Hondo Country Club/Golf Course and little Crawford Park (6.5). There are restrooms and water here as well as a playground. The next two miles are through areas surrounded by commercial/industrial facilities with little to offer in the way of scenery. For example, the outdoor "Bandini Planter Mix" factory near Imperial Hwy. is one of the trip "highlights" in this segment! The route passes Firestone Blvd. (6.8), a trans-river cable car (7.1), Southern Ave. (7.2), Garfield Ave. (7.6), a railroad tressel underpass (7.9), and reaches the confluence of the Rio Hondo and Los Angeles Rivers (8.2). Just south of the junction is Imperial Hwy. (8.4).

Hollydale Park. A quarter mile beyond Imperial Hwy. is the north edge of Hollydale Park. This park is a mixture of people-playground and horse-playground. To the north are playgrounds and equestrian show areas which give way to tennis courts and recreation fields to the south (9.0). There is sparse tree cover here, as well as water, providing a chance to rest up for the return trip.

CONNECTING TRIPS: 1) Continuation of the Upper Rio Hondo Bike Trail (Trip #19) - continue the trip north from Whittier Narrows; 2) continuation of the Lario Trail (Trip #20B) - continue south from Hollydale Park; 3) connection with the L.A. River Trail (Trip #21) - cross the L.A. River at Imperial Hwy. Just beyond the bridge on the north side of the street, follow the bike trail sign onto the west levee.

TRIP #20B - LARIO TRAIL: HOLLYDALE PARK
TO LONG BEACH HARBOR

GENERAL LOCATION: South Gate, Paramount, North Long Beach, Long Beach

LEVEL OF DIFFICULTY: One way - easy; up and back - moderate
Distance - 10.9 miles (one way)
Elevation gain - essentially flat

GENERAL DESCRIPTION: This Class I trip starts near the midpoint of the Lario Trail at Hollydale Park and proceeds to the trail's end in Long Beach Harbor. The route passes a couple of pleasant parks on the way south and provides some excellent views near the lower trip segment. These views include the Long Beach city skyline, Long Beach Harbor, Dominguez Hills, and a long-distance view of San Pedro Hill. There are some points in the trip where the bike route dips into the river bottom. If there is much water, the biker may be required to exit the river trail and cross fast-moving roadways, with no nearby pedestrian intersections, if he wishes to continue the trip (Rosecrans Ave., Compton Blvd., Alondra Blvd., and Del Amo Blvd.).

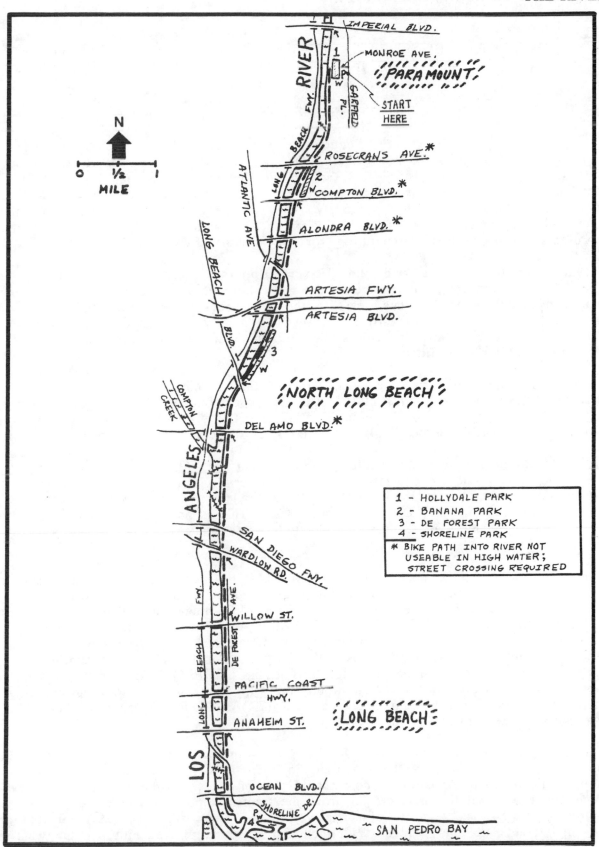

TRIP #20B - LARIO TRAIL: HOLLYDALE PARK TO LONG BEACH HARBOR

BICYCLE RIDES: LOS ANGELES COUNTY

TRAILHEAD: From the Long Beach Fwy., exit east on Imperial Hwy. and continue 0.5 mile to Garfield Place (Ruchti Rd. to the north). Turn right and drive 0.6 mile to Monroe Ave. Turn right (west) and continue to the parking lot at Hollydale Park.

Bring a moderate water supply or fill up at the park. Note that there is no near-trail water supply for the last 7.0 miles before reaching the harbor.

TRIP DESCRIPTION: **North Segment.** At the south end of the park, there is an asphalt entry path up to the Lario Trail. Once up on the Los Angeles River east levee, head south past a horse pasture (0.3) and an old blocked off railroad bridge (0.7); there is a short bike-walking segment nearby. The path continues through a commercial/industrial area with a "lovely" view of the Long Beach Fwy. across the river and a concrete riverbed to boot. Next there is a torn out bridge which probably represents construction in preparation for the Century Fwy. (1.1).

The Middle Segment and the "River Dippers." The tour passes Rosecrans Ave. In low water, take the marked bike route into the riverbed and in high water, choose between options: 1) head east to the next pedestrian crossing and return via the sidewalk; or 2) cross the street directly with a very cautious eye for fast-moving traffic. Do not cross directly with small children or if you are short on either mobility or biking confidence!

Next is a long, thin park that has various athletic courts, playgrounds, play areas, and water (near the south end) (1.4). This is "world famous" Banana Park which runs between Rosecrans Ave. and Compton Blvd. (1.9). The bikepath at Compton Blvd. and Alondra Blvd. which follows (2.4) are also "river dippers" like Rosecrans Ave.

The route passes by horse stables and a training area (2.7), crosses Atlantic Ave. (2.9), and passes another equestrian area. In succession, the bikeway crosses the Artesia Fwy. (3.2), Artesia Blvd. (3.4), passes a "trailer city," and meets up with the ultimate thin strip of park, De Forest Park (3.7). This is another nice rest spot with water (the last water until Long Beach). Both water and restrooms are at the south end of the park.

Beyond the park, the path parallels a marsh for the next 2-1/2 miles; stop and look for awhile, as there are some interesting plants and other wildlife. Shortly afterward, the bikepath crosses Long Beach Blvd. (4.6); there is a nice view of Dominguez Hills to the right (west). Next is Del Amo Blvd., another "river dipper" (5.5). In 0.3 mile is the river confluence with Compton Creek. The route proceeds under a railroad crossing (6.0), passes the Virginia Country Club and continues alongside a lovely residential area in the hills to the east (6.4). Next is the San Diego Fwy. (6.9) and Wardlow Rd. (7.2), where the trip reenters residential surroundings. There is a passenger cable car over the river (7.4) and another group of horse corrals and training area (7.8).

Southern Segment and the "Real" Los Angeles River. Finally comes the trip juncture where the riverbottom transitions from "C-for concrete, to N-for natural" (thank goodness!). The most scenic part of the trip follows. There is year-round water and wildlife not too far from the transition point. The route passes Willow Ave. (8.4) and Pacific Coast Highway (9.1). There are views of the harbor area and the Gerald Desmond Bridge. Within another 0.6 mile at Anaheim St., the waterway transitions into a deep channel that reminds one of a "real" river.

At Seventh St., there is an excellent view of the Long Beach city skyline and Long Beach Harbor (10.1). In 0.6 mile, the bikepath reaches Ocean Blvd. There are ski-boaters and water-skiers everywhere. In a short distance the Lario Trail reaches a gated area with a sign marking the trail end (10.9). There is a nice lookout into the Queen's Way Bridge and the Long Beach Harbor area from this point.

<u>CONNECTING TRIPS</u>: 1) Continuation with the upper Lario Trail segment (Trip #20A) - continue north from the trip origin at Hollydale Park; 2) continuation with the Long Beach Shoreline Park tour (Trip #14) - continue south through the parking lot at the Lario Trail terminus and steer toward Queen's Way Landing (Catalina Boat Terminal); 3) connection with the Long Beach Harbor:Southeast Basin Trip (Queen Mary, Harbor Scenic Dr.) (Trip #11) - hand carry your bike up the steps at the northwest end of the Queen's Way Bridge and continue across. Follow the road signs.

TRIP #21 - LOS ANGELES RIVER TRAIL

<u>GENERAL LOCATION</u>:   Southgate, Cudahy, Bell

<u>LEVEL OF DIFFICULTY</u>:   One way - easy; up and back - easy
Distance - 5.6 miles (one way)
Elevation gain - essentially flat

<u>GENERAL DESCRIPTION</u>: This is a short Class I trip along the Los Angeles River starting just south of its confluence with the Rio Hondo. There is little scenery and broken glass at spots along the bikeway. This may be an excellent trip someday if the route is ever extended northward. However, for now, it is a segment for bikers who want to "see it all" or who want to build up an appreciation for other bike routes.

<u>TRAILHEAD</u>: From the Long Beach Fwy., exit west on Imperial Hwy. Turn left (south) at Duncan Ave. and find parking subject to the local laws.

Bring a light water supply for this short venture. No public supply was found.

<u>TRIP DESCRIPTION</u>: Bike to Imperial Hwy, cross that roadway and continue right (east) on the north sidewalk over the Long Beach Fwy. Carefully cross the freeway entrance ramp. Turn left (north) at the bike trail sign that appears just before reaching the bridge over the L.A. River (0.3).

In a short distance, the path passes a viewing point of the river confluence, heads under the Long Beach Fwy. (0.6), and then under a railroad crossing. In further succession, the route passes Firestone Blvd. (1.7), a second railroad crossing, Clara St. (2.7), and Florence Ave. (3.2). Northbound, the trail passes under a railroad tressel, Gage Ave. (3.8), crosses Slauson Ave., and veers northwest before reaching Atlantic Ave. and the trip terminus (5.6).

In the 3-1/2 mile river stretch, there is a continuous line of industrial plants, commercial businesses, and mini-junk yards. The one breath of fresh air is just south of Clara St. at Cudahy Neighborhood Park.

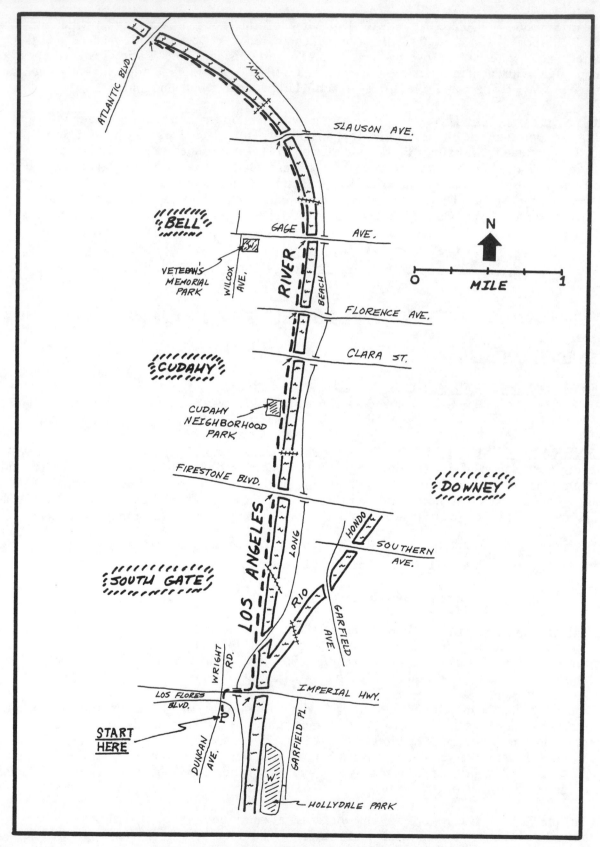

TRIP #21 - LOS ANGELES RIVER TRAIL

CONNECTING TRIPS: Connection with the Lario Trail (Trip #20) - at the trip origin, bike across the Imperial Hwy. bridge over the L.A. River (stay on north sidewalk).

TRIPS #22A-#22E -SAN GABRIEL RIVER TRAIL

The San Gabriel River Trail is probably the premier single river trail in this book. The route captures Southern California from the sea through the inland valley to the mountains, all in one continuous 38 mile shot. Taken in the winter after a cold storm, this trip is one of the best in every sense. The general area map is provided below.

The first segment (#22A) explores the river outlet near Seal Beach, a wildlife area to the north, and ends at super El Dorado Park. The connection segment (#22B) visits no less than five parks and finishes at Wilderness Park in Downey. The next northerly segment (#22C) leaves Wilderness Park, travels alongside some fine San Gabriel river bottom, and ends at one of the tour highpoints, the Whittier Narrows Recreation Area. Trip #22D starts at that fabulous recreation area and ends at another, the Santa Fe Dam Recreation Area. The most northerly segment (#22E) leaves from that dam and ends in the foothills at the entrance to San Gabriel Canyon.

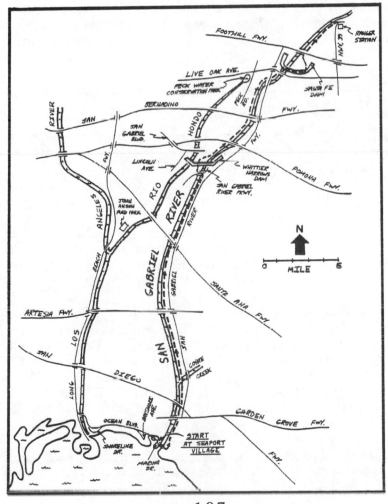

TRIP #22A - SAN GABRIEL RIVER: SEAL BEACH TO EL DORADO PARK

GENERAL LOCATION: Seal Beach - Long Beach

LEVEL OF DIFFICULTY: One way - easy; up and back - easy
Distance - 5.6 miles (one way)
Elevation gain - essentially flat

GENERAL DESCRIPTION: This is the starting segment of one of the most varied and interesting trips in this book, the San Gabriel River Trail. This is a completely Class I bike route that starts at the scenic lower section of the San Gabriel River near the the Long Beach Marina and winds up at classic El Dorado Park. The early part of the trip provides a look at "recreation city" with water, boats, water skiers, and jet skiers. The trip transitions into a nature area that is rich in wildlife and ends in a park that is so inviting that it could serve as a separate family excursion.

TRAILHEAD: Free public parking is available at the Long Beach Marina along Marina Dr. in Naples or along First St. in Seal Beach. From Pacific Coast Highway (PCH) in Seal Beach, turn west on Marina Dr. (2-3 blocks from Main Street in Seal Beach) and continue roughly 0.5 mile to First St. In another 1/4 mile, cross the San Gabriel River and continue a short distance into the marina near Seaport Village for parking. The trailhead is at Marina Dr. at the east end of the bridge over the San Gabriel River.

Only a light water supply is needed for this short trip. There are public water sources at the trip origin and terminus.

TRIP DESCRIPTION: **The Scenic Lower River Segment.** The first part of the trip provides views of boaters, water skiers, and an interestingly-developed shoreline. The natural river basin then passes PCH (0.4), the Westminster Ave. access, and the Haynes Steam Plant (electricity generation). At (2.2), a small alternate Class I bikepath leads off to the east along a 1.2-mile shaded route to Seal Beach Blvd. In this stretch of the river, up to the concrete portion (3.5), one has views of the large bird population that includes pelicans, egrets, and the ever-present seagulls. The trip passes under the Garden Grove Fwy. (2.3) and San Diego Fwy. (3.5). In this part of the bikepath are many "freeway orchards" -- those freeway-locked areas under the power poles filled with containerized plants.

The River Crossing and El Dorado Park. In 0.4 mile, the trip crosses a signed bikeway/walkway bridge across the river. Do not miss the bridge unless you've decided to change plans and see Coyote Creek (Trip #24). Once across the bridge, there are views across the river to the El Dorado Golf Course and El Dorado Park West. At 0.7 mile from the bridge crossing, the route reaches Willow St. and skirts the edge of the Nature Study Area which is the south end of El Dorado Park East (5.0). Shortly afterward, the bikepath reaches Spring St. and the entry to Areas I and II of the park (5.6).

There is a myriad of bikepath options just within the park. This portion of the trip is worth a good exploration effort in itself.

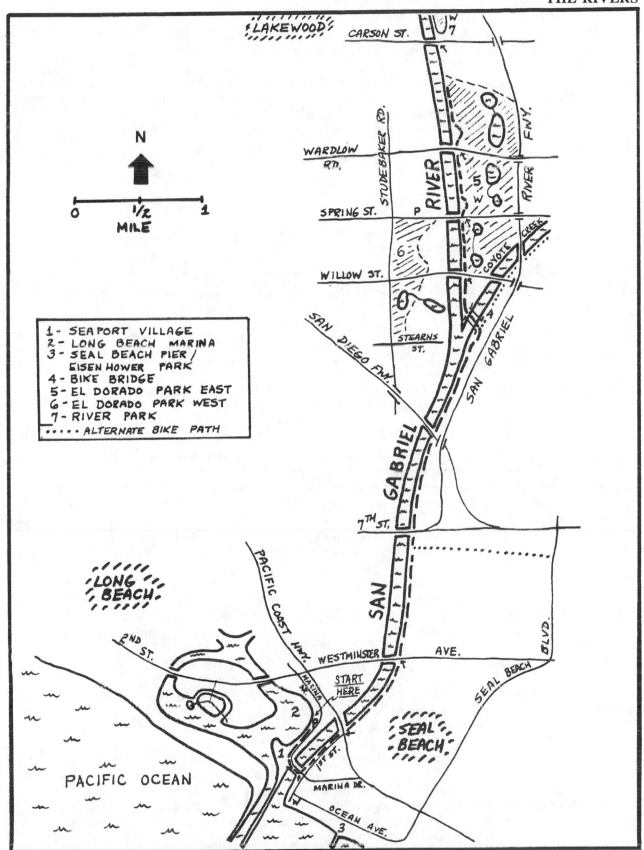

1- SEAPORT VILLAGE
2- LONG BEACH MARINA
3- SEAL BEACH PIER / EISENHOWER PARK
4- BIKE BRIDGE
5- EL DORADO PARK EAST
6- EL DORADO PARK WEST
7- RIVER PARK
•••• ALTERNATE BIKE PATH

TRIP #22A - SAN GABRIEL RIVER: SEAL BEACH TO EL DORADO PARK

CONNECTING TRIPS: 1) Connection with the San Gabriel River Trail (Trip #22B) - continue north beyond El Dorado Park toward Wilderness Park; 2) connection with the El Dorado Park tour (Trip #16) - cruise through the park at the trip terminus; 3) connection with the Coyote Creek Trail (Trip #24) - at the eastern end of the bike bridge across the San Gabriel River, stay on the eastern river bank; 4) connection with the Belmont Shores/Naples Tour (Trip #15) - from the origin, bike north on Marina Dr. to Second St. Turn left (west) and continue over the bridge to Naples Island.

TRIP #22B - SAN GABRIEL RIVER: EL DORADO PARK
TO WILDERNESS PARK

GENERAL LOCATION: Long Beach, Lakewood, Cerritos, Norwalk, Downey

LEVEL OF DIFFICULTY: One way - easy; up and back - moderate
Distance - 9.7 miles (one way)
Elevation gain - essentially flat

GENERAL DESCRIPTION: This is a segment of the Class I San Gabriel River Trail that has direct access to five major parks. In particular, this trip should not be completed without a tour of El Dorado Park. In addition, River Park provides a pleasant diversion from the river route, and Wilderness Park is a fine rest stop with a small pond/lagoon to dip the toes into before returning to the trip origin. There are also horse corrals and equestrian trails alongside the bike route in some sections. This is a fine workout section as the bike and foot traffic is very light.

TRAILHEAD: From the San Diego Fwy., turn north on Palo Verde Ave. and drive 0.9 mile to Spring St. Turn right (east) and continue about 0.8 mile to free parking along Spring St., just west of the bridge over the San Gabriel River. Other options are to continue over the bridge and park in the Nature Center parking area (turn south at the park entrance), or to continue up Spring St., make a U-turn and return to the Area II park entrance to the north (right). The latter two options are pay parking.

From the San Gabriel Fwy., turn west on Willow St. (Katella Ave. in Orange County), continue about one mile to Studebaker Rd. and turn right (north). Continue 0.3 mile to Spring St. and turn right. Follow the parking instructions above. For direct entry at Area II (pay parking) from the southbound freeway, exit at Spring St. and turn right at the park entrance.

Bring a light water supply. There is plenty of water and many restroom facilities at the parks along the way. El Dorado Park is a particular delight! Bring some barbecue food and enjoy the munchies at the park after a "tough" bike ride.

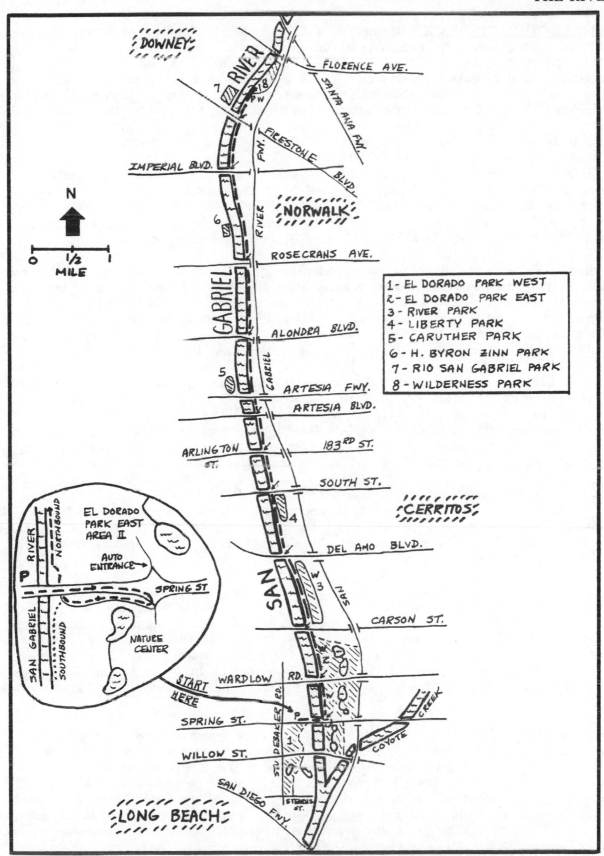

TRIP DESCRIPTION: El Dorado Park. From the parking area on Spring St., ride over the bridge and turn right (south) at the Nature Center entrance. Make another sharp right and continue parallel to Spring St. (but in the opposite direction) along the Nature Center roadway. Continue 0.2 mile to the fence along the San Gabriel River Bike Route. Rather than passing through the fence entry, follow the roadway as it turns to the right and passes under Spring St. The road enters Park Area II.

Stay to the left rather than bike into El Dorado Park. Pass through the fence and head right (north) along the San Gabriel River Trail (0.6). The first part of the trip parallels Park Area II. The path leaves the river again and follows the roadway under Wardlow Rd. (1.1). Again, stay to the left and pass through a fence which returns the biker to the river trail (the other option is to bike through Park Area III and rejoin the trail 0.5 mile later). The path continues alongside a stand of trees and passes the end of Park Area III (1.6) near the weapons firing range.

River Park. The route passes a pedestrian bridge which crosses over to De Mille Junior High School and then passes Carson St. (2.0). For the next 0.7 mile, the biker cruises alongside fun River Park. The park boasts tree cover, horse stalls and corrals, horse trails, a little footbridge leading to a connecting alternate bike trail (which reconnects near Del Amo Blvd.), baseball diamonds, and water (near the baseball fields). The shady park area ends near Del Amo Blvd. (3.0).

The Middle Trip Section. For the next half mile, the trip highlight is the clever (and in some cases, not so clever) graffiti on the concrete river walls. In 0.8 mile, the route reaches little Liberty Park, which is effectively a grassy rest area. Just beyond the park is South St. (3.8), followed by a passage below 183rd St. through a narrow tunnel (4.5). (Reduce speed and keep an eye "peeled" for oncoming bikers.) The route then passes more horse stalls.

The path dips down into the riverbed to cross under Artesia Blvd. (4.9). If the biker misses the marked route, there is an option to walk (crouch) the bike under the roadway. There is a short section where the bikes must be walked across a railroad crossing, followed by passage under the Artesia Fwy. (5.3). The first of many river spillways is near this junction.

The trail passes the Cerritos Ironwood Golf Course; nearby is the pedestrian bridge across the river that leads to Caruther's Park (5.6). However, the reference path stays on the east levee and enters a several mile pleasant residential stretch beyond Alondra Blvd. where there are horses in many of the backyards (we even spotted a llama). The route passes Rosecrans Ave. (7.0), another walk bridge over the river, and a new bridge that is part of the Century Fwy. (7.8). In 0.3 mile, the path reaches Imperial Hwy. and later dips down nearer the river, passing below a railroad tressel (8.7).

Wilderness Park. At (9.0), the bike trail passes Firestone Blvd. In a short distance, the route reaches the transition to a natural river bottom after 11 solid miles of concrete. There is Rio San Gabriel Park across the river and a small spillway. There is some excellent river bottomland north of this area (see Trips #22C and #22D). In about 0.7 mile, the trip reaches a refreshing terminus at Wilderness Park. This is a half-mile strip of park that offers water, restrooms and shade just for starters. There are also sports and recreation areas, playgrounds, a small pond, and a lovely decorative water fountain.

CONNECTING TRIPS: 1) Continuation with the San Gabriel River Trail south to Seal Beach (Trip #22A) from the trip origin, or north to the Whittier Narrows (Trip #22C) from the trip terminus; 2) continuation with the El Dorado Park tour (Trip #16) at the trip origin.

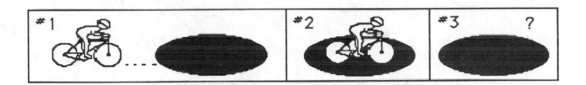

TRIP #22C - SAN GABRIEL RIVER:
WILDERNESS PARK TO LEGG LAKE

GENERAL LOCATION: Downey, Santa Fe Springs, Whittier, Pico Rivera

LEVEL OF DIFFICULTY: One way - easy; up and back - moderate
Distance - 7.7 miles (one way)
Elevation gain - 50 feet (Whittier Narrows Dam)

GENERAL DESCRIPTION: This is a pleasant segment of the San Gabriel River Trail that starts at Wilderness Park, visits Santa Fe Springs Park, and ends at the trip highlight in the Whittier Narrows Recreation Area. A short diversion at Whittier Blvd. also leads to Pio Pico State Historical Park. The Whittier Narrows area sports a ride on the dam, a visit to a wildlife refuge area, and a trip at the terminus to relaxing Legg Lake. This is one of the few river segments that is predominantly natural river bottom and there are some lush areas that beckon for rest stops. This is 99% Class I trail (one street crossing) with light bike traffic south of the Whittier Narrows Dam.

TRAILHEAD: From the San Gabriel River Fwy., exit west on Florence Ave. A short distance west of the freeway, turn left (south) on Little Lake Rd. This roadway also leads back onto the southbound freeway; therefore, in a few hundred feet, turn right onto Little Lake Rd. proper. Continue on this roadway to the free parking area at Wilderness Park. From the Santa Ana Fwy., exit west on Florence Ave. Pass under the San Gabriel Fwy., and follow the directions above.

Bring a moderate water supply. There is no enroute water supply between Santa Fe Springs Park and the Whittier Narrows Recreation Area. (Water sources near the recreation area are at Legg Lake and the Nature Center).

TRIP DESCRIPTION: **Wilderness Park to Santa Fe Springs Park.** From the south end of the parking lot, skirt the south edge of Wilderness Park and follow the path to the river entry. Turn right (north) and continue past Florence Ave. (0.2) and the first of many spillways 0.2 mile further. There are some trees and a great deal of brush along the path, and the riverbed is built up into holding basins. At (0.7), the tour reaches Santa Fe Springs Park, where there are play areas, shade, recreation fields, and restrooms. Fill up with water here if you are running low.

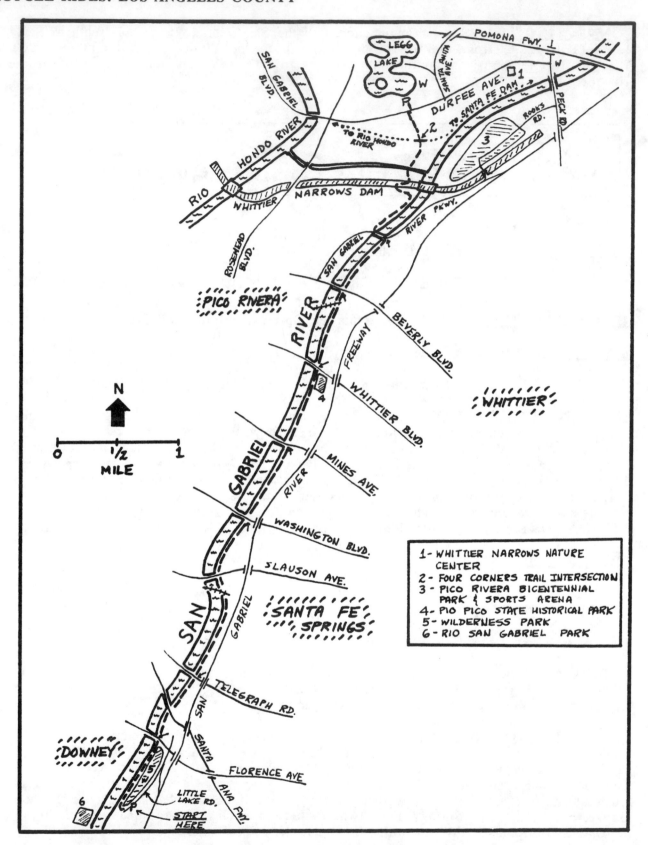

TRIP #22C - SAN GABRIEL RIVER: WILDERNESS PARK TO LEGG LAKE

The Railroad Route and Pio Pico Historical Park. About 0.4 mile from the park, the route crosses Telegraph Rd. At (1.4) the bikeway passes the highest (about six feet) spillway on this segment of the river. In this area, there is a stand of eucalyptus trees and a collection of horse stalls tucked between the river and the San Gabriel Fwy. At (2.1), the route passes under a railroad tressel. Soon after another railroad track comes in from the east and parallels the bike route for several miles. There is a high liklihood of having a train for company on this stretch.

In a short distance the route passes under another railroad tressel which, in turn, lies below the highly-elevated Slauson Ave. overpass (2.3). The riverbed and greenery in the riverbed continue, while there is brush and railroad tracks to the right. At (3.0) is Washington Blvd. and the beginning of a long, exposed stretch of bikeway. At (4.7) the bikepath meets Whittier Blvd.; it is a 0.2-mile diversion to the right (east) to visit Pio Pico Historical Park.

Our route trucks onward and reaches a point where the riverbed begins developing into a mini-forest. This continues up to the Whittier Narrows and beyond and is one of the loveliest stretches of the river. At (5.3), the path heads under another railroad tressel; the paralleling railroad tracks fuse with that track and the merged track leaves the river heading east. In another 0.2 mile is Beverly Blvd. Further north is a spillway with a large enough collecting basin to support a flock of young water frolickers. There is also a view into Rose Hills at this point.

Whittier Narrows Dam. The trip reaches a junction where the trail changes from asphalt to dirt at San Gabriel River Pkwy. (6.1). The dam is viewable at this point. Continue ahead if you have a wide tire bike and a desire to see Pico Rivera Bicentennial Park and Sports Area. Otherwise, return to the roadway and cross the river to the west side. This is the "advertised" route to the Whittier Narrows Dam. Continue north and observe the lush tree-filled river bottom. The route passes the Pico Rivera Golf Course (6.7) and makes a hard left at the dam base. From this point, there is a short, steep path up to the top of the dam (6.9). Stop and take in some of the excellent sights viewable from this area.

Whittier Narrows Nature Center. Continue down the meandering concrete bikeway on the backside of the dam. The path crosses a water run-off channel and reaches the marked Four Corners Trail Intersection (7.2).

Continue straight ahead and pedal another 0.4 mile through the lush bottomlands to Durfee Ave. Turn right (east) and continue a few hundred feet to the Legg Lake parking area within the Whittier Narrows Recreation Area (7.7).

CONNECTING TRIPS: 1) Continuation with the San Gabriel River Trail south to El Dorado Park (Trip #22D) - from the trip origin, bike south; 2) continuation with the San Gabriel River Trail north to Santa Fe Dam (Trip #22D) - from the Four Corners Trail Intersection, turn right (east) at the junction; 3) connection/continuation with the Whittier Narrows/Legg Lake Trail (Trip #26) - from Legg Lake, return to the Four Corners Trail Intersection and turn right (west).

TRIP #22D - SAN GABRIEL RIVER:
LEGG LAKE TO SANTA FE DAM

GENERAL LOCATION: Whittier Narrows, El Monte, Baldwin Park, Irwindale

LEVEL OF DIFFICULTY: One way - easy; up and back - moderate
Distance - 11.4 miles (one way)
Elevation gain - 50 feet (Santa Fe Dam)

GENERAL DESCRIPTION: This is one of our favorite segments of the river trips. The San Gabriel River in the Whittier Narrows region is river stomping at its best; there are trees, thickets, clear running water and readily visible wildlife in and around the river. The Whittier Narrows Recreation Area offers a wildlife sanctuary, Legg Lake, vista points from the top of the dam, and a diversion trip to the Pico Rivera Bicentennial Park and Sports Area. The Santa Fe Dam Recreation Area offers an expansive, pleasant picnic and recreation area at the edge of the lake, as well as superb lookout points from the top of the dam. Set aside a few hours and fully explore these territories. The best time to take this trip is within several days of a cold winter storm when the snow level in the nearby mountains is low. The route is nearly 100% Class I.

TRAILHEAD: From the Pomona Fwy., exit at Rosemead Blvd. south, travel about 0.8 mile to San Gabriel Blvd./Durfee Blvd. and turn left. Continue on Durfee Ave. 0.6 mile and turn left into the pay parking area at Legg Lake. Find a tree under which to park your car. Bring four quarters for the parking area fee.

Bring a moderate water supply. There are rest and water stops directly on the route and at the Santa Fe Recreation Area terminus.

TRIP DESCRIPTION: **Whittier Narrows Recreation Area.** Leave the parking area and cross Durfee Ave. a few hundred feet west of the parking area. Pass through the signed gate and pedal down a small asphalt road through an area surrounded by bushes, plants, trees, and brush. In a short distance is a junction; to the left through a sometimes-locked gate is the Whittier Narrows Nature Center. However, our route proceeds to the right and meets the Four Corners Trail Intersection (0.5). There is a nice view into the backside of the Whittier Narrows Dam from this area.

Turn left (east) and follow the path as it turns northward and rejoins the San Gabriel River (0.7). There are permanent horsetrails to the left (west) and also "find-your-way" paths in the lush river bed; both are well used by horseriders, the latter accompaning our path for the next couple of miles. In this area, there are excellent views of Rose Hills to the east.

The Unofficial Recreation Area/San Jose Creek Confluence. The route passes the first of many spillways that stair-step their way up the river (1.4). Small children slide down the rounded portion of the spillway into a holding basin below and even a swimming dog might be seen. In another 0.4 mile is Peck Rd. and a second spillway with a large pool backed up behind it. (There are gas stations and restaurants not too far from the river at this exit.)

116

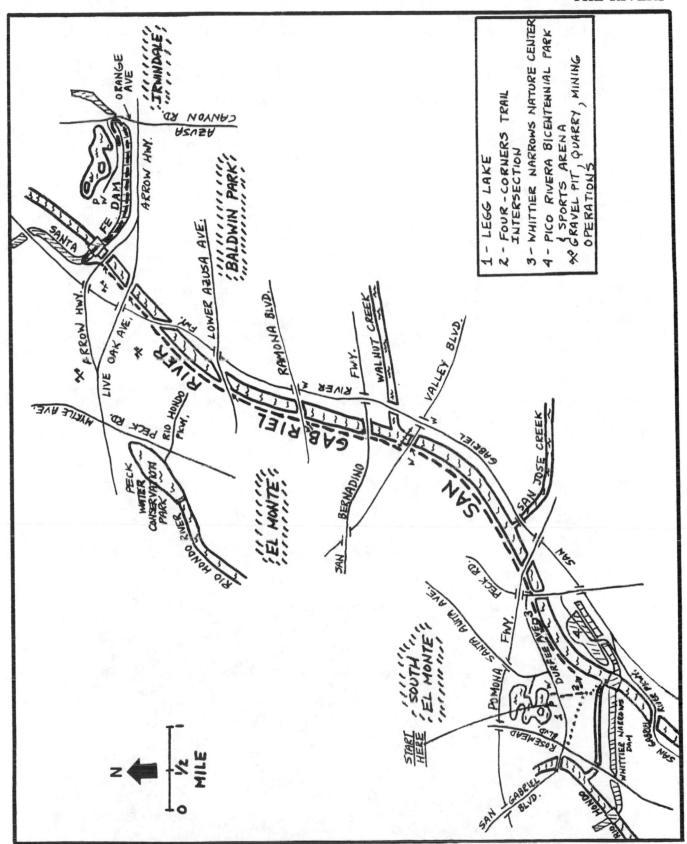

TRIP #22D - SAN GABRIEL RIVER: LEGG LAKE TO SANTA FE DAM

The trail passes the Pomona Fwy. (2.0) and then the third spillway, which has some fishermen and a few swimmers using the upstream water pool. In 0.3 mile is the confluence with San Jose Creek and one of the most used unofficial recreation spots on the river. There are inner-tube riders, swimmers, fishermen, horses with riders crossing the river, and even some off-road bicycling.

The Middle Segment. At (2.7) is a small rodeo ring where bikers have a free chance to watch the trainers work with horses or, with luck, to watch a mini-rodeo. Just beyond is one of the highest spillways on the river (about ten feet) with a holding basin stretched across the river on the downstream side. The route continues alongside residential areas, passes Mountain View High Athletic Field (3.9) and reaches Valley Blvd. (4.1). There is a small bike rest stop here with a simple pipe water fountain. On a clear day, there is a striking view into the San Gabriel Mountains from this point.

The bikepath travels under a railroad bridge and later meets the Walnut Creek junction (4.3). From this point north, the water level drops significantly and the river bed is much less interesting. At this junction, to the left (west) of the trail, is a corral that holds brahma bulls and a buffalo. Continuing onward, the bikeway passes the San Bernardino Fwy. (4.7) and then meets another biker rest area at Ramona Blvd. (5.6).

The Gravel Pits. At (6.5), the route passes the first of several large gravel dredging operations (to the right). In 0.2 mile, the trip passes Lower Azusa Rd. There is a large, open, water-filled gravel pit to the left (west) (5.9), followed by a "granddaddy" gravel pit across the river to the right (6.4). There are several highly visible above-ground mining operations in this area.

Atop Santa Fe Dam

118

Santa Fe Dam and Recreation Area. At (7.5), the path crosses under the San Gabriel River Fwy. and stares directly into the Santa Fe Dam face. The route passes a power station (7.0), Live Oak Ave. and appears to dead-end at Arrow Hwy. (8.8). Follow the signed path left and continue to the base of the dam. Pass through the bike entry opening in the fence and continue up a short, steep grade to the top of the dam (9.2).

From the top of the dam in winter are views into the San Gabriel Mountains that are awe-inspiring! There are also views into the San Jose Hills to the southeast and Puente Hills to the south. The cities of the foothills are spread out all the way to the western horizon.

There is a trail left (northwest) that dead-ends near the west levee terminus. However, our route goes right and continues another 1.9 miles along the top of the dam providing other fine views, including those down into the Santa Fe Recreational Area. The dam trail ends at the bike trail access gate and proceeds 0.2 mile further to the auto access road to the recreation area (Orange Ave. which is named Azusa Canyon Rd. south of Arrow Hwy.). The mileage at this point is (11.4).

The recreation area itself is a charmer. To get there, make a hard left onto the automobile roadway access just downhill of the auto pay gate. There are bikepaths and a slow moving, lightly travelled roadway that can be linked into a couple of miles of biking route. The entire park is built alongside a lake and comes equipped with picnic areas, swimming area with a sand beach, playgrounds, fire pits, shaded pogodas (group area at the western end of the lake), boat rental and a snack bar.

Also, there are dirt bicycle roadways beyond the west end of the lake. (Note that, as we sadly found, there is no reasonable entry back up to the top of the dam coming from this direction.) By the way, there are also restrooms and drinking water here.

CONNECTING TRIPS: 1) Continuation with the southbound San Gabriel River Trail to Wilderness Park (Trip #22C) - from the Four Corners Trail Intersection, head south and over the Whittier Narrows Dam; 2) continuation with the northbound San Gabriel River Trail to the San Gabriel River Canyon (Trip #22E) - at the recreation area auto access, continue north (nearly straight ahead) and follow the bike trail signs.

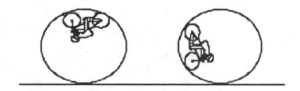

TRIP #22E - SAN GABRIEL RIVER: SANTA FE DAM
TO SAN GABRIEL CANYON

GENERAL LOCATION: Irwindale, Azusa

LEVEL OF DIFFICULTY: One way - easy; up and back - moderate
Distance - 7.5 miles (one way)
Elevation gain - 50 feet (Santa Fe Dam)

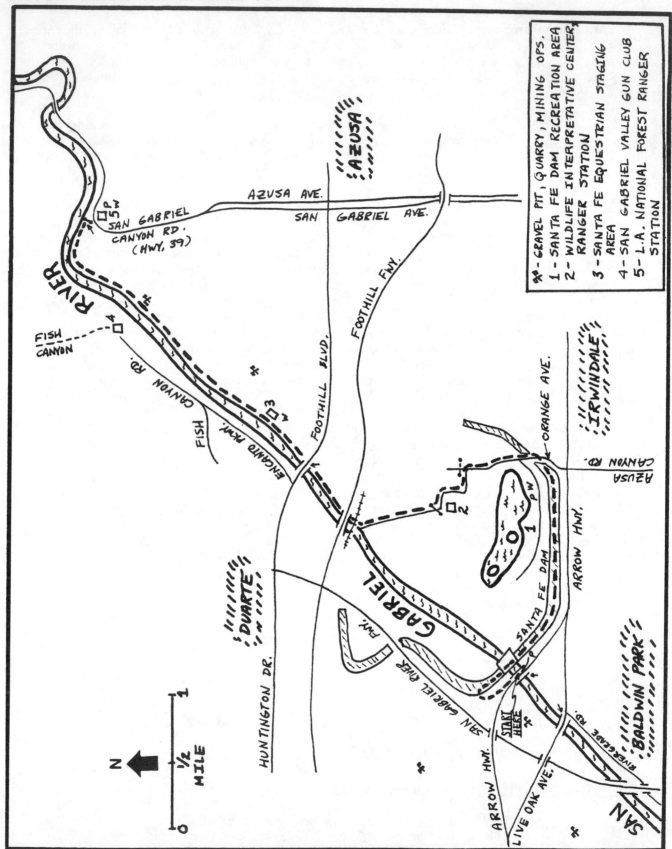

* - GRAVEL PIT, QUARRY, MINING OPS.
1 - SANTA FE DAM RECREATION AREA
2 - WILDLIFE INTERPRETATIVE CENTER, RANGER STATION
3 - SANTA FE EQUESTRIAN STAGING AREA
4 - SAN GABRIEL VALLEY GUN CLUB
5 - L.A. NATIONAL FOREST RANGER STATION

TRIP #22E - SAN GABRIEL RIVER: SANTA FE DAM-SAN GABRIEL CANYON

GENERAL DESCRIPTION: This 100% Class I trip starts downstream of the Santa Fe Dam, then climbs onto and follows the dam levee. The route continues from the dam upstream to the San Gabriel River terminus at the Los Angeles National Forest Information Center in San Gabriel Canyon. Along the way, the path traverses the Santa Fe Dam Nature Area, where there is a natural river bottom cactus garden. There are also spectacular close-up views of the foothills and surrounding mountains. These views are absolutely great after a cold winter storm. The stretch north of the dam is little used and makes for a good work-out trip.

TRAILHEAD: From the San Gabriel River Fwy., exit east on Live Oak Ave. and continue 0.9 mile to the junction with Arrow Hwy., making a U-turn onto Arrow Hwy. Continue in the reverse direction about 0.8 mile to free parking near the dam outlet.

Another option is to use pay parking in the Santa Fe Dam Recreation Area. This is particularly useful if the biker wishes to avoid riding up onto the dam and wants to start from the recreation area. Exit on Live Oak Ave. (east) as above, but continue one mile past the junction of Live Oak and Arrow Hwy. Turn left (north) at the Recreation Park entrance at Orange Ave. (named Azusa Canyon Rd. to the south).

TRIP DESCRIPTION: **Santa Fe Dam.** From the free parking area, pedal to the bike entry through the fence to the west of the spillway near the dam base. Follow the bike trail signs and pedal up the steep roadway to the top of the dam (0.2). From the top, there is a great 360-degree view. Most prominent are the San Gabriel Mountains to the north and the San Jose Hills and Puente Hills to the southeast and south, respectively. The view into the mountains is a real "heart grabber" when the snow level is down to low elevations and the sky is clear.

There is a route to the left (northeast) that dead-ends near the west levee terminus. Our route goes right and travels another 1.9 miles on the dam top, providing more interesting views, including a look down into the Santa Fe Dam Recreation Area (see Trip #22D). The dam trail ends at a bike access gate and proceeds 0.2 mile to the pay gate/auto access road into the recreation area (2.3).

Head downhill and turn sharply left below the pay gate to visit the developed park (southern) section of the Santa Fe Dam Recreation Area. However, our route follows the signed bike route and proceeds straight ahead.

Northern Santa Fe Dam Recreation Area. Follow the roadway to the dead-end at a nice little walled park-like area (2.8). Turn left and continue following the well-marked road 0.2 mile until it turns right (north) again. In another 0.2 mile, the route reaches the Wildlife Interpretive Center; there are both picnic and tent camping areas near the roadway intersection (3.2). Turn left again and proceed a few hundred feet to the ranger station. There are two bike route options at this point, plus marked walking/nature trails which tour the wildlife area. All routes head west and meet an old north-south asphalt roadway in a short distance. Follow the bike trail marker and turn right (north) on that old road.

The roadway passes through an interesting ecological area which is surrounded by a wide variety of cactus. At (3.8), the roadway reaches the top of a small rise; from this point is a nice view which includes a good look at the surrounding bottomland, the backside of the Santa Fe Dam, and a view north to the Foothill Fwy. In 0.4 mile, the bikepath returns to the San Gabriel River and shortly thereafter passes under the Foothill Fwy. (4.3).

The Gravel Pits. At (4.8), the bikeway passes a trans-river passenger cable car. In 0.1 mile is Huntington Dr./Foothill Blvd. Next is the Santa Fe Equestrian Staging Area where there are restrooms and water (5.2). There is a large above-ground gravel mining/processing works in the background. The river bed is boulder- and brush- filled with a spillway breaking the continuity of the scene every half-mile or more.

At (5.5), the path goes by an old closed-off railroad bridge. There is a budding residential area across the river with the homes continuing up into the nearby foothills. There are more gravel operations along the roadway to the right (east) with one sand and gravel operation lying right next to the trail (6.1). The route also passes a large water-filled gravel pit (6.5).

San Gabriel Canyon Entrance. The trail heads into a progressively more well-defined canyon environment. At (6.8), the route passes Fish Canyon in the hills to the left (west). There is an exquisite series of waterfalls (wintertime) several miles back into the canyon called Fish Falls. (Sorry, this is hiking country only.) At this point on the bike trail, there is also a firing range, the San Gabriel Valley Gun Club. The hills echo the sounds, providing a "Gunfight at the OK Corral" aura.

Just beyond, the trail dead-ends at a fence (7.5). A small trail to the right leads to Hwy. 39 and the L.A. National Forest Ranger Station. There is water and parking here should the biker want to start from this direction.

<u>**CONNECTING TRIPS**</u>: 1) Continuation with the San Gabriel River Trail south to Whittier Narrows (Trip #22D) - cross Arrow Hwy. and bike east a few hundred feet (in front of the spillway); 2) continuation with a very strenuous Class X "gut-buster" up San Gabriel Canyon Rd. - we <u>observed</u> a few hearty bikers working their way up the several miles of continuous steep grade.

TRIP #23 - SAN GABRIEL, RIO HONDO, L.A. RIVER
LOOP - - "THE BIG BANANA"

<u>**GENERAL LOCATION**</u>:   Long Beach to San Gabriel Canyon to Peck Water
Conservation Park to Long Beach

<u>**LEVEL OF DIFFICULTY**</u>: Loop - very strenuous
Distance - 83.5 miles (loop)
Elevation gain - 150 feet (three dams)

<u>**GENERAL DESCRIPTION**</u>: This trip starts from the Pacific Ocean, visits the foothills of the San Gabriel Mountains, and returns to the ocean in one big loop. The route tours the San Gabriel, Rio Hondo and Los Angeles Rivers. Along the way are some of the finest parks and recreation areas in Southern California, e.g., El Dorado Park, Whittier Narrows and Santa Fe Dam Recreation Areas.

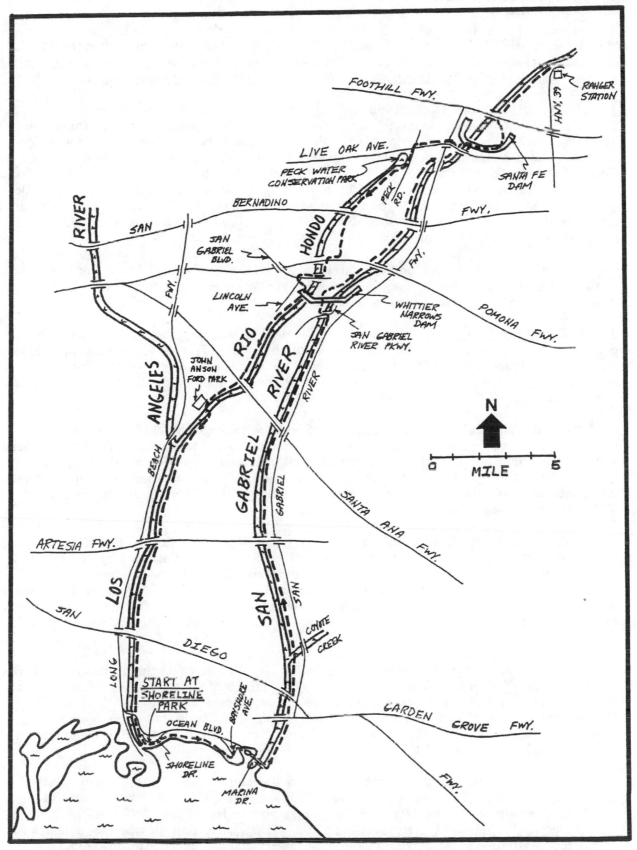

TRIP #23 - SAN GABRIEL, RIO HONDO, L.A. RIVERS -- "THE BIG BANANA"

Portions of the route are little known to most Angelenos (and Orange "Countyers"), such as the San Gabriel Canyon segment and the Upper Rio Hondo segment, including the Peck Water Conservation Park (reservoir). <u>Taken soon after a cool, wet winter storm, this may be the most scenic and inspiring trip in our book!</u>

TRAILHEAD: From Ocean Blvd. in Long Beach, turn south (towards the harbor) on Pine St. and continue to that street's end. There is free public parking around the Shoreline Park Lagoon (see Trip #14). From the Long Beach Fwy., continue south and take the Downtown Long Beach exit. Take this turnoff to Convention Center/Catalina Island and continue along Shoreline Dr. past the Golden Shore exit. Turn right (south) on Pine St. For busy days, pay parking is available between Ocean Blvd. and Shoreline Dr. An option is available to park for free along the north-south streets above Ocean Blvd. and then bike to the trailhead. Check parking signs carefully if the latter option is used.

Bring a couple of water bottles and load up at the trailhead. There are many water stops along the way, but having plenty of water lessens the number of required stops. Start this trip in the early morning.

TRIP DESCRIPTION: The trip description will detail only the new or confusing portions of the loop. The tour starts at Shoreline Park (Trip #14), travels to Marina Dr. in Seal Beach (Trip #15), proceeds north up the San Gabriel River (Trip #22), transitions west to Peck Water Conservation Park and returns to Long Beach via the Rio Hondo and Los Angeles Rivers (Trips #19 and #20).

Long Beach-Seal Beach. Exit the Shoreline Village parking area and follow the parking access roadway that parallels Shoreline Dr. Continue past the overhead walkway, along the perimeter of Shoreline Village, and turn left at the street's end (0.3). Bike through the easternmost village parking area on roadway which parallels Shoreline Dr. At the end of the parking lot, follow the bikepath north toward the Villa Riviera Hotel (0.8).

At the first bikepath junction just beyond, turn right and follow the Class I oceanfront path three miles to its terminus at Bay Shore Dr. Follow Bay Shore Dr. 0.3 mile and turn right on 2nd St. (4.1). Cross the two Naples Island bridges and just beyond the second bridge, turn right on Marina Dr. (5.2). Follow Marina Dr. around the marina periphery and near the Seaport Village entry, turn left (6.3). Just across the bridge (southeast side) is the bike entry to the San Gabriel River (see Trip #22A) (6.4).

San Gabriel River. Proceed 3.9 miles to the "Y" river channel junction. Cross the bike-pedestrian bridge across the river (see Trip #22A). Continue along the east levee of the San Gabriel River and make two short passages along the edge of El Dorado Park (13.0). The next major decision point is about 14 miles down the road where the path crosses to the west side of the river at the San Gabriel River Pkwy. (see Trips #22B, #22C) (27.1).

The path leads to the top of the dam, then downhill to the Four Corners Trail Intersection (28.2). Turn right (east) and follow the river on the west levee to the river outlet at the Santa Fe Dam (36.5). Cross Arrow Hwy., turn left (west), then follow the trail up to and across the dam top. The outlet trail passes the automobile entry fee station, heads downhill and continues straight ahead (north) (39.1).

The junction to the left enters the Santa Fe Dam Recreation Area. Follow the bike trail signs and rejoin the river on the east levee (41.0). Continue another 3.3 miles to the trails end at the entry to San Gabriel Canyon. Reverse the route and return to the base of Santa Fe Dam at Arrow Blvd. (51.8).

Santa Fe Dam - Peck Water Conservation Park. Continue west on Arrow Hwy./Live Oak Ave. 1.9 miles to Peck Rd. Turn left (south) and ride 0.8 mile on Peck Rd. and turn right at Rio Hondo Pkwy. into Peck Road Water Conservation Park (54.5). Continue to the south end of the parking lot and follow the small path on the west side of the reservoir. At the spillway is a sign noting the start of the formal bike trail (54.9).

Rio Hondo and Los Angeles River. Follow the Upper Rio Hondo bikeway 5.2 miles to Whittier Narrows Recreation Area "A" (see Trip #19). Pedal to the very south end of the recreation area and find the trail that is almost right next to and parallels the Pomona Fwy. Follow the route under the freeway to the point where it leaves the river at San Gabriel Blvd. (61.8).

Ride west on the bridge over the river and continue 0.3 mile to Lincoln Ave. Turn left at Lincoln Ave. and turn immediately left again into the bike trail entry. Follow the path another 0.6 mile to a point at the western edge of the west levee of the Whittier Narrows Dam (next to Lincoln Ave.). This is the official beginning of the Lario Trail (Trip #20) (62.7).

Continue east across the top of the dam 0.4 mile and take the path down the south side (spillway side) of the dam (see Trips #20A and #20B). Pedal another 5.4 miles on the west levee of the Rio Hondo and cross the river on a bike bridge that is near John Anson Ford Park (68.2). The route reaches the confluence with the Los Angeles River at (70.9)

Continue on the east levee of the Los Angeles River all the way into Long Beach to the end of the Lario Trail (82.6). If the water is high, bikers may have to leave the river and make on-street crossings at Rosecrans Ave., Compton Ave., Alondra Blvd., and Del Amo Blvd. in this segment of the trip. Just beyond the signed end of the Lario Trail, ride through the parking lot, then follow the shoreline around the Queen's Way (Catalina Cruise) Landing and under the Queen's Way Bridge. Follow the perimeter (left-most) trail around Shoreline Park and return to the starting point (83.5).

"Small Banana" Trip Option. A fifty-mile version of this trip is to park at De Forest Ave. just north of Willow St. and proceed on that street over Signal Hill to the San Gabriel River. Follow the river trail north to the Whittier Narrows Dam, Four Corners Trail Intersection, San Gabriel River and exit at Peck Rd. Turn on Durfee Ave., tour Legg Lake, then follow Durfee Ave./San Gabriel Blvd. to Lincoln Ave. and join the Lario Trail along the Rio Hondo River. Follow the Rio Hondo and L.A. Rivers back to the starting point.

CONNECTING TRIPS: See individual trip writeups.

TRIP #24 - COYOTE CREEK TRAIL

GENERAL LOCATION: Long Beach - Seal Beach/Cerritos

LEVEL OF DIFFICULTY: One way - easy; up and back - moderate
Distance - 9.2 miles (one way)
Elevation gain - essentially flat

GENERAL DESCRIPTION: Another of the river trails, this is a 100% Class I route. The trip starts at the scenic lower section of the San Gabriel River outlet near the Long Beach Marina and proceeds to the Coyote Creek junction. The Coyote Creek path is well maintained, but lightly used.   The 4.3 mile Coyote Creek section is not highly scenic, unless one enjoys "window shopping" into backyards of the adjoining homes and apartments.   It is a fine workout bikeway, however.   The trip terminates at La Palma Ave./Del Amo Blvd. (at a previously locked, but now open, gate). A short trip from the terminus leads to the Cerritos Regional County Park.

TRAILHEAD: Free public parking is available on Marina Dr. in Long Beach or along First St. in Seal Beach.   From Pacific Coast Highway (PCH) in Seal Beach, turn west on Marina Dr. (2-3 blocks from Main Street in Seal Beach) and continue roughly 0.5 mile to First St.   In another 1/4 mile, cross the San Gabriel River and continue a short distance along the marina for parking.   The trailhead is located at Marina Dr. at the east end of the bridge over the San Gabriel River (near Seaport Village).

Bikers should have a filled water bottle since the trip is waterless up to the terminus at Cerritos Regional Park.   An option is to ride south about 0.3 mile from the trailhead to use restrooms at the beach.   The side trip may also serve as a very pleasant scenic diversion.   After the ride, Shoreline Village at the marina edge may serve as a nice dining spot, watering hole, or place to shop.

TRIP DESCRIPTION: **The Scenic Lower Segment.**   The first part of the trip provides views of boaters, water skiers, and an interestingly-developed shoreline. The natural river basin then passes the PCH access, the Westminster Ave. entry (1.2), and the Haynes Steam Plant (electricity generation).   At (2.2), a small diversion Class I path leads off to the east along a 1.2-mile shaded route to Seal Beach Blvd.

In this stretch of the river, up to the concrete portion at about (3.5), one has views of a large bird population that includes pelicans, egrets, and the ever-present seagulls.   The trip passes under the Garden Grove Fwy. (2.3) and the San Diego Fwy. near the San Gabriel Fwy. interchange (3.5).   In this portion of the path are many "freeway orchards" -- those freeway-locked areas under the power poles which are used for growing containerized plants.

Coyote Creek.   At (3.9), a marked bridge over the river takes bikers to the connecting portion of the San Gabriel River Bike Trail (Trip #22A).   However, at this junction, our route continues along the east side (stay to the right) of the channel and passes the Katella Ave. entry, the San Gabriel River Fwy., and the Cerritos Ave. access (5.2).   Nearby, the channel junctions to the north (no easy access at this junction was found on the return trip), although our reference route stays along the east side of the channel.

126

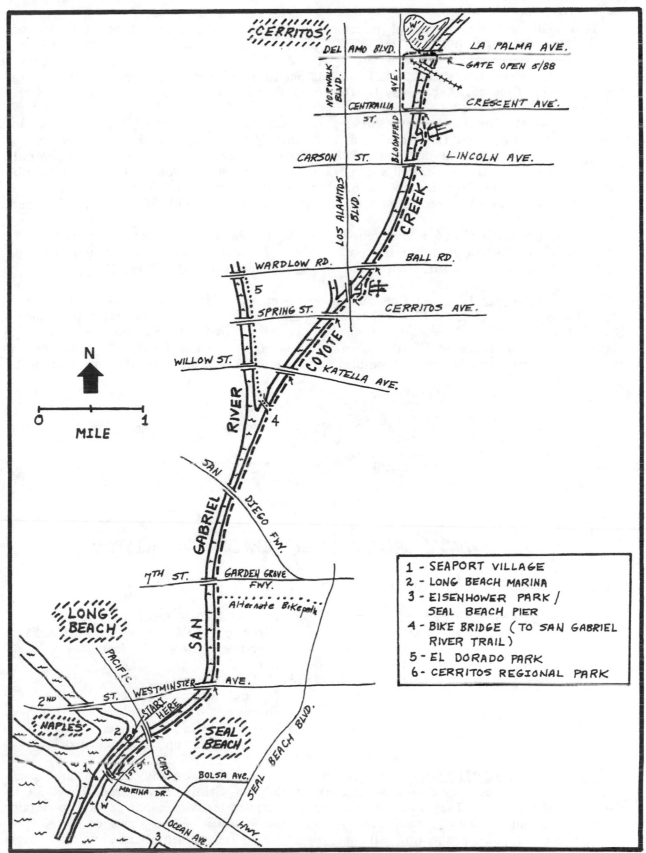

1 - SEAPORT VILLAGE
2 - LONG BEACH MARINA
3 - EISENHOWER PARK / SEAL BEACH PIER
4 - BIKE BRIDGE (TO SAN GABRIEL RIVER TRAIL)
5 - EL DORADO PARK
6 - CERRITOS REGIONAL PARK

TRIP #24 - COYOTE CREEK

Two additional small channel junctions to the east were encountered at (5.6) and (7.3). However, both junctions are closed off by locked gates and the main Coyote Creek path crosses those junctions via small overpasses. The Los Alamitos access is at about (5.6). Pass Ball Rd., a small walking-only bridge across the creek at (6.3), Lincoln Ave., Crescent Ave., and the Del Amo Blvd./La Palma Ave. terminus at (8.2).

Cerritos Regional County Park. To reach Cerritos Regional County Park, bike west a short distance on Del Amo Blvd. and turn right. If the gate at La Palma Ave. is not open (it <u>was</u> open on our Oct. 1988 revisit), backtrack to Crescent Ave./ Centrailia St. and proceed west on Centrailia St. 1/2 mile to Bloomfield Ave. Turn right (north) and continue to Del Amo Blvd, then bike east to the park (9.2). There are water fountains and restrooms, recreation fields and a limited amount of shade at this park.

Do not use the railroad bridge crossing at the La Palma Ave./ Del Amo Blvd. terminus as a shortcut route to the park. There are real live trains that use that bridge and there is not sufficient room for <u>big</u> trains and <u>little</u> bikers!!

<u>CONNECTING TRIPS</u>: 1) Continuation to lower and middle portions of the San Gabriel River tour (Trips #22A and #22B) - take major access streets west over the San Gabriel River Fwy. noting that distance between Coyote Creek and the San Gabriel River increases the further north one goes on Coyote Creek; 2) connectors to the lower portion of this trip along the San Gabriel River are described in Trip #22A.

TRIP #25 - WEST FORK, SAN GABRIEL RIVER

<u>GENERAL LOCATION</u>: Angeles National Forest

<u>LEVEL OF DIFFICULTY</u>: **Glen Camp Loop:** Up and back - moderate
Distance - 13.4 miles (up and back)
Elevation gain - 450 feet

Cogswell Reservoir Loop:
Up and back - strenuous
Distance - 15.0 miles (up and back)
Elevation gain - 800 feet
(sheer grade up to reservoir)

<u>GENERAL DESCRIPTION</u>: This is one of the most natural scenic rides in our book. This trip follows the meandering West Fork of the San Gabriel River from Hwy. 39 to Cogswell Reservoir. The route is through a forrested canyon along a well-maintained service road and is Class I since it is closed to public traffic. The views of the surrounding canyon, connecting streams, and the abundant floral and wildlife are wonderful. There are plenty of good fishing and swimming holes along the way.

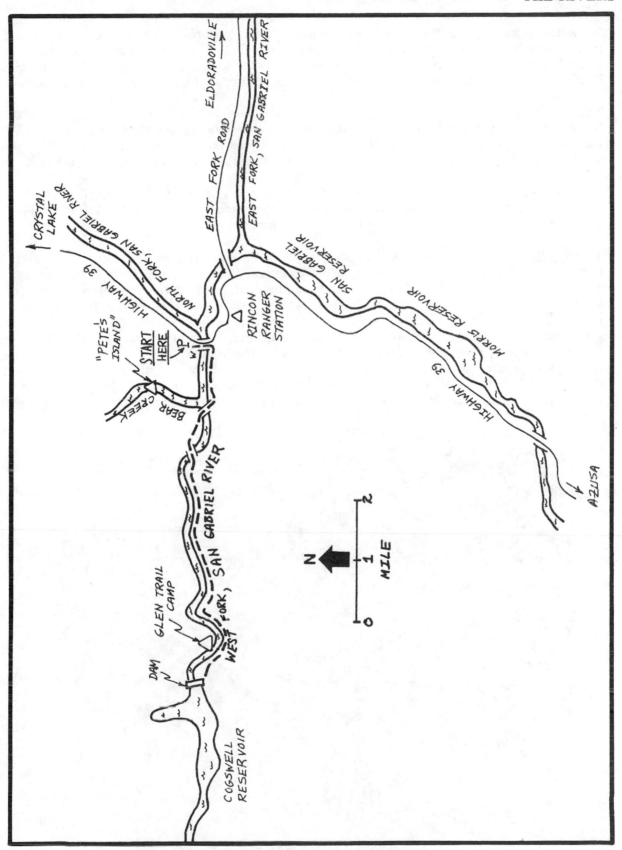

THE RIVERS

TRIP #25 - WEST FORK, SAN GABRIEL RIVER

After light rains, there are spectacular small waterfalls over the surrounding bluffs which fall near the trail itself; conversely, this trail is dangerous immediately after heavy rains. There are two trip options, one to the relatively flat trip to Glen Trail Camp, the other a trip extention up the sheer grade to Cogswell Reservoir.

TRAILHEAD: Exit the Foothill Fwy. at Azusa Ave. (Hwy. 39) and drive north about 8-1/2 miles to the road junction at the north end of the San Gabriel Reservoir. Stay to the left and continue up Hwy. 39 about 1-1/2 miles, then cross the bridge over the river. Just beyond the bridge and to the left (west) is a public parking area.

There are public facilities at the parking area. Fill up with water here (two water bottles recommended if you plan to "dawdle") as there are sometimes bacterial problems with the river water in the local mountains.

TRIP DESCRIPTION: **Trail Entry to Bear Creek.** Recross the bridge to meet West Fork Rd., lift your bike over the entrance guard (motorized bikes and public automobiles are not allowed). The trip begins with a moderate uphill along an open section of the river. Within a short distance, several small water runoffs cross the road. (These little dribbles pass a lot of water after a heavy rain.) The route passes a small waterfall which is across the river (0.5), then crosses a small bridge over the San Gabriel River at the pleasant junction with Bear Creek (0.9). A short hike up Bear Creek leads to some very scenic territory, as well as a "private" camping spot that we call "Pete's Island." From this bikepath junction, most of the journey is alongside a lush, tree-lined river with sporadic tree cover and a canyon wall to filter the sun.

West Fork Near Glen Trail Camp

130

At (1.5), the route recrosses the river and enters the West Fork Wild Trout Area (no bait, no barbs on hooks, and fish must be thrown back). In about another mile (2.6), the trip passes alongside a steep bluff through a large open area. Another steep bluff is passed in one more mile (3.5), with two small waterfalls flowing over the bluffs. The most westward waterfall cascades down a series of stair steps before dropping within feet of the trail. Just beyond is an area where the road is washed out for a few hundred feet; a look up the landsided cliff area hints that during heavy rains, the water must be funneled down the cliffside at a frightening rate!

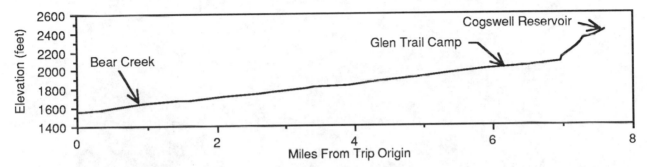

Glen Trail Camp. In 1/2 mile, the route enters an area where high canyon walls enclose the trail for about 0.5 mile. Just beyond is a small creek which spills across the roadway and a solitary, private residence along the roadway (4.5). The route follows the meandering river and crosses a small bridge over an unnamed creek (5.7). A half-mile further is Glen Trail Camp, a pleasant rest stop. The camp has a shaded section near the river and an open field across the trail. There are picnic tables, fire stoves, and plenty of spots to pitch tents (permits required).

Cogswell Reservoir. Returning to the parking area from this point results in a 13.4 mile round-trip. An option is to continue another 0.4 mile to the bottom of a steep roadway which leads up to Cogswell Reservoir (6.6). This roadway remains as steep as it looks at this point, rising roughly 350 feet in the remaining 0.7 mile up to the spillway. This is steep for walking, and exhaustive for biking for all except those bikers in excellent condition.

On the way up, the route passes a heliport and a private residential area (quiet please, as a courtesy). Once at the spillway, the road left leads steeply up West Fork, Red Box Rd. There is a 360-degree vista from the area just beyond the junction with views back down into the river canyon and into the reservoir itself. The trail crosses the dam and ends at the opposite side (7.5) -- for all but those with mountain bikes. A return to the trailhead from this point results in a round-trip distance of 15 miles.

<u>**CONNECTING TRIPS**</u>: Mountain bikers should try the riverbed recreation area just 1/2 mile south of this trip origin. For the truly serious mountain biker, head back into the East Fork, San Gabriel River, from the Eldoradoville Ranger Station. For the latter option, check first with the Rangers.

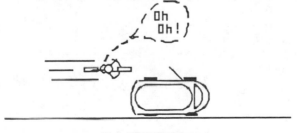

131

THE INLAND TRAILS

Rose Bowl in Pasadena

TRIP #26 - WHITTIER NARROWS/LEGG LAKE TRAIL

GENERAL LOCATION: Montebello, Pico Rivera (Whittier Narrows Recreation Area)

LEVEL OF DIFFICULTY: Round trip - easy
Distance - 11.2 miles (round trip)
Elevation gain - essentially flat

GENERAL DESCRIPTION: This fiendishly clever route allows the biker to explore nearly the entire Whittier Narrows Recreational Area on a Class I bikeway. It includes a tour around Legg Lake, a visit to the bottomland behind Whitter Narrows Dam, a cruise along the Rio Hondo River, and a "secret passage" under the Pomona Fwy. to the northern recreation and picnic area. This is a family special that involves crossing only one street and one intersection. There are also other options to ride up on the east levee of the Whittier Narrows Dam and to connect up with the San Gabriel River.

TRAILHEAD: From the Pomona Fwy., exit at Rosemead Blvd. south, travel about 0.8 mile to San Gabriel Blvd./Durfee Blvd. and turn left. Continue on Durfee Ave. 0.6 mile and turn left into the Legg Lake pay parking area. Bring four quarters for parking.

Bring a light water supply; there is plenty of water enroute. There are also food stands open on weekends at Legg Lake. As a precaution, bring some bug spray for gnats if you plan to picnic near the lake in the summer months.

TRIP DESCRIPTION: **Legg Lake.** The lake trip is entirely on well-compacted dirt. It is easily rideable with any type of bike, but some care is needed in a couple of fine gravel or wet areas. Leave the parking lot and head north toward the lake. Veer right for the counterclockwise tour. The route passes a roofed picnic area, continues by a little spillway into the lake, and visits a giant sandy play area with a ten-foot high cement octopus (0.2).

Shortly after, the route passes a food stand and boat rental area. There are numerous ducks and geese in the area. Further on is a "rocket" playground and some lovely shaded picnic sites that are situated right at the lake edge (0.4). Just beyond is a trail junction. If the biker diverts to the left, the route crosses a bridge between the northernmost lake and the main lake. However, our trip continues right and passes around the north lake through the green, natural, tree-covered surroundings. On this southbound segment the path meets the other end of the junction route between the lakes at (1.6). This area is one of the fishermen's favorites.

In another 0.1 mile, the bikepath passes a spillway near the western end of the lake, one of the few areas of the lake where motor traffic is highly visible. In a short distance, we passed a group of ducks sleeping on the grass not six feet away from a hard-at-work fisherman. The route turns eastward later and roughly parallels Durfee Ave. (2.1). The final stretch continues to wind along the lake edge and returns to the trip origin in another half mile (2.6).

Dam Bottomland/Wildlife Sanctuary. Leave the parking area and cross Durfee Ave. a few hundred feet to the west. Pass through a signed gate and pedal on a small asphalt road through an area surrounded by bushes, plants, trees, and brush.

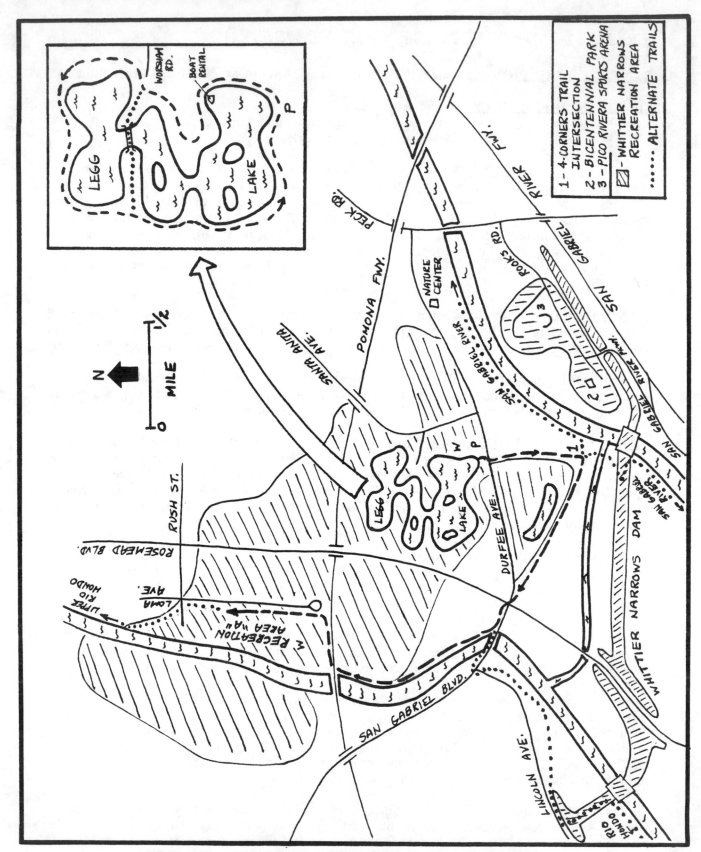

TRIP #26 - WHITTIER NARROWS/LEGG LAKE TRAIL

There are also many nature exhibits and other animals in this area. In a very short distance, the route junctions. To the left is a gate which, when open, leads to the Whittier Narrows Nature Center (if closed, an alternate is to take the Class II route down Durfee Ave.). Our reference route goes to the right and continues through the lush greenery to the "Center of the Universe," commonly known as the "Four Corners Trail Intersection." This is a pleasant, open area with a nice view of the backside of the Whittier Narrows Dam.

At that intersection, the route at the left (east) meets the San Gabriel River and heads north, while the route dead ahead (south) heads back to the dam and the south San Gabriel River segment. Our route turns right (west) and roughly parallels the dam, passing alongside some very interesting vine-covered trees. In a half mile, there is a nice look back into Rose Hills (3.7). The trail crosses a small footbridge over a wash and reaches Durfee Ave. in 0.1 mile. The trip remains Class I and continues 0.2 mile to the intersection of Rosemead Blvd. and Durfee Ave./San Gabriel Blvd.

Upper Rio Hondo Trail Segment. Cross the intersection to the northwest side and continue on the Class I San Gabriel Blvd. route to the bike entry to the Rio Hondo River (just before the bridge) (4.1). Ride along a pleasant, natural tree- and brush-lined stretch of the river. The growth is so dense that the river view itself does not open up for a quarter mile or so. The bikepath passes under the Pomona Fwy. (5.0) and then parallels that freeway at road level for another 0.6 mile before reaching the recreation area entrance.

Whittier Narrows Recreation Area "A." The bike entrance to the park is at its south end. The biker can cruise both the bikeways and slow-moving, lightly-travelled roads within the recreation area. The park is roughly one-half mile north-south and a quarter mile east-west, providing plenty of room to roam. The park is moderately treed and has restrooms and water. There are also picnic areas, recreation fields, model airplane flying and model car racing areas. This recreation area, combined with Legg Lake, is certainly on par with such fine recreation/biking areas as El Dorado Regional Park in L.A. County (Trip #16) and Mile Square or Irvine Regional Parks in Orange County.

<u>**CONNECTING TRIPS**</u>: 1) Continuation with the Upper Rio Hondo Bike Trail (Trip #19) - continue north on the west park edge on Loma Ave. for the north-heading segment (the south-heading segment of Trip #19 is part of this trip); 2) connection with the San Gabriel River Bike Trail (Trips #22C and 22D) - from the Four Corners Trail Intersection, bike east to reach the north-heading segment or bike south toward the dam to meet with the south-heading segment.

TRIP #27 - HACIENDA HEIGHTS LOOP

GENERAL LOCATION: Hacienda Heights

LEVEL OF DIFFICULTY: Loop trip - moderate
Distance - 5.6 miles (loop)
Elevation gain - periodic moderate grades

GENERAL DESCRIPTION: This loop trip around the eastern end of Hacienda Heights combines a Class II tour along lightly-developed Colima Ave. and a Class III tour through local residential neighborhoods.   There are some nice views into the San Gabriel Mountains on the route's western segment on Stimson Ave.   Additonal trip highlights are Stimson County Park and the Puente Hills Mall.   The route is well-laid out and well marked.   The bike route does contain one workout upgrade leading to the southwestern point near Colima Ave. and Stimson Ave.

TRAILHEAD: Exit the Pomona Fwy. south at Azusa Ave. and turn left into the Puente Hills Mall.   The Park and Ride area is near Pepper Brook Way at Azusa Ave.

Bring a light water supply.   There is water at Puente Hills Mall (a nice place for munchies and shopping after your tour) and Stimson County Park.   There is also water at the public schools along the bike route, if you're willing to search for it.

TRIP DESCRIPTION: **Colima Road and the Trip Crest.**   Exit the parking area and head south on Azusa Ave. 0.1 mile to Colima Rd.   A left turn here leads to Otterbein State Recreation Area, where there is some fun hill hiking and possible off-road bicycling (balloon-tire bikes).   Our route turns right and proceeds down a Class II bikeway alongside some heavy traffic.   There are hills to the left (south) and a light mix of commercial and residential development in this area.   The bike route starts uphill (0.4) passing Countrywood Rd. (0.6) and Dawnhaven Rd./Halliburton Rd. (0.8).   The upgrade continues and steepens into a stiff workout grade just before reaching the crest near Punta Del Este (1.4).   This is the highest elevation point of the trip.

Stimson Ave. and Stimson Park.   Just beyond, the path heads back downhill and flattens out near Stimson Ave. (1.8).   Turn right and continue downhill on a Class II bikepath.   There are some fine views into the San Gabriel Mountains from this area.   There is a long running downgrade with hillsides to the left and residential areas at road level to the right.   The downhill runout continues past La Monde St. (2.6) and flattens out in the vicinity of Stimson Park (3.2).   There are restrooms, water, recreation areas, and some nice shaded, grassy rest spots in this pleasant park.

The Residential Circuit.   In 0.2 mile and just before reaching the Pomona Fwy., turn right at Garo St.   Note that the marked bikepath also continues down Stimson Ave.   This segment of bikeway is Class III in light traffic residential areas. The route turns right (south) at Glenelder Ave. (3.8) and left at Cedarlane Dr. in front of a school (the sign had been twisted when we passed by this turnoff).   Continue down this street and turn right at Fieldgate Ave. (4.2).

In a short distance, turn left on Wedgeworth Dr. and pass in front of Wilson High School.   There are some nice views into the local hills to the north in this area.

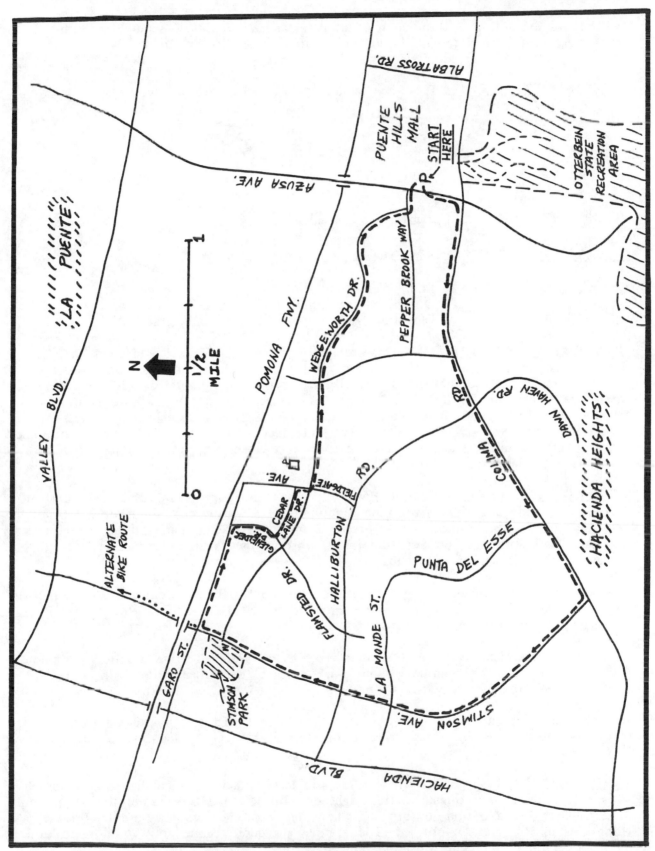

TRIP #27 - HACIENDA HEIGHTS LOOP

The route continues through residential areas past another school, crossing a small creek just beyond (5.1). In 0.3 mile, turn left on Pepper Brook Way. Cross Azusa Ave. and return to the loop starting point (5.6).

CONNECTING TRIPS: There are numerous local spurs off the described route.

TRIP #28 - SAN MARINO TOUR

GENERAL LOCATION: San Marino

LEVEL OF DIFFICULTY: Loop - moderate (hill loop)
Distance - 6.8 miles (hill loop)
Elevation gain - periodic moderate grades

GENERAL DESCRIPTION: This stately San Marino tour is not a bikepath or bike route. It is entirely Class X and just too good not to include. Almost the entire route is through residential neighborhoods on lightly travelled, generally wide roadways. There are some hills in the first 1-1/2 miles of the trip, but the biking is primarily flat or downhill beyond that point. The tour sports stately mansions and well-groomed, expensive neighborhoods.   The reference route passes by the Huntington Library and Botanical Gardens, and provides a selected number of view points into the hills and San Gabriel Mountains.

TRAILHEAD: From the Foothill Fwy., exit south on Sierra Madre Blvd. Drive about 2-1/2 miles and turn right (west) on Huntington Dr. Continue about one-half mile and turn right at St. Albans Rd. Drive 1/2 mile further and park on the street near the Lacy Park entrance; be very careful to observe the local parking laws. Note that the park is not open on weekends.

From the San Bernadino Fwy., exit north at Atlantic Blvd. Continue 2-1/2 miles to Huntington Blvd., turn right (east) and drive 3/4 mile to St. Albans Rd. Turn left (north) and continue as described above.

From the Pasadena Fwy., exit south at Fair Oaks Ave. and drive a mile to Monterey Rd. Turn left (east) and continue about 1-1/2 miles to St. Albans Rd. Turn left and continue several hundred yards to parking just outside Lacy Park.

Bring at least one filled water bottle. We did not find any public water supply other than at Lacy Park. Also bring a roadmap as a backup since this is not a marked bicycle path and it is easy to miss the described route.

TRIP DESCRIPTION: **The Hills.** The trip leaves Lacy Park and heads north on St. Albans Rd. In a short distance, turn right on Mill Rd. and bike uphill to Virginia Rd. (0.2).   There is an option to turn right here and take the less hilly optional route along Euston Rd. and Oxford Rd. The prettier and more challenging route is to turn left and continue uphill to Rosalind Rd. (0.4).

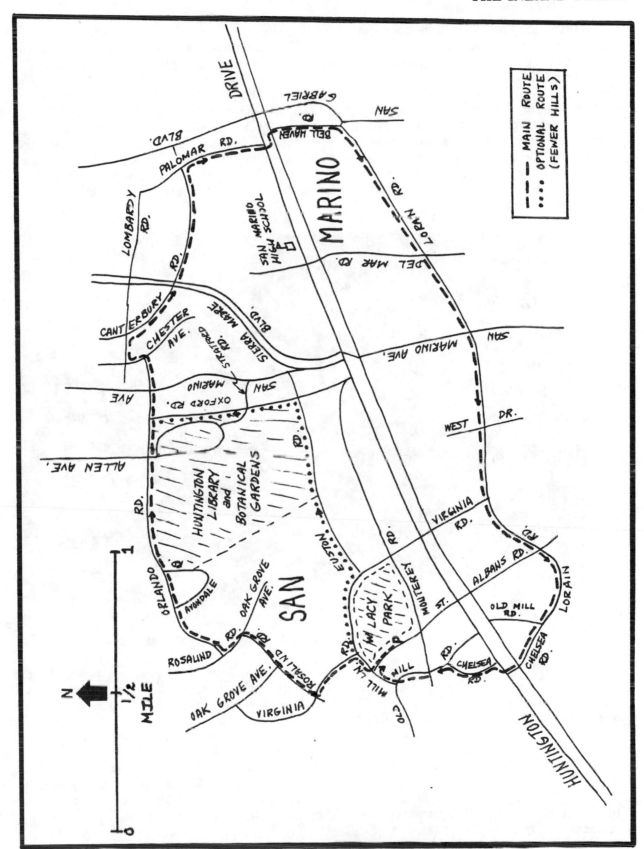

TRIP #28 - SAN MARINO TOUR

Turn right on Rosalind Rd. and continue through a rural setting where most residential grounds seem like mini-parks. The roadway winds downhill, junctions with one segment of Oak Grove Ave., turns a hard left and proceeds on another upgrade (0.7).

The route flattens out, then turns right on Orlando Rd. and proceeds uphill again (0.9). A refreshing downhill segment follows. There is a nice view into the San Gabriel Mountains from this area. The bikepath continues through well-groomed residential areas, proceeds up another short upgrade (the last workout for a long time) and passes the Avondale Rd. loop (1.0-1.1). Next the path cruises along the periphery of the Huntington Botanical Gardens, which shelters several magnificent set-back private residences.

San Marino Along Old Mill Road

Huntington Library and the Botanical Gardens. The route proceeds past the Allen Ave. entry to the Huntington Library Gallery and Botanical Gardens (1.7). Biking is not allowed within the grounds; note also that the grounds are open only on afternoons, Tuesday through Sunday, with limited public access on Sunday. If you wish to see the Huntington Library, call first for special instructions.

Northeast San Marino. The level route crosses Oxford Rd. (1.9), San Marino Ave. (2.0), and dead ends at Chester Ave. (2.2). Turn left at Chester Ave. then right at Lombardy Rd. and cruise downhill to Canterbury Rd. (2.3). Follow this street across busy Sierra Madre Blvd. and continue through a less shaded and less spectacular residential area to Palomar Ave. (3.1).

"The Southside." Proceed downhill to Huntington Dr. passing the beautiful Saint Felicities and Perpetua Church (3.4). After crossing Huntington Dr., the route zig-zags a short distance to the left (east) to Bell Haven Rd. and proceeds downhill about 0.3 mile. South of Huntington Dr. is the "other side of the tracks," where the mansions and oversized lots reduce to merely well-groomed expensive residences. Turn right on Lorain Rd. (3.8) and bike on flat terrain through more residential neighborhoods past busy Del Mar Ave. (4.3), San Marino Ave. (4.7), Virginia Rd. (5.2), and St. Albans Rd. (5.5). In 0.2 mile at Sherwood Rd., veer left (not a hard left) and bike up a light upgrade on Chelsea Rd.

The Estates. Cross Huntington Dr. (6.0) and follow a short jig-jog to the right (north) to continue on Chelsea Rd. Stop and admire some of the lovely estates along the roadway. The road veers right and dead ends at Old Mill Rd. (6.4). Turn left and bike up a mild grade to Mill Ln. The historic El Molino Viejo (The Olde Mill) is just up the hill on Old Mill Rd. However, our route turns right on Mill Ln. and continues 0.1 mile to St. Albans Rd. Turn right and return to the trip starting point (6.8).

CONNECTING TRIPS: There is an option to visit the San Gabriel Mission and Grapevine Park about two miles south of the West Dr./Loraine Rd. intersection. About 0.4 mile west of San Marino Blvd. on Lorain Rd., turn left (south) on West Dr. West Dr. becomes Mission Dr. and leads directly into the mission.

TRIP #29 - ARROYO SECO BIKE TRAIL

GENERAL LOCATION: Montecito Heights

LEVEL OF DIFFICULTY: Loop - easy
Distance - 7.5 miles (includes excursion trips)
Elevation gain - 0.1 mile steep upgrade (walk bikes)

GENERAL DESCRIPTION: This bike trip combines a pleasant ride along the Arroyo Seco and into two parks with excursion trips to several points of interest. The bikeway visits two separate sections of pleasant, shaded Arroyo Seco Park and touches the periphery of massive, hilly, and pretty Ernest E. Debs County Regional Park.

Excursions include visits to Heritage Square (restored Victorian mansions), the Lummis Home and Casa de Adobe (historical sites), and the Southwest Museum. Most of the route is on a marked bikeway (Class I or Class III), with some Class X on generally lightly travelled roadways. A large section of the Arroyo Seco path is flooded during winter storms.

Plan trip timing to be at Heritage Square in the afternoon if you can. Hours and dates of operation vary and should be checked ahead of time.

TRAILHEAD: Exit the Pasadena Fwy. east on Ave. 43. Drive two blocks and turn left (north) at Homer St. Continue to the end of Homer St. and park within the Montecito Heights Recreation Center parking lot.

141

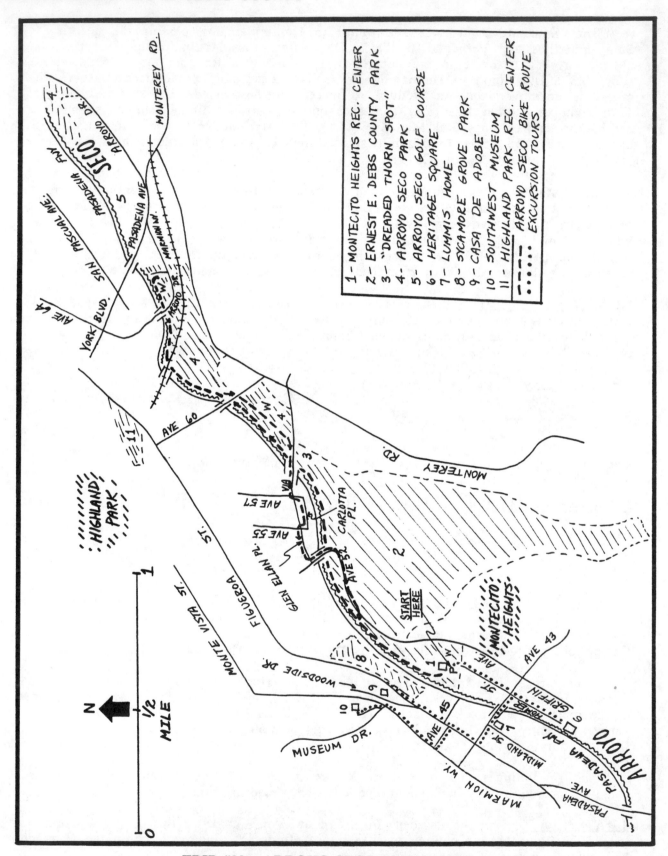

Legend:
1 – MONTECITO HEIGHTS REC. CENTER
2 – ERNEST E. DEBS COUNTY PARK
3 – "DREADED THORN SPOT"
4 – ARROYO SECO PARK
5 – ARROYO SECO GOLF COURSE
6 – HERITAGE SQUARE
7 – LUMMIS HOME
8 – SYCAMORE GROVE PARK
9 – CASA DE ADOBE
10 – SOUTHWEST MUSEUM
11 – HIGHLAND PARK REC. CENTER
- - - ARROYO SECO BIKE ROUTE
······· EXCURSION TOURS

TRIP #29 - ARROYO SECO BIKE TRAIL

142

Bring a light water supply. Water is available at the parks and some of the excursion sites.

TRIP DESCRIPTION: **Arroyo Seco Outward Bound.** Exit the parking lot at the west end and follow the tree-shaded path along the Arroyo Seco. Watch for broken glass near any path sections that are around park picnic areas. In 0.3 mile, there is a junction (referred to as "reference" junction later in the text) with the right-hand path proceeding up to Ave. 52 within the park. Our route proceeds to the left and down into the Arroyo Seco riverbed. The route leaves the freeway sounds at this point and drops into a quiet riverbed that is sheltered by trees for much of the trip. In another 0.4 mile is the Ave. 52 overcrossing. In this area there is a collection of varied types of graffiti that may classify as artwork. Also there are some nifty views into the local hills.

The route passes Via Marisol (1.1), Ave. 60 (1.4), and the Ave. 60 on-ramp (1.5), where there are nice views of the distant foothills. In another 0.1 mile, the path ducks under a railroad tressel, then the Arroyo Dr. off-ramp and Ave. 64/Marmion Way overpass (1.9). In 0.2 mile, the bikepath climbs out of the river to Arroyo Seco Park, where there is a shaded cul-de-sac, the Arroyo Horse Stables, and a nice picnic area with water about 0.2 mile further down Arroyo Dr.

Arroyo Seco Return Route. Returning from the picnic area, the route backtracks along the Arroyo Seco to the Ave. 60 overpass (3.2). Just before reaching the overpass, take the trail out of the riverbed; follow the path under the roadway to the southernmost segment of Arroyo Seco Park.

There is a bikeway/walkway that leads back up to Ave. 60; however, our route tours the pleasant shaded park past nice picnic areas, tennis courts and restrooms. Bike through the park and turn right at Via Marisol (3.6). Do not explore the territory across that street, even by walking bikes, as there are thorns on the ground that are guaranteed tire and tube wreckers (we know!).

Cross the Pasadena Fwy. and follow the signed Class III bike route as follows: Left on Ave. 57 (3.7), left on Carlota Blvd. (3.8), right on Ave. 55 (4.0), left on Glen Ellen Pl. (4.1), and left on Ave. 52 (4.3). Continue on this Class III roadway which recrosses the freeway and becomes Griffin Ave. In another 0.7 mile, the route meets the reference junction. Turn right at that junction and follow the Class I bikepath back to the starting point (5.2).

Excursion Tours. Return south on Homer St. Cross Ave. 43 and bike another 0.2 mile to the street's end at Heritage Square (5.6). There are several Victorian mansions here in various states of restoration. Return north to Ave. 43, turn left (west), and bike 0.1 mile to the historic cobblestone Lummis Home, "El Alisal" (5.9).

Continue another 0.1 mile on Ave. 43 and turn right (northeast) on Figueroa St. Follow that street about 0.2 mile just past Woodside Dr. to Casa de Adobe, a replica of an 1850's California hacienda (6.2).

Return 0.1 mile to Ave. 45 and turn right (northwest), continuing a short distance to Marmion Way (6.4). Turn right again and follow that street 0.2 mile to Museum Dr. Turn left and angle right almost immediately, following a very steep uphill (probably a walking stretch) to the Southwest Museum (6.6). This museum contains an extensive collection of Southwestern Indian artifacts.

143

Return 0.9 mile to the park area (7.5).

CONNECTING TRIPS: 1) Connection with the Highland Park Loop (Trip #30) - at the Southwest Museum turnoff, continue north on Marmion Way; 2) connection with the Kenneth Newell Bikeway (Trip #31) - from the trip terminus, head northeast on Arroyo Dr., which becomes Marmion Way. Continue 0.2 mile on Pasadena Ave. to Arroyo Dr., turn left (north) and proceed about 1-1/4 miles to the northernmost section of Arroyo Seco Park.

TRIP #30 - HIGHLAND PARK LOOP

GENERAL LOCATION: Highland Park

LEVEL OF DIFFICULTY: Loop - easy
Distance - 7.6 miles (loop)
Elevation gain - periodic moderate grades

GENERAL DESCRIPTION: This primarily Class III loop tours the periphery of Montecito Heights, traverses a series of rolling hills through the first half of the trek, and returns via the parks along the Arroyo Seco. There are numerous side trips, including visits to Heritage Square, Casa De Adobe, and the Southwest Museum (see Trip #29). Primarily in a residential area, most of this trip is on lightly used roads. The areas on either side of the Pasadena Fwy. are an interesting contrast, the western side having relatively light tree cover and a high density residential area, while the east is heavily treed, light residential, and packed with lovely parks.

TRAILHEAD: Exit the Pasadena Fwy. east on Ave. 43. Drive two blocks and turn left (north) at Homer St. Continue to the end of Homer St. and park within the Montecito Heights Recreation Center parking lot.

Bring a light water supply. Water is available at the parks along the way. There are also several gas stations.

TRIP DESCRIPTION: **Western Segment.** Exit the Montecito Heights Recreation Center area by returning south on Homer St. (continue straight ahead to visit Heritage Square). Turn right on Ave. 43 and proceed over the Pasadena Fwy. 0.3 mile to Figueroa St. (continue on Figueroa St. to visit Casa De Adobe and Sycamore Grove Park). Turn right and bike 0.1 mile to Ave. 45, turn left and right again on Class III Marmion Wy. Follow the mile upgrade past Museum Dr. (0.7) (turn left here to visit the Southwest Museum) and turn left at Shanley Ave., then right at Malta St. Continue to Ave. 50 and turn left (1.4).

Pedal on this Class III road through the residential community situated in rolling hills, cross York Blvd., and turn right one street beyond at Meridan St. (2.4). Follow the 0.8 mile upgrade through the quiet residential area which crests near Milwaukee Ave. Continue another 0.7 mile and turn sharply right at Ave. 63, skirting the covered water reservoir and passing shady, green Garvaya Park. Turn left at Repton St., right on Ave. 64, then continue to York Blvd. (4.4).

144

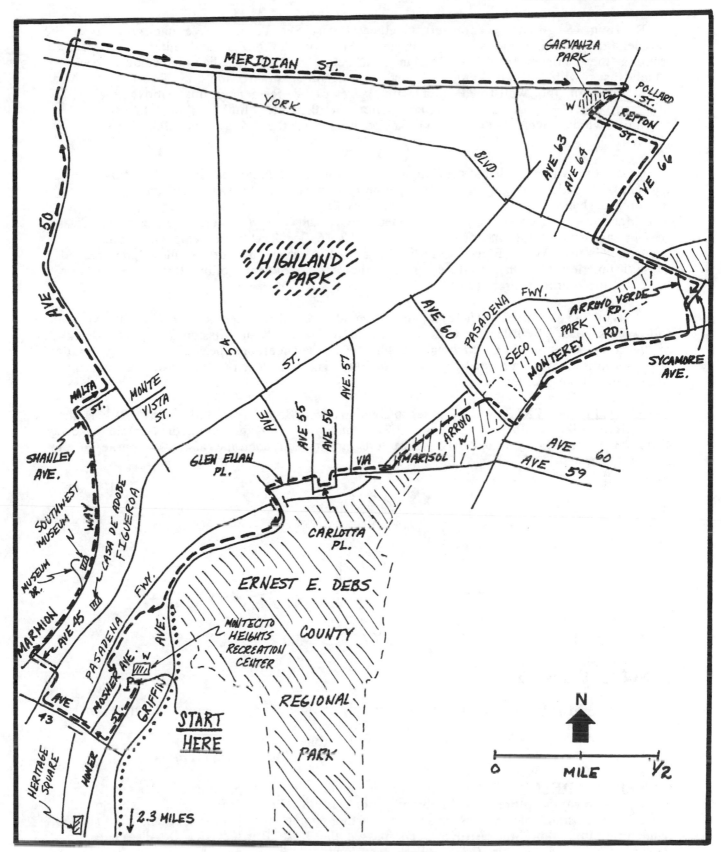

TRIP #30 - HIGHLAND PARK LOOP

Eastern Segment. Turn left (southeast) past San Pascual Ave and cross over the Pasadena Fwy. using the signed walkway. Stop on the bridge and admire the riders training their horses in the equestrian area below. Bike up shady Sycamore Ave. which fuses with Arroyo Verde Rd. and turn right again at Monterey Rd. (4.9). Pedal uphill through the well-treed area with large rustic residences just above the northern Arroyo Seco Park segment. After the 0.3-mile climb, follow the nice downhill which levels near Ave. 60 and continue to the bridge over the Arroyo Seco (5.6).

Cross the street and pass through the motorized vehicle barrier and follow along the Class I path through the lovely southern segment of Arroyo Seco Park. There are restrooms, shade, tennis courts, and many inviting rest spots in this cozy park. At Via Marisol (6.1). cross over the Pasadena Fwy. and follow several well marked Class III zig-zags, recrossing the freeway at Ave. 52 (6.7). The road veers right and becomes Griffin Ave. Bike 0.7 mile along Griffin Ave. and turn right at the marked Class I junction trail that leads down into the Arroyo Seco. Follow this path 0.2 mile back to the parking area (7.6).

Griffin Ave. Spur. There is an option at 7.4 mile to remain on Griffin Ave. and follow this road 2.3 miles on Class II road to it's terminus at Mission Rd. at the backside of the L.A. County/U.S.C. Medical Center. This segment has periodic moderage grades with a limited winding roadway; the roadway is in primarily residential areas with reasonable bike room.

CONNECTING TRIPS: 1) Connection with Arroyo Seco Bike Trail (Trip #29) - at the trip origin, bike south on Homer St.; 2) connection with the Kenneth Newell Bikeway (Trip #31) - at San Pascual Ave., turn left (north) and continue about one mile to the northern segment of Arroyo Seco Park.

TRIP #31 - KENNETH NEWELL BIKEWAY

GENERAL LOCATION: Pasadena

LEVEL OF DIFFICULTY: One way- easy (north to south), moderate (south to north); up and back - moderate
Distance - 6.8 miles (one way)
Elevation gain - periodic moderate upgrades

GENERAL DESCRIPTION: One of the premier inland trips, this popular, well-marked bikeway explores an interesting north-south slice of Pasadena. The route passes picturesque old homes near the starting point, follows a pleasant tree-shaded residential area along the Arroyo Seco, passes the Rose Bowl, visits Devil's Gate Reservoir and Oak Grove County Park, and ends at Jet Propulsion Laboratories (JPL).

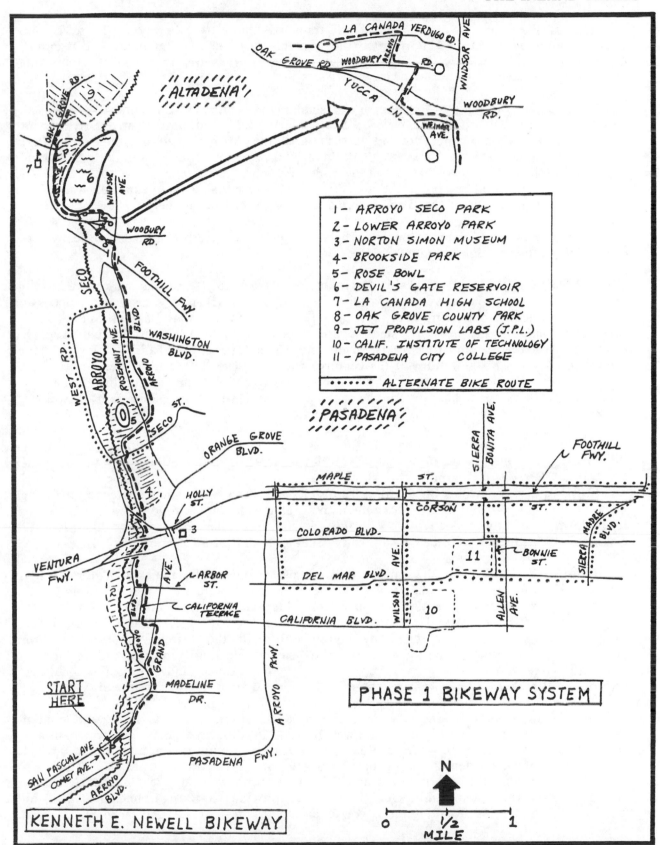

LA CANADA VERDUGO RD.

OAK GROVE RD.

WINDSOR AVE.

WOODBURY ALCADO RD.

YUCCA LN.

WEIMAR AVE.

WOODBURY RD.

ALTADENA

9

8

P

7

6

WINDSOR AVE.

WOOBURY RD.

FOOTHILL FWY.

SECO

WEST RD.

ARROYO

ROSEMONT AVE.

ARROYO BLVD.

WASHINGTON BLVD.

SECO ST.

5

4

ORANGE GROVE BLVD.

HOLLY ST.

3

VENTURA FWY.

10

ARBOR ST.

CALIFORNIA TERRACE

GRAND AVE.

ARROYO BLVD.

START HERE

1

MADELINE DR.

ARROYO PKWY.

SAN PASCUAL AVE.

COMET AVE.

ARROYO BLVD.

PASADENA FWY.

1 – ARROYO SECO PARK
2 – LOWER ARROYO PARK
3 – NORTON SIMON MUSEUM
4 – BROOKSIDE PARK
5 – ROSE BOWL
6 – DEVIL'S GATE RESERVOIR
7 – LA CANADA HIGH SCHOOL
8 – OAK GROVE COUNTY PARK
9 – JET PROPULSION LABS (J.P.L.)
10 – CALIF. INSTITUTE OF TECHNOLOGY
11 – PASADENA CITY COLLEGE

• • • • • • ALTERNATE BIKE ROUTE

PASADENA

MAPLE ST.

SIERRA

BONITA AVE.

FOOTHILL FWY.

CORSON ST.

COLORADO BLVD.

WILSON AVE.

11

BONNIE ST.

SIERRA MADRE BLVD.

DEL MAR BLVD.

ALLEN AVE.

10

CALIFORNIA BLVD.

PHASE 1 BIKEWAY SYSTEM

N

0   1/2   1
MILE

KENNETH E. NEWELL BIKEWAY

TRIP #31 - KENNETH NEWELL BIKEWAY

Most of the route is on roomy, lightly-travelled Class III bikeways. There is one workout upgrade (south to north) that places this trip at the "moderate" difficulty rating upper limit. There is an additional option to link this route with an unnamed inner city bikeway.

TRAILHEAD: From the Pasadena Fwy. southbound, exit west on York Blvd. (Pasadena Ave. to the east), continue 0.2 mile to San Pascual Ave., and turn right. Drive about 3/4 mile just beyond Comet St. and just short of the Arroyo Seco overcrossing. Park in the Arroyo Seco Park parking lot. From the northbound direction, exit at Marmion Way, turn left and follow that street over the freeway. Continue on a road now named Ave. 64 to York Blvd. Turn right and drive to San Pascual Ave. Turn left (north) and continue to the Arroyo Seco Park parking lot as described above.

Bring a moderate water supply. There is one strategically located public water source at Brookside Park near the Rose Bowl.

TRIP DESCRIPTION: **Classic Residential Pasadena.** Exit the parking area and turn right (north). In a very short distance, the Class III path crosses in succession the Arroyo Seco, Stoney Dr. near a recreation field, and the San Pascual Stables. The rural area path climbs a short, steep uphill which crests at the San Pascual Ave. terminus at Arroyo Blvd. (0.2). Turn left (north) and pedal past a collection of lovely fenced estates with their turn-of-the-century homes. The bike route here is in a quiet, tree-shaded, rural setting which is just outright pleasant. Continue past Madeline Dr. (0.5) and junction to the right at Grand Ave. (0.7). The path is well-marked at this, as well as all upcoming junctions.

Continue up a moderate upgrade for 0.3 mile, which becomes rather steep the next 0.1 mile. Turn left at California Blvd. (1.2) and turn right 0.1 mile down the road at California Terrace. Continue the slow, steady uphill in continued shaded, classic residential areas to Arbor St. (1.6). Turn left and in a very short distance, turn right back onto South Arroyo Dr. The path is now alongside the Arroyo Seco and offers a look down into Lower Arroyo Park. Just beyond, the bike route passes historical La Casita Del Arroyo, a replica of an early Southern California hacienda (1.8).

Brookside Park. In 0.2 mile, the route passes under the majestic Colorado Blvd. bridge. Up the hill from this area is a fine view of the classic Federal Building. Nearby, but out of view, is the Norton Simon Museum of Art. Another 0.1 mile beyond, the path passes under the massive Ventura Fwy. bridge. There is a "window" view to the mountains achieved by sighting through the bridge supports northward and down the canyon. The bike route heads steeply downhill for 0.2 mile, flattens out, and passes under Holly St. (2.3). The flat roadway continues past the southern portion of Brookside Park, where there is a nice covered picnic area and water (2.5).

Rose Bowl. In 0.3 mile, the path crosses Seco St., jogs to the right, and continues north alongside the east side of the Rose Bowl. In this area, there are recreation fields and restrooms (3.0). Cross Rosemont Ave. and continue on a workout upgrade through tree-lined residential areas past Westgate St. and Everts St. (3.7). The upgrade eases and the route continues 0.2 miles further to a great turnout/vista area which overlooks the Brookside Golf Course and provides a look around the local hills. The path then crosses Washington Blvd. to an uphill crest at La Cresta (4.5).

The "Maze." Cross over the Foothill Fwy. and turn left at Weimar Ave., just before Woodbury Rd. (4.9). Follow a well-marked route to Yucca Ln. and turn right, then left on Woodbury Rd. near a cul-de-sac, right on N. Arroyo Blvd., and left on La Canada Verdugo Rd. (5.2). Continue downhill to the road's end at a cul-de-sac (5.4).

Residential Area Along Arroyo Boulevard

Devil's Gate Reservoir and Oak Grove County Park. Follow the Class I path across Devil's Gate Reservoir (5.7) and bike downhill above the reservoir area. There are some fine views into the San Gabriel Mountains from here. Cruise past a little shady park with benches into the main area of Oak Grove County Park. The path continues 0.3 mile along the park periphery past a junction to the right (west), which leads to the lower picnic area. At (6.3), the route meets Oak Grove Dr. Turn right and continue 0.5 mile to the Jet Propulsion Laboratories (6.8).

<u>CONNECTING TRIPS</u>: 1) Connection with the Arroyo Seco Bike Trail (Trip #29) - from the junction of San Pascual Ave. and Arroyo Dr., continue about 1-1/4 miles south on Arroyo Blvd./Pasadena Ave. and turn left at Marmion Way. Turn right in 0.2 mile at Arroyo Verde and proceed to the Arroyo Seco; 2) connection with the Highland Park Loop (Trip #30) - at the trip origin, bike one mile south to York Blvd.; 3) connection with the Pasadena inner city bikeway shown on the eastern portion of the trip map.

TRIP #32 - ARCADIA LOOP

GENERAL LOCATION: Arcadia

LEVEL OF DIFFICULTY: Four loop trips - moderate to strenuous; Highland Oaks segment of Rancho Oaks Loop - strenuous

Distance - 29.4 miles (not including the 3-mile strenuous Highland Oaks segment)

Elevation gain - periodic moderate grades (Rancho Oaks Loop); single extended, steep upgrade (Highland Oaks segment)

GENERAL DESCRIPTION: The delightful Arcadia bikeway system consists of four well laid out, well marked loops. Most of the route is Class III on lightly used roadways with plenty of bike room. The route is generally flat, except for the northern portions of the Rancho Oaks Loop, particularly the steep upper segment of Highland Oaks Dr. The biker can follow individual marked loops or free-lance among the loops. The Rancho Oaks Loop is the longest and most varied, including such major points of interest as the Los Angeles Arboretum, Santa Anita Race Track, Arcadia Park, Wilderness Park, and the elegant residential neighborhoods in the foothills.

TRAILHEAD: From the Foothill Fwy., exit south at the Michillinda Ave. off-ramp. Follow Colorado St. to Michillinda Ave., turn right (south) and drive one mile to Huntington Dr. Turn left and continue 0.4 mile to Golden West Ave. Turn left and find parking in this residential area subject to local parking regulations.

From the San Bernardino Fwy., exit north on Rosemead Blvd. and drive about four miles to Huntington Dr. Turn right and continue 3/4 mile to Golden West Ave. Turn left and park as stated above.

Bring plenty of water unless you are willing to search or beg and borrow along the way. There may be water at some of the parks that we did not visit.

TRIP DESCRIPTION: The individual loops should be biked in the direction shown since the bikepath signs are only posted in one direction. Bring a map along on this trip as a backup, whether following the signed routes or "free-lancing." The following are general highlight descriptions of each loop.

Hugo Reid Loop. The shortest of the four loops, the counterclockwise three-mile route cruises a pleasant, quiet, well-manicured residential area which is bordered by Baldwin Lake and the L.A. Arboretum on the east. This area is neatly tucked away, isolated from the busy roadways to the north, west and south. Peacocks wander this territory at will. There are some light upgrades on this loop and several views into the San Gabriel Mountains, particularly from Altuna Rd. looking back.

Lucky Baldwin Loop. This counterclockwise 6.8 mile loop enfolds a major portion of the Hugo Reid Loop. From the parking area, the route crosses Huntingtron Dr. into a more modest residential neighborhood, passing Tripolis Park (0.3) and meandering as far south as Camino Real. The route heads north at El Monte Ave. (2.1) on a Class II bike route and turns left (west) at Duarte Ave., returning to Class III biking. The path zig-zags north and west, passing the lovely Holy Angels Church and crossing Huntington Dr. near the exquisite Rose Garden (2.9).

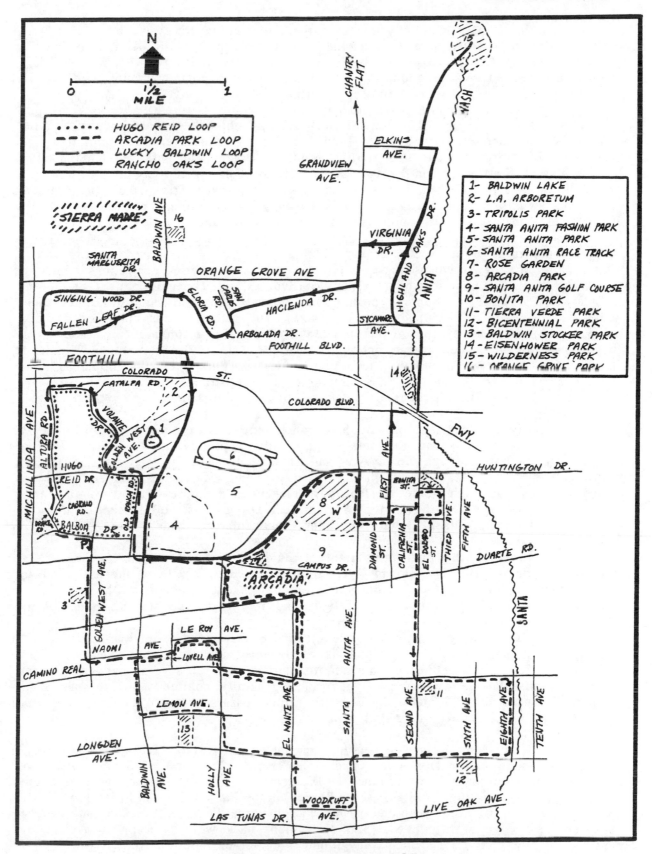

TRIP #32 - ARCADIA LOOP

The bike route passes directly south of the Santa Anita Raceway; there is a great mountain backdrop from here. Next, the path cruises past Santa Anita Fashion Park (shopping center) (3.4), crosses Baldwin Ave., and heads north on Old Ranch Rd. (3.8). Just beyond this junction, the bike route shares a common route with the Hugo Reid Loop, returning to the starting point (6.8).

Rancho Oaks Loop. The longest of the loops, this counter-clockwise 9.9 mile favorite is described starting at Hugo Reid Dr. and Baldwin Ave. The parking previously described is near this starting point or bikers can park at Santa Anita Fashion Park. Start south on Baldwin Ave. and turn left on Huntington Dr. (0.8). The path follows that roadway as it passes the Santa Anita Race Track, the Rose Garden (1.2), and swings north alongside Arcadia City Park. There are recreation and picnic areas, trees and grassy rest spots, together with water and restrooms.

The route turns right (south) at Santa Anita Ave. (2.3) and passes an arts and crafts exhibit area. At Diamond St., a left turn leads to a series of jig-jogs which lead to a Foothill Fwy. undercrossing at Colorado Blvd. (3.5). The path cruises by Eisenhower Park and a shopping center near Second Ave. and Foothill Blvd., then works its way over to Highland Oaks Dr. (4.2). The path proceeds uphill on a workout grade. The route heads toward the mountains through a residential area and meets Virginia Dr. (4.7). There is an option to continue 1-1/2 miles further on Highland Oaks Dr. on a steep, gutty uphill to rustic Wilderness Park (trees, picnic areas, restrooms, nature trails) -- this is a strenuous to very strenuous workout! The compensations are fine vistas and a feeling of accomplishment.

For everyday mortals like us, the bike route turns left, proceeds uphill for a short distance, and works its way to some exceptionally impressive residential areas starting just south of Orange Grove Ave. and Santa Anita Ave. at Hacienda Dr. (5.2). At Baldwin Ave. (6.7), the bikepath jig-jogs over to Santa Marguerita Dr. and proceeds mostly downhill through some of the most elegant and impressive residential areas in L.A. County. The Singingwood Dr./Fallen Leaf Dr. area is well stocked with mansions and large, elegant homes on huge, immaculately tended lots.

Reality returns as the path turns right at Baldwin Ave. (8.6) and proceeds downhill to Foothill Blvd. Baldwin Ave. continues about 0.2 mile to the east, and soon passes under the Foothill Fwy. The bike route passes one entrance to the L.A. Arboretum just south of Stanford Ave. (9.4) and returns to the starting point (9.9).

Arcadia Park Loop. This 9.7 mile clockwise route is described as starting at Huntington Dr. and Holly Ave., which is easily reachable from the described trailhead parking area. Other options are to start at one of several parks along the route. This is the flattest route of the group, generally confined to less spectacular territory than the other loops. Most of the route passes through modest residential areas which are liberally sprinkled with parks.

Proceed along Huntington Dr. passing the Santa Anita Race Track, the Rose Garden, and swing north alongside Arcadia City Park. Turn left at Santa Anita Ave. (1.1) and left again in a short distance at Diamond St. The bike route goes through a series of jig-jogs passing Bonita Park (1.9) and proceeding south on Second St. The tour heads left at Camino Real and passes Tierra Verde Park (3.2). The path reaches its easternmost edge at Eighth St. (3.7), then loops back west on Longden Ave., passing Bicentennial Park (open playground and tennis courts) (4.3).

The bike tour turns left (south) on Santa Anita Ave., passes near the southern Arcadia city limits on Woodruff Ave. (5.4), winds its way north and west on Class II El Monte Ave., and returns to Class III Longden Ave. (6.4). The path turns right (north) on Holly Ave., left on Lemon Ave., and passes Baldwin Stocker Park (6.9). There are covered picnic areas, restrooms and a playground at the park.

In a short distance, the bikepath turns right (north) on Baldwin Ave. and continues to Camino Real (7.6). From this point, the route shares a path with the Lucky Baldwin Loop. The path jig-jogs north and east, eventually reaching El Monte Ave. (8.9). To return to the starting point (9.7), the path proceeds north on El Monte Ave., left (west) on Durate Rd., and north again on Holly Ave.

CONNECTING TRIPS: There are numerous combinations of possible routes just within the four loops described.

TRIP #33 - GRIFFITH PARK

GENERAL LOCATION: Hollywood Hills, Griffith Park

LEVEL OF DIFFICULTY: **Griffith Park Dr. Loop** - moderate to strenuous
Distance - 8.8 miles (loop)
Elevation gain - single long, moderate-to-steep grade

Zoo Dr. Up and Back Trip - easy
Distance - 8.2 miles (up and back)
Elevation gain - periodic light grades

GENERAL DESCRIPTION: This is a pleasant ride in a rural setting through one of Los Angeles County's finest parks. One option is the loop route which includes Griffith Park Dr. and a half mile strenuous upgrade. (This is the reference option described below.) Another option is to take the Zoo Dr. route up and back, avoiding Griffith Park Dr. completely. A third option is to plan a route that includes all but the strenuous upgrade.

153

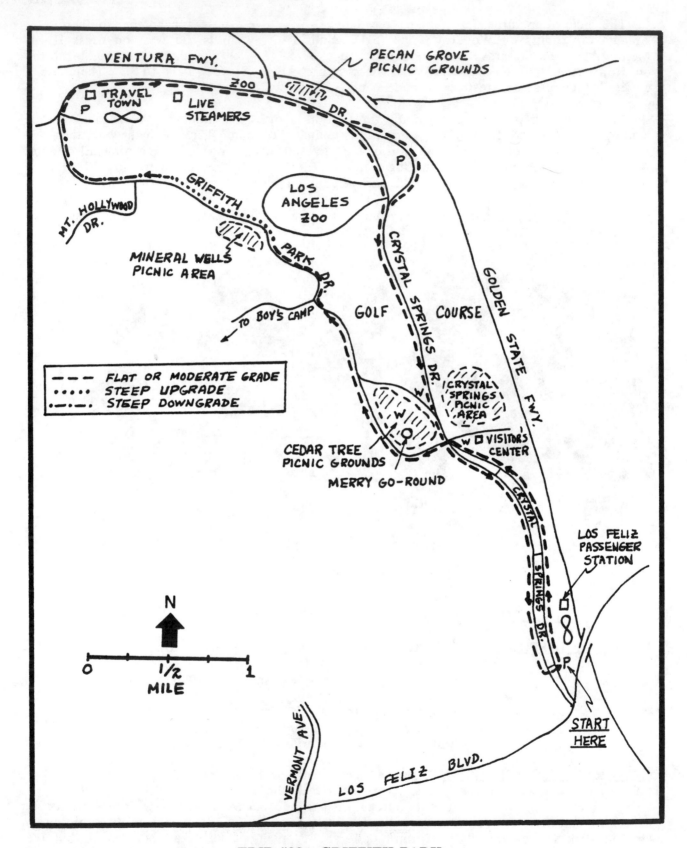

VENTURA FWY.

PECAN GROVE
PICNIC GROUNDS

ZOO

P   TRAVEL   ∞   Live
TOWN   STEAMERS

DR.

P

LOS
ANGELES
ZOO

GRIFFITH

MT. HOLLYWOOD
DR.

CRYSTAL SPRINGS DR.

PARK DR.

MINERAL WELLS
PICNIC AREA

GOLDEN STATE FWY.

GOLF   COURSE

TO BOY'S CAMP

CRYSTAL
SPRINGS
PICNIC
AREA

- - - - FLAT OR MODERATE GRADE
· · · · · STEEP UPGRADE
-·-·- STEEP DOWNGRADE

W
W   W

W ☐ VISITOR'S
CENTER

CEDAR TREE
PICNIC GROUNDS

MERRY GO-ROUND

CRYSTAL SPRINGS DR.

LOS FELIZ
PASSENGER
STATION

N

0   1/2   1
MILE

8
P

START
HERE

VERMONT AVE.

LOS FELIZ BLVD.

TRIP #33 - GRIFFITH PARK

Regardless of the option, the tree-lined route passes numerous picnic areas and sightseeing attractions such as the L.A. Zoo, Travel Town, and the Griffith Park Merry-Go-Round. Griffith Park Dr. is effectively a Class III roadway, while the remainder of the bikepaths are Class II. The Zoo Dr. up-and-back option is a nice family ride for all but inexperienced or very young bikers.

TRAILHEAD: Exit the Golden State Fwy. at Los Feliz Blvd. and turn west. Continue about a quarter mile and turn right (north) at Crystal Springs Rd. Within a short distance, park in the area just off the roadway, preferably in a shady spot.

Bring a light water supply. There is plenty of water in the main picnic areas surrounding Crystal Springs Dr. near the Griffith Park Dr. junction. Also there are water fountains at most park attractions, although bikers must leave the bike trail to gain access to them.

TRIP DESCRIPTION: **Lower Crystal Springs Drive.** Leaving the parking area, Crystal Springs Dr. starts on a mix of moderate upgrades and flats. In 0.1 mile, the roadway passes the Los Feliz Passenger Station, the point of departure for rides on the mini railroad. The route continues above and alongside the Golden State Fwy. until it transitions to an area above grassy knolls and horse stables (0.8). The entire Griffith Park area is crisscrossed with some of the finest horse trails in the county. In a short distance, the roadway passes alongside the Visitor's Center/Ranger Station and just beyond meets the junction with Griffith Park Dr. (1.1).

Mineral Wells Picnic Area. Continue straight ahead (north) on Crystal Springs Dr. for the easier family bike route. However, for the reference loop trip, turn left (west) on Griffith Park Dr. and bike up a short, steep upgrade. Continue on the roadway past the car roadblock and around the edge of the Cedar Tree Picnic Grounds parking area. The road passes above the Griffith Park Merry-Go-Round and a pleasant grassy, shaded picnic area (1.5) which extends for about another 1/4 mile.

At the junction north of the picnic area, bear left and continue alongside the golf course. The route passes the Boy's Camp turnoff (2.4), golfer's clubhouse/restaurant, driving range (2.6), and then heads uphill to the Mineral Wells Picnic Area (2.8). This is one of the most natural and scenic picnic areas in the park.

The "Roller Coaster." Beyond the picnic area, the route steepens. For the next half mile, the biker faces a gritty uphill that levels off near a high development area. This is the segment that leaves some question as to whether the route is moderate or strenuous. Just beyond the flat, the roadway twists and winds steeply downhill passing Mt. Hollywood Dr. (3.5) and then leveling out in another 0.6 mile.

Travel Town. Just beyond is the turnoff to Travel Town (4.2). There are miniature train rides here, as well as stationary, life-size steam trains. The bikepath continues past Travel Town, makes a turn to the right (east) and becomes Zoo Dr. Zoo Dr. passes alongside the live "Steamer" area (4.3), a small open picnic area (4.5), Riverside Dr. (5.3), and the Pecan Grove Picnic Area (5.4).

L.A. Zoo and the Return Loop. In 0.3 mile, the route meets a junction where the bikeway splits. A left turn leads around the edge of the L.A. Zoo parking lot, while our route continues straight ahead. The trail passes under a walking bridge (6.1) and continues along a eucalyptus-lined route which separates two golf courses.

In a short distance, the route passes alongside the eastern edge of the Cedar Tree Picnic Area and later returns to the Griffith Park Dr. junction (7.7). The final segment follows Crystal Springs Dr. southbound through a series of small rolling hills back to the parking area (8.8).

CONNECTING TRIPS: 1) There are other connecting trips in the Hollywood Hills area which are extremely hilly and on Class X roadways. These routes are only for experienced bikers in excellent condition; 2) connection with the Burbank Bikeway (Trip #36) - at Zoo Dr. and Victory Blvd., follow the latter street across the freeway.

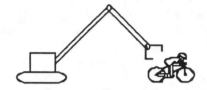

TRIP #34 - ELYSIAN PARK

GENERAL LOCATION: Elysian Park (Central Los Angeles)

LEVEL OF DIFFICULTY: Loop - strenuous
Distance - 6.4 miles (loop)
Elevation gain - periodic steep grades

GENERAL DESCRIPTION: Elysian Park provides a natural setting tucked away in the middle of the city of Los Angeles. The trip boasts parks, trees, hills and vistas -- all in a lightly travelled area (baring a major event at nearby Dodger Stadium). The key word is vistas. Few places in L.A. county provide more spectacular views per bike mile. While "gut-busting" on Elysian Park Dr., there are rewarding views back into the park area, the hills across the L. A. River, the L.A. city skyline, and views to the west that include Dodger Stadium. The price paid is some strenuous hill climbing and an entire route on Class X roadway. There are options to link additional loops and thus expand the trip mileage.

TRAILHEAD: From the Pasadena Fwy., exit at Stadium Way and follow that roadway southwest and parallel to the freeway (do not drive up into Dodger Stadium). Continue about 1-1/4 miles past the point where Stadium Way takes a 90-degree bend to the northwest. At Academy Rd., drive straight into the park on Chavez Ravine Dr. (do not take the jog to the right, which is the continuation of Stadium Way).

From the Golden State Fwy., exit at Stadium Way. Drive 1-1/2 miles to Academy Rd. and turn right. Just beyond, turn right into the Chavez Ravine Dr. parking area.

Bring a moderate water supply. Bikers will use plenty of water, but resupply is available at several sites within the park.

TRIP DESCRIPTION: **Elysian Park Road (West) and Grace E. Simons Lodge.** The biker leaves a well-treed picnic area with benches, barbecues, playground, restrooms, and water and continues south along Stadium Way. Just across Academy Rd. is a similar picnic area that is slightly more hilly. In 0.1 mile, there is a smaller park area with a blocked uphill entry to Old Lodge Rd.

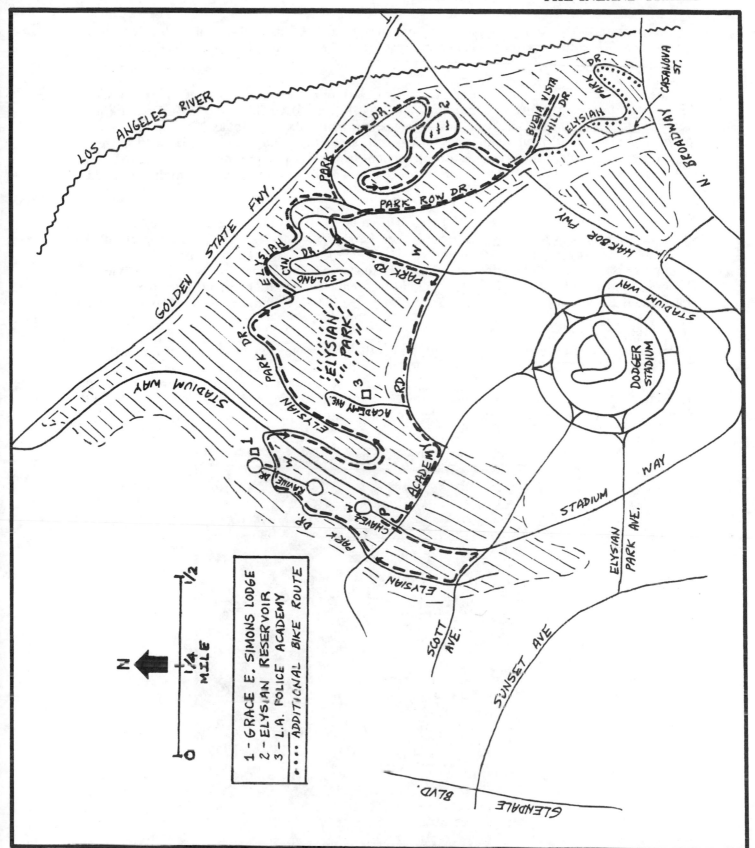

TRIP #34 - ELYSIAN PARK

Just beyond, the route turns right (northwest) and heads uphill on Scott Rd. (0.2). In another 0.1 mile of steep uphill, the path turns right on Elysian Park Rd. and parallels Stadium Way.

The tour continues on a moderate upgrade through shaded roadway with views down into the picnic area and crosses Academy Rd. (0.6). This is a favorite parking area for folks taking a workday lunch break or just "playing hooky." The path reaches a crest (0.9) and soon passes a small arboretum and picnic area with water. In another 0.1 mile, there is a short diversion trip to a nice group picnic area and the Grace E. Simons Lodge. The path proceeds downhill past a small picnic/playground area and returns to Stadium Way (1.3).

The "Workout" and the Vistas. The route crosses that street and begins a strenuous 0.9 mile winding grade on Elysian Park Dr. This is the toughest part of the trip! The first of several vista points is 0.2 mile beyond with a nice park overlook. Following is a great 180-degree view that includes the "backside" of the L.A. Civic Center (1.7), a view down into the Police Academy Firing Range and into the Hollywood Hills (2.0) and, at the crest, a fine overlook of Dodger Stadium and the San Gabriel Mountains (2.2).

Following a flat stretch and steep downhill, the route reaches a junction with Park Row Dr. (2.7). Stay to the left and enjoy the fine view down into the L.A. River and across to the local hills. In 0.2 mile, there is another junction (referred to as the "reference" junction) with the same street. Stay left again and bike to an automobile turnout that has an exceptional 180-degree view into the L.A. Civic Center (3.3).

Elysian Park Near Chavez Ravine Drive

Elysian Reservoir and the "Other" Elysian Park. Elysian Park Dr. begins a steep, winding downhill, passing the Elysian Reservoir (4.0), and a small shaded park area with restrooms just beyond. In a short distance is a short, steep upgrade that leads to a third junction with Park Row Dr. Turn left and cross over the Pasadena Fwy. to the park's southeastern section. There is a short, steep spur trip up Buena Vista to a tree-walled cul-de-sac (4.4). For the very determined, there is also a steep 1/2 mile spin down Elysian Park Dr. to the N. Broadway exit (take the left fork at the first junction on the downhill).

However, our trip returns over the bridge and continues straight ahead on Park Row Dr. on a steep 0.3 mile upgrade. Just beyond the crest, the route returns to the reference junction (4.9) and continues to the left. There is a short downhill to another junction; either a left or right turn leads, in a short distance, to the Park Row Dr. terminus at Park Dr. (5.3). Turn left at Park Dr. and bike past picnic areas, tennis courts, and a water fountain to reach the Academy Rd. intersection (5.5).

L.A. Police Academy. Turn right (northwest) and pedal up a steep 0.3 mile upgrade past the Elysian Park Recreation Center. Just beyond the crest, the route passes Academy Dr. and the L.A. Police Academy (5.9). In another 0.2 mile, the roadway turns a hard right and descends 0.3 mile further to Stadium Way. Proceed across Stadium Way to the parking area (6.4).

CONNECTING TRIPS: For those in the mood for further punishment, there are numerous alternate routes within the park, including the Dodger Stadium "spoke."

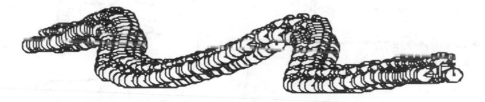

TRIP #35 - GLENDORA BIKEWAY

GENERAL LOCATION: Glendora

LEVEL OF DIFFICULTY: Loop trip - moderate
Distance - 8.3 miles (loop)
Elevation gain - periodic moderate grades

GENERAL DESCRIPTION: This predominantly Class III tour is essentially a loop trip around the South Hills of Glendora. The route has some nice views into the local foothills and San Gabriel Mountains, particularly on the northern trip segment. The general route is well laid out, primarily in residential neighborhoods on lightly travelled roadways. The route is well marked and has many potential spurs and connectors which were not investigated by the authors.

TRAILHEAD: From the Foothill Fwy., exit north at Grand Ave., continue about 1/2 mile north to Foothill Blvd. and turn right (east). Drive 0.5 mile to Wabash Ave., turn left and then turn right at Meda Ave. in 0.2 mile. Continue into the Finkbiner Park area and park on Minnesota Ave., subject to the posted laws.

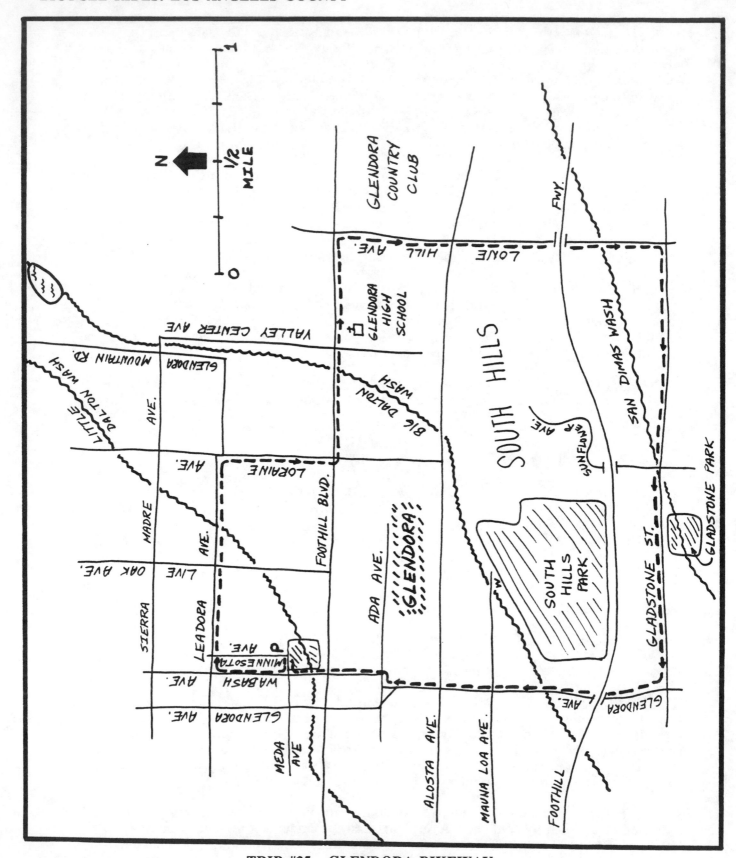

TRIP #35 - GLENDORA BIKEWAY

Bring a moderate water supply. There is water at the origin, South Hills Park (spur trip), and some of the schools along the route.

TRIP DESCRIPTION: The North Segment. From the park, ride west to Wabash Ave. and turn right. Follow this Class III roadway as it passes through a residential neighborhood past Bennett Ave., Whitcomb Ave. and a market, and reaches Leadora Ave. (0.4). Turn right (east) and begin a steady uphill while taking in the foothills and San Gabriel Mountains to the north. The Class III path continues past Live Oak Ave. and a school (0.9), crosses Little Dalton Wash (1.1), and dead ends at Loraine Ave. (1.4) near the crest.

Turn right (south) and continue on a moderate downgrade 0.5 mile past a school to Foothill Blvd. Turn left and follow a tree-lined and busier roadway on a Class II bikepath crossing Big Dalton Wash (2.4), Valley Center Ave., and passing by Glendora High School (2.5). Start uphill and continue to a crest just short of Lone Hill Blvd. (3.0). Instead of proceeding up the nasty looking hill straight ahead, breathe a sigh of relief and turn right at Lone Hill Blvd.

East Segment. Follow a long downhill on a Class III route in a more exposed, more residential area than Foothill Blvd. There is a slight uphill just before Alosta Ave. (3.5) and in 0.4 mile, the path passes under the Foothill Fwy. There is a San Dimas Wash crossing just beyond and the route is now alongside some large agricultural fields. The South Hills are clearly visible to the right (west) in this area.

South Segment. The bike route turns right at Gladstone St. (4.5) and proceeds on a flat Class II roadway alongside open fields. In 0.5 mile, the route crosses Valley Center Ave. and again enters a residential area. The bike route crosses Sunflower Ave. (5.5), the San Dimas Wash, Gladstone Park (5.8), and reaches Glendora Ave. in another 0.7 mile.

West Segment. Turn right (north) and pass under the Foothill Fwy., cross the Big Dalton Wash (7.0), pass Baseline Rd., and meet up with Mauna Loa Ave. (7.3). A right turn here leads 0.3 mile to South Hills Park where there is a dead end. There is a small grassy playground with a restroom, together with lots of local hills to hike.

However, our Class III route continues down Glendora Ave. past Alosta Ave. where the road narrows considerably. In 0.2 mile, the route junctions. Follow the bike sign right to Vista Bonita and right again (east) on Ada Ave. Pass through a shaded residential area to Wabash Ave. and turn left (7.9). Cross Foothill Blvd., pass the Glendora Ranger Station (8.1), ride across the Little Dalton Wash, and turn right on Meda Ave. Continue through the park to the starting point (8.3).

CONNECTING TRIPS: Numerous spurs off our basic trip were observed. Bikepath signs were noted on Bennett Ave., Live Oak Ave., Alosta Ave. and extensions to our basic route were found at Loraine Ave., Foothill Blvd., Gladstone St., and Glendora Ave. Connection with the Baseline Road tour (Trip #45) - at Lone Hill Blvd. and Gladstone St., continue east on the latter road.

TRIP #36 - BURBANK BIKEWAY

GENERAL LOCATION: Burbank

LEVEL OF DIFFICULTY: Peripheral loop - moderate to strenuous
Distance - 14.8 miles (loop)
Elevation gain - continuous moderate-to-steep grades in
    foothills, essentially flat elsewhere

GENERAL DESCRIPTION: This fifteen mile extravaganza is one of the better inner city tours in our book. The Burbank Bikeway actually consists of four separate Class III inner loops and a fifth, peripheral loop. The latter loop is described here. The route initially tours the foothills below the Verdugo Mountains in the northeast trip sector; there are several nice parks and excellent San Fernando Valley views in this segment. The long and sometimes steep upgrades in this area are also what give the trip the borderline "strenuous" label.

The route drops out of the foothills, passes through "Beautiful Downtown Burbank" and proceeds southwest as far as the Los Angeles Equestrian Center along the Los Angeles River. The path continues past the Disney Studios and NBC Television Studios, visits the relaxing, lightly-trafficked residential area on Burbank's west side, then returns to the trip origin via busy Buena Vista St.

TRAILHEAD: From the Golden State Fwy., exit at Buena Vista St. From the northbound freeway exit, turn south on Buena Vista St. (back toward the freeway) and turn left (east) on Winona Ave. Drive several blocks to Keystone St. and find parking subject to the posted parking laws. From the southbound exit, turn left upon reaching Buena Vista St. and drive north back under the freeway; turn right on Winona Ave. and continue as above.

Bring a moderate water supply. There are water sources strategically located throughout the trip.

Follow the route map carefully as some turns are not clearly marked (e.g., at the intersections of Kenneth Rd./Providencia Ave. and Santa Anita Ave./Lake St.). In addition, bring a street map as a backup, should you lose your way. Because some of the route is tricky, this trip is written with more than the usual number of turns described.

TRIP DESCRIPTION: **The Foothills.** From the Winona Ave. intersection, pedal north (toward the hills) through a shaded residential area on Keystone St. The path proceeds on varying grades of uphill for 0.9 mile before reaching Scott Rd. Turn right and puff another 0.2 mile before reaching a level area below Brace Canyon Park.

Just beyond is Haven Way, a diversion route up to the park, which has shade, restrooms, picnic area, recreation fields, playground, and a mesh of walkways/bikeways throughout. However, our reference route continues downhill on Scott Rd., turns left on Kenneth Rd. (1.3), curves southeast, and proceeds moderately downhill to Cambridge Dr. (2.1).

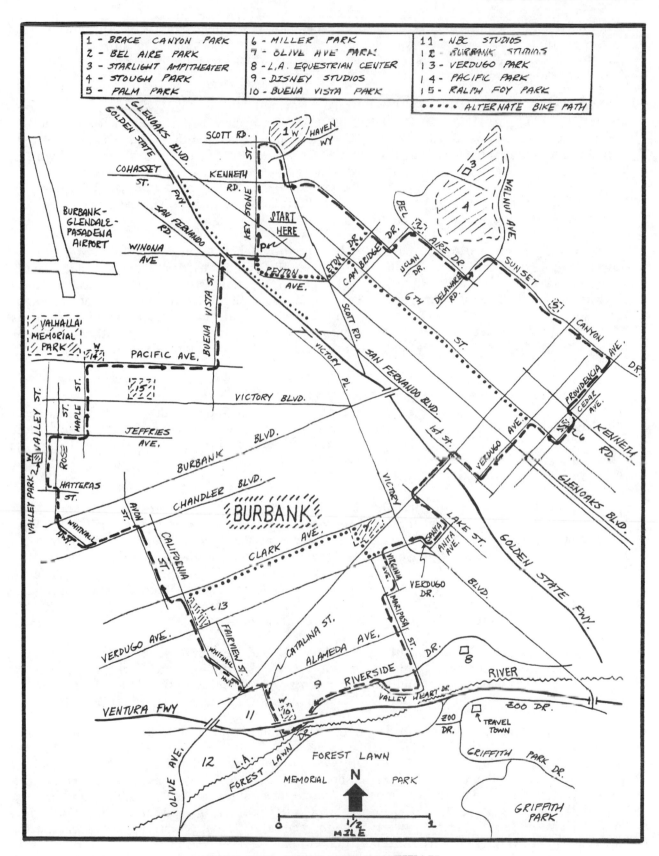

1 - BRACE CANYON PARK	6 - MILLER PARK	11 - NBC STUDIOS
2 - BEL AIRE PARK	7 - OLIVE AVE PARK	12 - BURBANK STUDIOS
3 - STARLIGHT AMPITHEATER	8 - L.A. EQUESTRIAN CENTER	13 - VERDUGO PARK
4 - STOUGH PARK	9 - DISNEY STUDIOS	14 - PACIFIC PARK
5 - PALM PARK	10 - BUENA VISTA PARK	15 - RALPH FOY PARK
		••••• ALTERNATE BIKE PATH

TRIP #36 - BURBANK BIKEWAY

163

BICYCLE RIDES: LOS ANGELES COUNTY

Now the fun begins! Pump up a steep grade for 0.3 mile to Bel Aire Dr. A nice lady living at this corner intersection watched us push our bikes up the hill and offered our tired, weary group of bikers some ice water--which we gladly accepted! Just across the street is a rest area at Bel Aire Park.

Turn right on Bel Aire Dr. and cruise downhill through this impressive residential area past UCLAN Dr. (yes,--UCLAN) and then pedal another steep uphill which crests at Delaware Rd. (2.9). Turn left and climb another "gut-buster" for 0.3 mile which crests near the junction where Delaware Rd. fuses into Sunset Canyon Dr. There are fine scattered views into the San Fernando Valley from this area, particularly on clear days. The route continues on a more moderate set of rolling hills through rural territory passing the De Bell Golf Course (3.3), Palm Park (3.7), and reaches Providencia Ave. at (4.3).

Downhill to Downtown. Turn right on Providencia Ave. and bike steadily downhill enjoying the view of the Hollywood Hills and Griffith Park straight ahead. Turn left (east) at Kenneth Rd. (4.6) and right at the next street which is Cedar Ave., skirting pleasant, little Miller Park. Turn right at Sixth St. (4.8) and left at Verdugo Ave. in another 0.2 mile. The route now enters one of the heavier commercial areas of town, passing Glenoaks Blvd. and reaching First St. (5.6). Turn right and continue to busy Olive St., turning left and passing over the Golden State Fwy. on a narrow sidewalk (6.0).

The Southern Segment and The Studios. Ride 0.3 mile to Lake St., turn left, bike to Santa Anita Ave. and turn left again (6.5). Continue to the end of the street, turn right on Verdugo <u>Dr</u>. and follow that street a short distance before turning left on Verdugo <u>Ave</u>. (6.9). Bike 0.2 mile and turn left on Virginia Ave., continuing to its terminus at Oak St. Turn right, continue one block to Mariposa St., and turn left on that tree-lined residential roadway (7.4).

The route continues another 0.5 mile through this pleasant residential area and crosses Riverside Dr. where the road narrows significantly. The roadway continues a short distance and ends at the Los Angeles River at the western edge of the L.A. Equestrian Center. Turn right on Valley Heart Dr. and return to Riverside Dr. (8.4), following that road left (west). The bikeway passes the Disney Studios, goes under the Ventura Fwy. (9.0) and cruises the southern segment of Buena Vista Park. There is a nice shaded rest area here with water and a fine view across the Los Angeles River into Forest Lawn, the Hollywood Hills and Griffith Park.

At the park's edge, turn right at Catalina St. and continue back under the freeway to the main body of Buena Vista Park. A creek runs through the park, which has shade trees, restrooms and picnic tables. Across the street are the NBC Television Studios complete with one of the KNBC helicopters and television vans (9.3).

The Residential Western Segment. Continue on Catalina St. to its terminus at Alameda Ave. and turn left (9.6). Bike almost to the Olive Ave. intersection. However, just short of that junction, use the Olive Ave. pedestrian crossing which leads across to Fairview St. Bike on that street a short distance and follow the one-way entry to Whitnall Hwy. as it angles left under the high tension power poles (9.9). Follow Whitenall Hwy. to its end at California St. (10.0), turn right, and cruise by Verdugo Park. Here is the California Swim Stadium and a park with restrooms, tennis courts, barbecue facilities, and a children's playground.

164

The remainder of the trip is through lightly trafficked residential areas with well-marked routes back to the trip origin. The highlights of that segment are provided below.

The route zig-zags its way northward and westward reaching its westernmost point along Valley St. (12.1). At Valley St. and Allan Ave. is Valley Park with shade, restrooms, tennis courts, picnic benches and a recreation field. The route then works its way northward on Maple St., reaching Pacific Ave. (13.2). At that junction, there is a terrific view of Valhalla Memorial Park and the gigantic mausoleum that resides within. This area is also directly under the Burbank Airport flightpath (an interesting contrast, no?).

The Return Leg. The bikepath travels by pleasant little Pacific Park with its shade trees, restrooms, tennis courts, and picnic tables (13.3). The route cruises through a mix of residential and light commercial zones in an area where there are splendid views into the nearby Verdugo Mountains and the more distant San Gabriel Mountains. Our path heads north on busy Buena Vista St. (14.0), passes under the Golden State Fwy. (14.6), turns right on Winona Ave. and returns to the trip origin (14.8).

CONNECTING TRIPS: 1) There are numerous combinations of possible routes just within the five loops mentioned. In addition, there is a linking Class I trail which parallels the Golden State Fwy. between Cohasset St. and Morgan Ave.; 2) connection with the Griffith Park ride (Trip #33) - at Mariposa St. and Riverside Dr., turn left (east) on the latter street, continue to Victory Blvd., and turn left.

Helmet   No Helmet

TRIP #37 - MULHOLLAND DRIVE

GENERAL LOCATION: Santa Monica Mountains

LEVEL OF DIFFICULTY: One way - very strenuous
Distance - 13.0 miles (one way)
Elevation gain - continuous steep upgrades

GENERAL DESCRIPTION: This roller-coaster tour along the crest of the Santa Monica Mountains provides some of the more spectacular vistas into the San Fernando and San Gabriel Valleys. There are separate views north across the valley to the San Gabriel Mountains and south to the ocean and the Palos Verdes Peninsula that are nothing short of breathtaking! A potential drawback of this Mulholland Dr. tour is that it is open and very hilly, i.e., sun-exposed and very physically exhausting. In addition, this Class X two-lane roadway is narrow in some areas with little or no separate shoulder for biking. In addition, some sections of roadway are in poorly maintained condition.

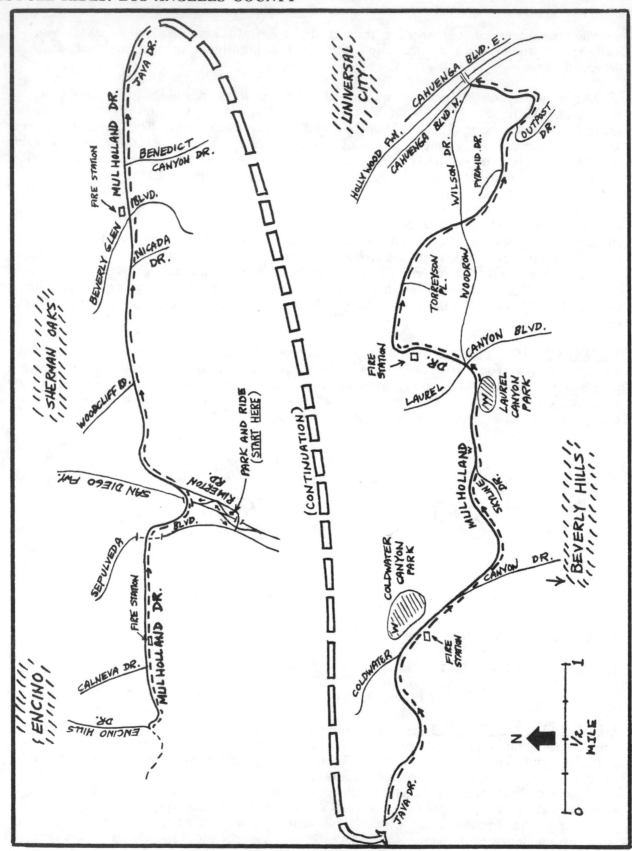

TRIP #37 - MULHOLLAND DRIVE

The one-way mileage for the trip is provided above. The trip can be started from either end. However, our tour starts with an up and back of the western Mulholland Dr. segment which covers the region from Sepulveda Pass to the end of the paved section of Mulholland Dr. This up and back is included as a "hint" that it might be wise to test a short segment of the trip before committing to the entire trip.

TRAILHEAD: From the San Diego Fwy. northbound, exit at Rimerton Rd. and make a right turn. Continue about a quarter mile to the Park and Ride area. From the southbound lanes, exit at Rimerton Rd. and turn left. Continue on the bridge over the freeway to the parking area.

Bring a large water supply and plenty of sun-protection gear. There is water at Coldwater Canyon Park, Vista Point, and Laurel Canyon Park, all concentrated in a two-mile stretch of the trip. Avoid taking this route during the week, particularly during the rush hours.

TRIP DESCRIPTION: **Western Segment.** From the Park and Ride area cycle back to Rimerton Rd. and turn left, crossing over the San Diego Fwy. and above the Mulholland Tunnel. Follow the uphill-downhill tour on an upgrade past Curtis School and just beyond, stop and admire one of many excellent overlooks of the San Fernando Valley/Encino area (0.7). Continue past the Bel-Air Church (note the great view from the north-facing parking lot), and continue the workout through a lovely residential area to Calneva Dr./Parklane Circle (1.4). The area takes on a less developed, more rural setting just beyond and begins a steady uphill climb for the next one-half mile. Near the top of the grade is the end of the paved section of Mulholland Dr. (2.1). Just beyond is mountain bike territory! Return to the San Diego Fwy. overpass. (Note that the one-way trip mileage for this segment is used below.)

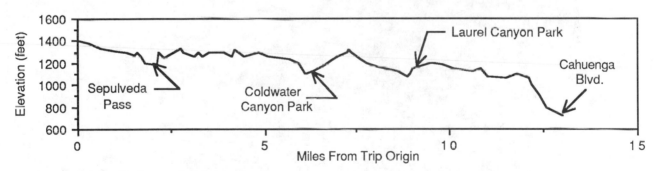

Eastern Segment. Rimerton Road to Coldwater Canyon Park. Cross over the freeway and begin a short, steep uphill that is followed by a steep, winding downhill (2.6). The route passes Woodcliff Rd. (3.1), cruises through some moderate rolling hills, and passes several overlooks into the Stone Canyon Reservoir to the south (3.4). In succession, the tour crosses Nicada Dr. and Beverly Glen Blvd. (4.3).

The journey proceeds uphill for about a half mile, crosses Benedict Canyon Dr. (4.7), and then continues the "rolling hills tradition." There are several interesting views into the San Fernando Valley to the left (north) and into the canyons and canyon residential communities to the right. In the stretch just beyond Java Dr. is the first of several well-separated "peeks" into the "backside" of central Los Angeles (6.2). The tour heads uphill and soon merges with Coldwater Canyon Dr. The route passes near pleasant, shady Coldwater Canyon Park, the home of the "Tree People" (6.5).

167

Coldwater Canyon Park to Laurel Canyon Park. The bike route continues for about 0.5 mile as a merged roadway; at this point Mulholland Dr. splits off to the left (east, if there is a single direction one can define on this winding road!). The roadway approaches a large radio tower placed high on the hillside and opens up into a view area with a turnout; hike out just beyond the parking area and take in one of the most sweeping, spectacular views of the San Fernando Valley and surrounding mountains (7.6).

There is a short downhill and a flat before reaching another fine vista in about another mile; this is the Fryman Canyon Overlook (and a water stop). Another section of very winding, steep downhill follows leading to pleasant Laurel Canyon Park (9.1) and in a short distance, Laurel Canyon Blvd. (9.3).

Laurel Canyon Park to Cahuenga Boulevard. Just across this intersection the roadway starts up a steep, steady, winding grade. Near the crest is an inspiring view of Universal City (10.1). In another half mile near Torreyson Pl. is the official "Universal City Overlook" with another fine view. The route heads downhill, crosses Woodrow Wilson Dr. (11.1) and then starts a steep upgrade where there are several views into the Los Angeles area.

Central Los Angeles From Mulholland Drive

At 0.4 mile from the Woodrow Wilson Dr. intersection is the most spectacular view into the central Los Angeles area and beyond that we've seen from a roadway! The roadway heads very steeply downhill through a series of curves and switchbacks, passes Outpost Dr. (12.3), and meets up with another fine view at the "Mulholland Scenic Vista Turnout" (12.6). The highway snakes its way steeply downward another 0.7 miles before reaching the trip end at Cahuenga Blvd.

168

CONNECTING TRIPS: Connection with the Old Sepulveda Hill Climb (Trip #5) - from the Park and Ride area, cross over the San Diego Fwy. at Rimerton Rd.; continue west to the intersection with Sepulveda Blvd.

TRIP #38 - SEPULVEDA DAM BIKEWAY

GENERAL LOCATION: Encino

LEVEL OF DIFFICULTY: Loop - easy
Distance - 9.1 miles (loop)
Elevation gain - essentially flat

GENERAL DESCRIPTION: This popular bike route is comprised of two separate loops within the Sepulveda Dam Recreation Area, a 3.8-mile western loop and a 5.3 mile eastern loop. Most of the route is Class I and with use of the Balboa Blvd. bike undercrossings, street travel is restricted to one short 0.3 mile segment. The bikeway tours lovely tree-lined routes in many areas, cruises around the Balboa Sports Center and several golf courses, and has several open areas with spectacular views into mountains to the east and south. There are several nice "R & R" areas along the route, including Woodley Park.

TRAILHEAD: From the Ventura Fwy., exit north on Balboa Blvd. Cross Burbank Blvd., continue several hundred yards further, and turn left into the tree-lined parking area.

From the San Diego Fwy., exit west on the Ventura Fwy. and drive about 2-1/2 miles to Balboa Blvd. Continue as above.

Bring a light water supply. Water is strategically located along the route.

TRIP DESCRIPTION: **West Loop.** Exit the parking lot and head north on a Class I bike route. Directly north is a nice view into the hills at the base of the Santa Susana Mountains. Continue past a small restroom facility and cruise alongside a large recreation area that is the eastern edge of the Balboa Sports Center. In a short distance, there is a junction with a bikepath segment heading across the recreation field (west) (0.2). Continue north along Balboa Blvd. and in 0.1 mile cross the bridge over the L.A. River. A look into the river reveals bikers on the Balboa Ave. bikeway undercrossing. To the east are views into the Verdugo and San Gabriel Mountains.

Continue north along open fields and turn left at Victory Blvd. (0.7). The route passes the USN/USMC Reserve Training Center and enters an open area with a fine view south to the Santa Monica Mountains. Continue past the cannon in front of the California National Guard Armory at Louise Ave. (1.3). Next is the San Fernando Valley Youth Center (there are biking activities for youngsters here) and an open agricultural area (1.5). Turn left at White Oak Ave. (1.7) and cross over the Los Angeles River.

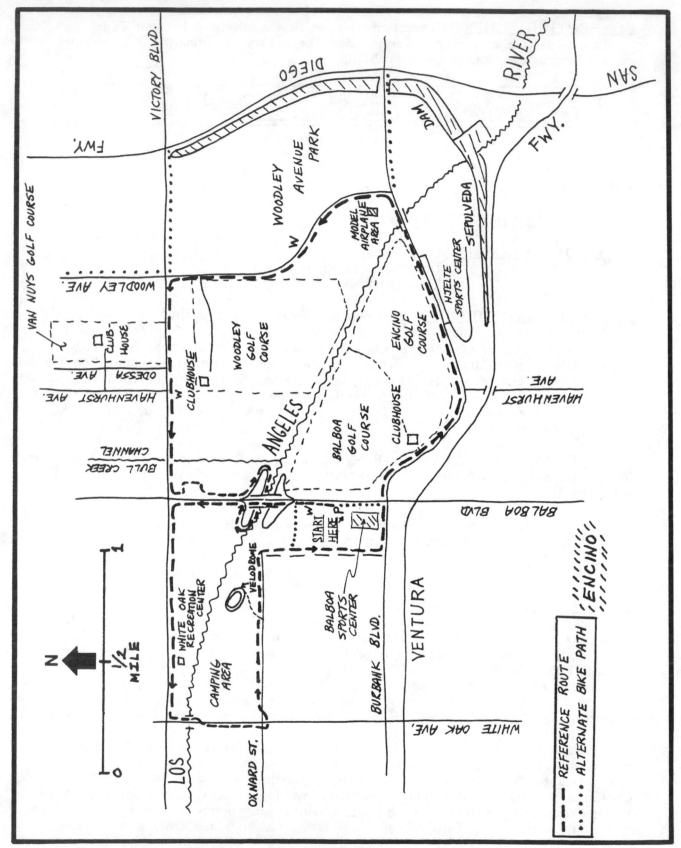

TRIP #38 - SEPULVEDA DAM BIKEWAY

170

Just beyond, the bikepath shifts over to the west side of White Oak Ave. (Class II) and proceeds 0.3 mile through a residential area to Oxnard St. The bike route turns left and returns to a Class I path alongside a small wash (2.2). The path continues along open fields to the left, and passes the entry to the Encino Velodrome (2.7).

In 0.2 mile, the bikeway curves to the right (south) and passes a junction with the path which crosses the recreation field (3.0). Continue past the junction to a picnic/play area with shaded picnic tables (3.4). Just beyond is Burbank Blvd., where the bike route turns left (east) and crosses Balboa Blvd. on a pedestrian cross-walk (3.8).

Sepulveda Dam Bikeway Near the Balboa Park Clubhouse

East Loop. This loop starts along the well-treed Balboa Golf Course, snakes through a parking lot along Burbank Blvd., and passes the Balboa Park Clubhouse (4.2). This is a convenient place to stop for water, food, or any number of "attitude arrangers." Just beyond, the path continues to maneuver between the golf course and Burbank Blvd.

At 0.8 mile from the East Loop starting point, the path crosses Havenhurst Ave. In 0.3 more mile is a roadway to the Hjelte Sports Center. The bikepath continues alongside the Encino Golf Course into an area where there are nice views into the San Gabriel Mountains (5.3).

In another 0.1 mile is a short upgrade just prior to crossing the L.A. River. At Woodley Ave. (5.6) there is an option to continue 0.4 more mile on a Class I path along Burbank Blvd. to the top of the Sepulveda Dam. However, this trip turns left on Woodley Ave. and continues past open fields into an area where there is a nice open 360-degree viewing area (6.0).

In a short distance and across Woodley Ave. is Woodley Park, where there are restrooms, cricket fields and an archery range (6.2). There is a Class III connector on Woodley Ave. which continues about 6-1/2 miles north to Granada Hills.

The route passes the entrance road to the Woodley Golf Course (6.8) and turns left at Victory Blvd. (6.9). There is an option to turn east and bike about a half mile to the dam edge. The reference route proceeds on a relatively exposed stretch alongside open fields, passing a mini-rest area with water at Havenhurst Ave. (7.3). In succession the path passes a lone rest bench, crosses over the Bull Creek Channel (7.7), and meets Balboa Blvd. (7.9).

Turn left (south) and follow a short path loop that leaves Balboa Blvd. for a short distance (8.1). In 0.3 mile, the route meets the L.A. River. Take the Balboa Blvd. undercrossing to the west side of Balboa Blvd. and backtrack a short distance to the starting point (9.1).

CONNECTING TRIPS: There are spurs off the main route as mentioned in the trip writeup.

TRIP #39 - CHATSWORTH TOUR/ BROWN'S CREEK BIKEWAY

GENERAL LOCATION: Chatsworth

LEVEL OF DIFFICULTY: Loop - easy
Distance - 6.3 miles (loop)
Elevation gain - essentially flat

GENERAL DESCRIPTION: This tour explores the Chatsworth area in the western San Fernando Valley. The trip combines a Class I segment along Brown's Canyon Wash with a Class X tour on lightly travelled roadways. The tour visits two excellent parks, Chatsworth Park North and Chatsworth Park South. There are interesting hills and rock formations there, as well as pleasant, shaded rest areas. There are also fine views into the surrounding hills throughout the trip.

TRAILHEAD: From the Simi Valley-San Fernando Valley Fwy., exit south at De Soto Ave. and continue about 1-1/2 miles to Lassen St. and turn right (west). Drive about a half mile to the Brown's Canyon Wash overcrossing and find parking nearby on Lassen St.

From the Ventura Fwy., exit north at Topanga Canyon Blvd. and continue about 5-1/2 miles to Lassen St. Turn right and drive about 0.4 mile to Brown's Canyon Wash.

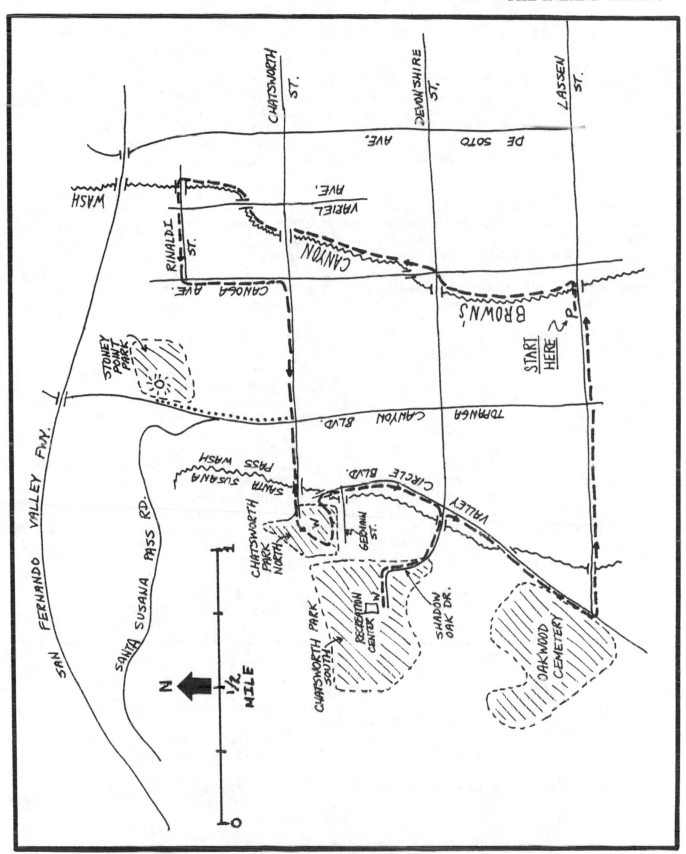

TRIP #39 - CHATSWORTH TOUR/ BROWN'S CREEK BIKEWAY

Bring a light water supply. This is a short trip with water along Brown's Creek Bikeway and at both Chatsworth Parks.

TRIP DESCRIPTION: Brown's Creek Bikeway. From Lassen St., follow the Class I bikepath which is on the east side of Brown's Canyon Wash. This is the Brown's Creek Bikeway. The path immediately passes a tightly packed group of kennels with a large canine greeting committee. The exposed path continues alongside the backside of a light industrial/commercial area. The bikeway leaves the wash diagonally, crosses Devonshire St. (0.4), and returns to the wash just north of that street.

The bikeway passes a nursery and then cruises through a neighborhood with apartments on the left and residences to the right. There is one section where bikers can pluck citrus off the the trees that overhang the bikeway (but don't do it, okay?). Further north is an aromatic area that is surrounded by small pens of farm animals and an area with riding horses (0.9). Just beyond, the path crosses Chatsworth St. and proceeds through a residential area. Near Chatsworth St. is a mini-rest area complete with bench, shade, and water fountain (1.1). In 0.2 mile, the path fuses with Variel Ave., where there is another mini-rest area (figure this one out!).

Chatsworth Street/Chatsworth Park North. Just beyond the bikeway ends at Rinaldi St. (1.4). The route proceeds left (west) on that wide, lightly-travelled roadway, passes trail-marked hills (foot or bicycle trails) in 0.2 mile, and reaches Canoga Ave. (1.8). There are nice views into the surrounding hills to the west and north in this area. The path turns right on Chatsworth St. (2.4) and reaches Topanga Canyon Blvd 0.3 mile further. Turn right (north) if a visit to Stony Point Park and Stoney Point is on your agenda.

Our route crosses Topanga Canyon Blvd., passes some horse stables and a parking lot to the left (2.9), and reaches a dead end at Chatsworth Park North (3.0). Follow the bikeway/walkway around the pretty, shaded park and investgate the rocky outcroppings at its periphery. There are picnic benches, barbecues and recreation areas, as well as a lovely lush field in the northernmost section of this park. Follow the path past the restroom and ride into the southern edge of the parking area. Just beyond the lot is the terminus (origin) of Valley Circle Blvd. (3.2).

Chatsworth Park South. Follow Valley Circle Blvd. 0.4 mile and turn right at Devonshire Blvd. Continue on that roadway as it changes name to Shadow Oak Dr. This is Chatsworth Park South. This larger park has lighter tree cover, but has nice picnic facilities, large grassy fields, tennis courts, hiking trails into the hills, and a recreation center (4.0).

Return Segment. Return to Valley Circle Blvd. and turn right (south). This segment leads to a more rural area of town and passes alongside the pretty, well-maintained Oakwood Cemetery (5.1). Just beyond is Lassen St., where the bike route turns left (5.3). The route transitions from rural to light commercial/industrial surroundings and returns to the starting point at Brown's Canyon Wash (6.3).

CONNECTING TRIPS: Connector trips were not specifically investigated; however, most of the roadway away from the center of town is lightly travelled by automobiles and of bikeable quality.

TRIP #40 - TORRANCE TOUR

GENERAL LOCATION: Torrance

LEVEL OF DIFFICULTY: Loop - moderate
Distance - 14.3 miles (loop)
Elevation gain - periodic easy-to-moderate grades

GENERAL DESCRIPTION: A fine city ride, this 14.3 mile loop trip tours the periphery of the larger Torrance bikeway system. The tour starts at the Torrance Civic Center, visits north Torrance, cruises the scenic Torrance Blvd. area of east Torrance, then bee-lines south to the Skypark Office Center area. This is followed by a 1.3 mile segment on action-packed PCH and a return via the pleasant residential area along Anza Ave. The tour is of mixed classes, though predominantly Class II.

TRAILHEAD: From the San Diego Fwy., exit south at Crenshaw Blvd. and drive two miles to Torrance Blvd. Turn right (west) and continue one mile to Madrona Ave./Prairie Ave. Turn right and turn right again at the first entry, which leads to a large parking area near the Torrance Recreation Center.

From the Harbor Fwy., drive west on Torrance Blvd. 3-1/2 miles to Madrona Ave./Prairie Ave. Turn right and continue as above.

Bring a filled water bottle. There is water at the Torrance Recreation Center and at scattered parks which are generally off the described route. There are also numerous gas stations along the way.

TRIP DESCRIPTION: **Northern Segment.** Follow the Class I path on the east side of Prairie Ave. to the intersection, then bike across Prairie Ave. on Class II Torrance Blvd. Pass the stately Marriott Hotel, Hawthorne Blvd., then shift over to the Class I sidewalk path just past Village Ln. Shift back to the Class II Torrance Blvd. path in 0.1 mile and turn right at Anza Ave. (1.0). Bike on the Class II route (the path is shared with parked cars for 0.7 mile) through residential area. Pass the small shopping center at Del Amo Blvd. and turn right on Class X 190th St. in 0.6 mile (2.3).

Pass a larger shopping center and bike on the tree-lined road segment, continue across Hawthorne Blvd., then pass under a railroad bridge. Continue on the road with generally wide bike shoulder and pass Columbia Park (recreation fields, playground, picnic benches, water, and a few trees). Pass Prairie Ave. (3.6), the Mobil Torrance Refinery entrance, then shift over to the Class I sidewalk path. Follow that path 0.9 mile to Crenshaw Blvd, then return to the Class X path and bike to Van Ness Ave. (5.0).

Southbound: 190th St. to Pacific Coast Highway (PCH). Follow the Class III road alongside the Mobil Refinery; there is a wide bike shoulder for most of the Van Ness Ave. segment. Bike through industrial/commercial area past Del Amo (5.9) and continue 0.4 mile to the point where Van Ness Ave. jogs left. Continue straight ahead on little Class X Arlington Ave. 0.1 mile to Torrance Blvd. and turn right.

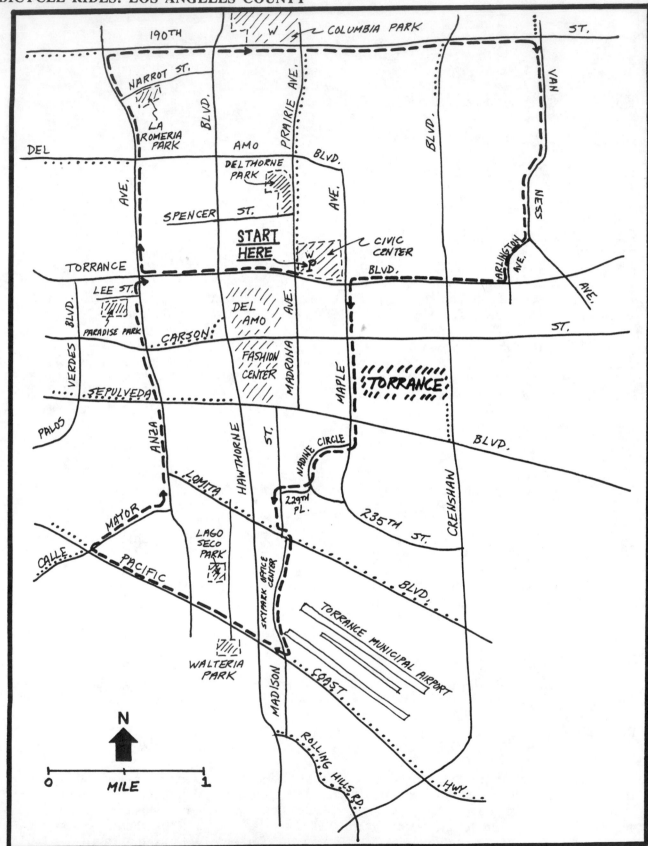

TRIP #40 - TORRANCE TOUR

Pedal on the Class II path (which is shared with parked cars) through the pleasant tree-lined residential/light commercial area past Crenshaw Blvd. and a couple of gas stations (6.9). Continue 0.6 mile, turn left on Class X Maple Ave., and bike 0.8 mile south on that lightly travelled residential street to Sepulveda Blvd. Continue past the shopping center and turn right at the first street, Nadine Circle.

Follow Nadine Cr. through the residential area 0.4 mile to 229th Pl., turn right, pass the Levy Adult School, and turn left on Madison St. (9.0). Continue to Lomita Blvd. and pedal against the traffic on the Class II path; cross Lomita Blvd (no traffic signal) and rejoin Madison St. Continue past the well-groomed Skypark Office Center, pedal under the Torrance Airport flight path, and follow the 0.2-mile upgrade to PCH.

Pacific Coast Highway. Turn right at PCH and follow the Class II path on this busy road across Hawthorne Blvd. (10.2), pass a cluster of fast-food businesses, and pedal 0.4 mile to Anza Ave. Pass a pair of shopping centers and the Donut Den (we could spend a lot of time talking about one of Don's big weaknesses, but we won't). Follow the upgrade past South Torrance High School, then bike another 0.3 mile on the short upgrade just before reaching Calle Mayor (11.4).

The Return Segment. Turn right and follow the steep downhill past the shopping center entry. Turn left in 0.6 mile at Anza Ave. and follow the Class III? road through the residential area to the short uphill segment at Sepulveda Blvd. The route transitions to Class II and continues another 0.7 mile to Torrance Blvd. (13.3). Turn right, veer right again, and follow the small road which parallels Torrance Blvd. In 0.3 mile at Ocean Ave., the bikeway transitions to Class II on Torrance Blvd. and continues across Hawthrone Blvd., Prairie Ave./Madrona Ave., then returns to the trip starting point (14.3).

CONNECTING TRIPS: 1) Connection with the South Bay Bike Trail (Trip #1A) and Palos Verdes Peninsula Loop (Trips #6A and #6B) - at PCH and Calle Mayor, bike southwest on the latter street 1-1/4 mile to Palos Verdes Blvd. Turn north for Trip #1A and south for Trips #6A or #6B; 2) connection with the Gardena/Dominguez Channel (Trip #41) - at 190th St. and Yukon Ave., bike north 1-1/2 miles on Yukon Ave. to Alondra Park.

TRIP #41 - GARDENA BIKEWAY/DOMINGUEZ CHANNEL

GENERAL LOCATION: Gardena

LEVEL OF DIFFICULTY: **Gardena City Loop** - easy
Distance - 7.0 miles (loop)
Elevation gain - essentially flat

Dominguez Channel: Round trip - easy
Distance - 5.2 miles (round trip)
Elevation gain - essentially flat

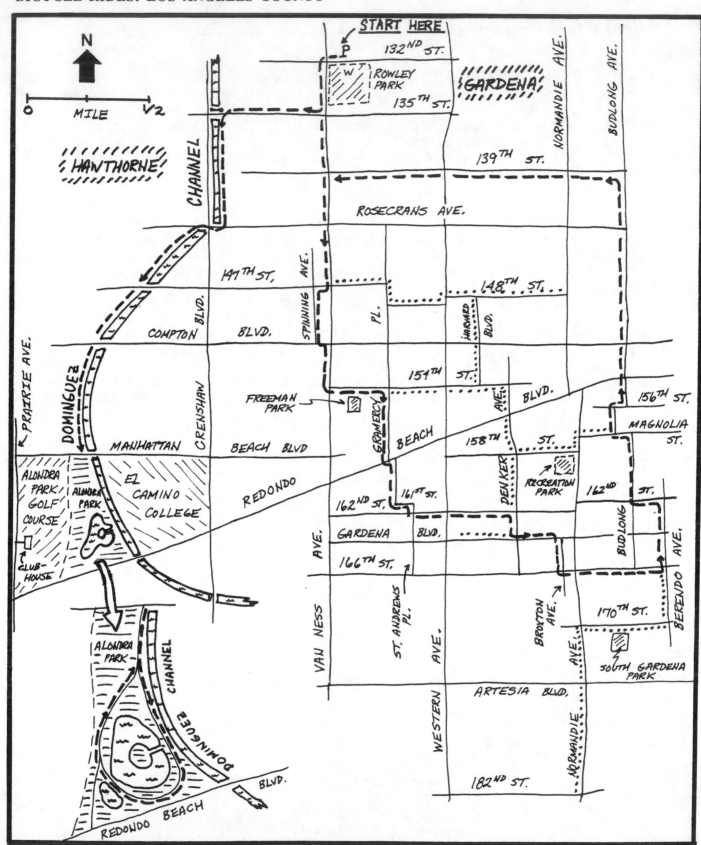

TRIP #41 - GARDENA BIKEWAY/DOMINGUEZ CHANNEL

GENERAL DESCRIPTION: Gardena City Loop. A well-marked Class III loop that explores the city of Gardena, this described trip is part of a larger city bikeway system. With the exception of the Van Ness segment, the bikeway is generally on relatively slow-moving residential or light commercial streets. The route is only modestly scenic, but does offer some nice parks which are scattered along the route.

Dominguez Channel and Alondra Park. There is also a Class I bikepath to the west along the Dominguez Flood Control Channel which is not directly connected to the Gardena loop. This 1.6 mile path starts at 135th St. and Crenshaw Blvd. and works its way south to its terminus at the Alondra Park entrance. There is an excellent Class I park tour beyond this point.

TRAILHEAD: Gardena City Loop. From the San Diego Fwy., exit east at Artesia Blvd. and drive 1-1/2 miles to Van Ness Ave. Turn left (north) and drive 2-1/2 miles to 135th St. Continue to 132nd St. and turn right. Find parking near Rowley Park (water, shade, recreation fields, and basketball courts).

From the Harbor Fwy., exit west at Rosecrans Ave. and drive 1-3/4 miles to Van Ness Ave. Turn right (north) and drive 3/4 mile to 132nd St. Continue as above.

Dominguez Channel. Start from Rowley Park as described above.

Bring a light water supply as there are public water sources at the parks along the trail.

TRIP DESCRIPTION: Gardena City Loop. The outer city loop in the accompanying trip map is described below. The western segment starts along narrow and highly trafficked Van Ness Ave., but leaves the busy road and cruises residential territory beginning at 154th St. There is an Army Reserve Center and Freeman Park nearby.

Once across busy Redondo Beach Blvd., the bikeway passes the civic center area on the 162nd St. southern trip segment. On this stretch is a miniature public Japanese Garden and the Rush Memorial Gymnasium. The eastern trip segment jig-jogs its way north through a residential area and passes near the Victorian-architectured St. John's Lutheran Church (163rd St. and Budlong Ave.). After recrossing Redondo Beach Blvd., the bikeway continues on a tree-lined segment of Budlong Ave. and passes the backside of the Normandie Club (24-hour gambling) near Rosecrans Ave.

The route heads west at 139th St., traversing a predominantly industrial area with relatively light traffic and returns to Van Ness Ave. in about 1-1/4 miles. A short one-half mile cruise to the north leads back to Rowley Park.

Dominguez Flood Control Channel. From Van Ness Ave. and 135th St., bike west 0.5 mile along the latter street to a bridge just before reaching Crenshaw Blvd. Pass through the extrance gate on the south side of 135th and bike 0.5 mile on the backside of an industrial area to Rosecrans Ave. Cross Rosecrans Ave. to the southwest side of the intersection and switch over to the west levee of the Dominguez Channel. Pedal through a residential area with street crossings at 147th St. (1.3), Compton Blvd. (1.6), and Manhattan Beach Blvd. (2.1). Note that there are roadway dividers on the latter two busy streets which make the crossings relatively easy---however, keep an eye on the traffic!

179

Friendship Stop at Alondra Park

Once across Manhattan Beach Blvd., follow the Class I path to the right of the divider fence into Alondra Park. (The downhill path to the left leads to the channel floor. We did not find a nearby downstream outlet.). Once inside the park, stay to the left, pass a restroom facility, and follow along the periphery of El Camino College through the green and shaded park. Veer right just before reaching Redondo Beach Blvd. (2.6) and follow the loop around the Alondra Park lake. Bring a few slices of bread and make friends with the ducks and geese! Bike past the large reservoir/swimming pool and follow the loop around the lake's west side, returning to Manhattan Beach Blvd. (3.1). Return to Rowley Park by reversing the incoming route (5.2).

Note: Alondra Park is certainly the tour highlight. An excellent option is to "set up camp" at this park and start the Dominguez Channel ride from there.

CONNECTING TRIPS: There are numerous local spurs off the Gardena City Loop.

TRIP #42 - DIAMOND BAR LOOP

GENERAL LOCATION: Diamond Bar

LEVEL OF DIFFICULTY: Loop - moderate
Distance - 10.4 miles (loop)
Elevation gain - periodic moderate grades

GENERAL DESCRIPTION: This pleasant predominantly Class II loop trip starts at rustic Sycamore Canyon Park and proceeds through a mix of flats and rolling hills on Diamond Bar Blvd. through Brea Canyon. Next is a short pump over the Puente Hills and a return via Colima Rd./Golden Springs Dr. There are varied views of the Puente Hills throughout the trip and an excellent view of the valley below and the San Jose Hills from the Brea Canyon Cutoff summit.

There is an interesting workout diversion tour up Grand Ave. which provides a dandy view of Diamond Bar. The Diamond Bar Loop easily can be connected to the San Jose Hills ride if the biker is interested in extending this hillside tour.

TRAILHEAD: The Orange and Pomona Fwys. merge for about a two-mile stretch near Diamond Bar. Exit at Grand Ave., turn right (east) and drive 0.4 mile to Golden Springs Dr. Turn left and continue 1/2 mile to the Sycamore Canyon Park entrance on the right and find public parking.

Bring a filled water bottle, especially on hot days. We found public water sources at Sycamore Canyon Park and at the Los Angeles National Golf Course. There are also gas stations peppered along the route.

TRIP DESCRIPTION: **Golden Springs Dr. Eastbound.** Before leaving the park, investigate the upper segment where there is a hiking trail through a lightly forrested area. Turn right onto Golden Springs Dr. and bike on the modest grade which crests and heads downhill to Diamond Bar Village with eateries and shopping. In 0.1 mile turn sharply right onto the wide expanse of Diamond Bar Blvd. (0.6).

Diamond Bar Blvd. Follow this road uphill through the treeless canyon-like setting to the crest at Tin Dr. Continue on the downhill past Steep Canyon Dr. to Grand Ave. and four-corners worth of shopping centers (1.9). Coast downhill on the long, slight grade past several small shopping plazas, then follow the steeper descent which leads to Mountain Laurel Rd. (2.6). Note the homes on the ridge above---we'll say more about the ridge area in "The Grand Ave. Diversion Trip."

Continue on the mile long downgrade through a residential setting past Pathfinder Rd., Shadow Canyon Rd. (4.0), and then bike uphill to the crest at Cold Spring Ln. Just beyond, the road passes Brea Canyon Rd. and a gas station, then tunnels under the Orange Fwy.; the road name then changes to Brea Canyon Cutoff.

Brea Canyon Cutoff. The setting returns to a less developed area of the Puente Hills on Class X roadway with a wide biking shoulder. Follow the 3/4 mile workout stair-step upgrade through the exposed canyon past Pathfinder Rd. (5.3). Just beyond at the summit is an excellent view into the valley below and the San Jose Hills across the valley. Next follow the steep, mildly winding downhill which lets out at Colima Rd. near a strategically-located delicatessen (6.9).

181

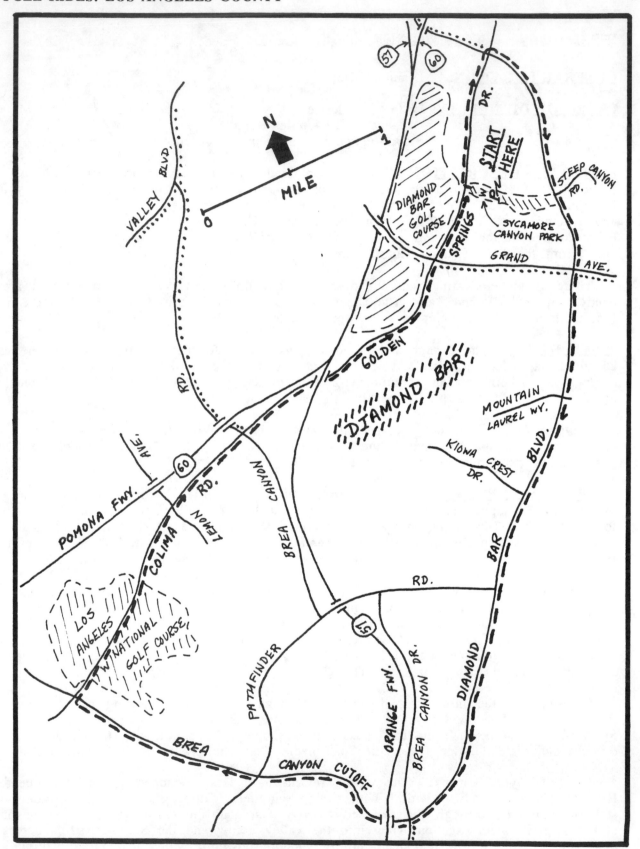

TRIP #42 - DIAMOND BAR TOUR

Colima Rd - Golden Springs Dr. Eastbound. Turn right (east) and bike on the Class X road between the two segments of the Los Angeles National Golf Course. Continue past the Los Angeles Royal Vista Restaurant and an area of the golf course to the right with a convenient water fountain (7.2). Continue on the flat, pass Lemon Ave., and begin the 0.3 mile uphill to an area with fast food restaurants and gas stations. Pass Brea Canyon Rd. (8.5) and begin the Class II ride under the freeway interchange on what is now Golden Springs Dr.

Just beyond is the stair-step upgrade which becomes testy just before reaching Gateway Dr. In this area there are bare hills and the freeway to the left and new commercial complexes to the right. In the next 0.6 mile is a ride on varying degrees of grade which reaches the crest at Grand Ave. at a shopping/industrial complex (9.9). Here is Casa O'Brien's with margueritas and great Mexican food. Across the street is the Diamond Bar Golf Course and just beyond is the Diamond Bar Country Club. In another 0.3 mile, turn right into the Sycamore Canyon Park (10.4).

Grand Ave. Diversion Trip. One look at the street map convinced us to bike up Grand Ave. east of Golden Springs Rd.; the ride on the ridge at the summit appeared to be too good to pass up. So we biked up steep Grand Ave. 0.7 workout mile to Shotgun Ln. only to find that the road access is gated---private property! However, we continued up to Summit Ridge Dr., turned left and biked 0.3 mile to the Summit Ridge Park turnoff. A short distance uphill is the park with water, restrooms, picnic tables and a tremendous view of the surrounding hills and valleys. The total round trip is 2.2 miles.

CONNECTING TRIPS: 1) Connection with the Hacienda Heights Loop (Trip #27) - at Brea Canyon Cutoff and Colima Rd., turn west at the latter road; 2) connection with the San Jose Hills ride (trip #43) - at Brea Canyon Rd., bike north 1-1/2 miles to Valley Blvd.; 3) connection with the Bonelli Regional Park tour (Trip #44) and the Baseline Road tour (Trip #45) - from the intersection of Golden Springs Rd. and Diamond Bar Blvd., bike north on the latter street, which becomes Mission Blvd. and meets little Humane Wy. in 2-1/2 miles; follow that road to Valley Blvd. and turn left (north) at the first major intersection (Ganesha Blvd.) beyond the Corona Expressway.

TRIP #43 - SAN JOSE HILLS

GENERAL LOCATION: Walnut, City of Industry

LEVEL OF DIFFICULTY: Loop - moderate
Distance - 12.9 miles (loop)
Elevation gain - periodic moderate-to-steep grades
(Amar Rd. and Temple Ave.)

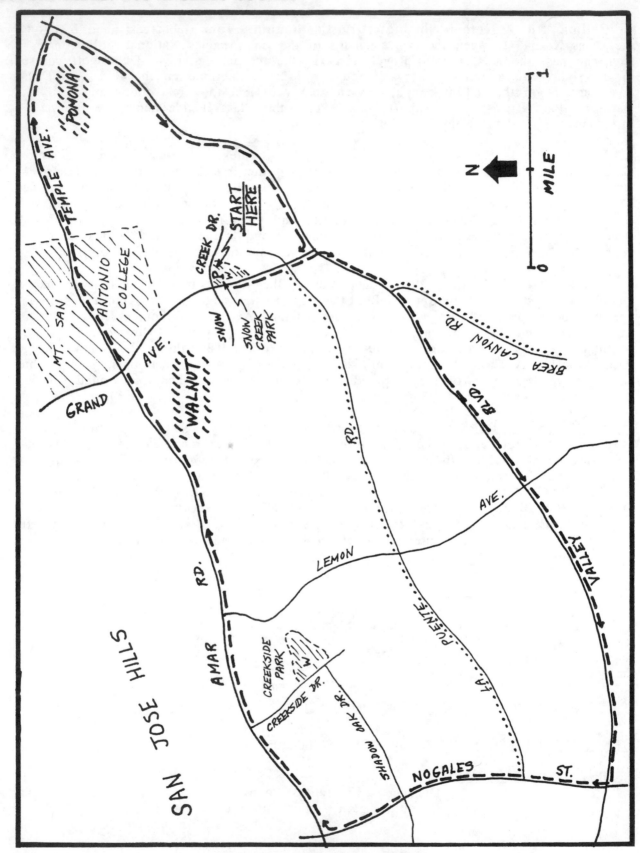

TRIP #43 - SAN JOSE HILLS

GENERAL DESCRIPTION: This is a dandy trip for "hillies." From Nogales St. to La Puente Rd. to the outlet at Temple Ave. and Valley Blvd. (6.7 miles), the biker is treated to a steady diet of ups and downs in the San Jose Hills. The trip is mostly on Class X roads with plenty of biking room. There are splendid views into the valleys and across to the Puente Hills at the higher elevations. For variety, the remaining half of the trip is in the valley flatlands.

On a hot, smoggy day this workout might budge the *strenuous* difficulty rating. More adventurous bikers might explore the surrounding hillside, residential communities, particularly on La Puente Rd., west Amar Rd. and north Grand Ave.

TRAILHEAD: From the Pomona Fwy., exit at Brea Canyon Rd. and drive north 1-1/2 miles to Valley Blvd., turn right and continue one-half mile to Grand Ave. Turn left and drive 0.6 mile to Snow Creek Dr. and turn right into Snow Creek Park.

From the Orange Fwy. south of Diamond Bar, exit at the Pomona Fwy. westbound and turn off at Brea Canyon Rd. Continue as described above. From the Orange Fwy. north of Diamond Bar, exit at Temple Ave. and drive 0.7 mile to Valley Blvd. Turn left and proceed 2-1/4 miles to Grand Ave. and turn right (north). Continue to Snow Creek Dr. as described above.

Bring a filled water bottle (two for hot days); no easily accessible public water sources were found.

TRIP DESCRIPTION: **Grand Ave.** Explore the well designed little Snow Creek Park before hitting the road. There are shade trees, picnic benches and a picnicker's pogoda, water, restrooms, sunken baseball field, and little Snow Creek on the park periphery. Return to Grand Ave. and bike downhill through the hills. In 0.4 mile the road passes La Puente Rd., then continues downhill 0.3 mile to Valley Blvd.

Valley Blvd. Outbound. Turn right and bike on the Class X road with wide biking shoulder through the flat and wide valley. The road parallels the Southern Pacific tracks and there is a reasonable liklihood of having a choo-choo for company along this stretch. The area along the tracks has scattered industy for the next several miles - this is part of the City of Industry (surprise!). Continue through varying and sparsely populated and developed areas (mixed residential and commercial) past Brea Canyon Rd. and reach Pierre Rd. with its small plaza, gas station and aromatic plant nursery (1.8). In another 0.7 mile is Lemon Ave. with a gas station, small shopping center and a few rolling hills for variety. Bike past Fairway Dr. and a shopping plaza complete with a German deli, Sentous Ave. with a gas station (3.2), then continue another 0.4 mile to Nogales St.

Nogales St. So you're wondering---where are these San Jose Hills? Nogales St. will be the biker's introduction. Bike 0.5 mile in a residential setting to La Puente Rd.; there is a nice three mile Class II bikeway to the east on this road. However, our trip starts uphill on tree-lined Nogales St., reaching the crest in 0.4 mile. The residential road continues on the flat for a short distance then starts a mild, steady uphill to Shadow Oak Dr. (4.9).

Just 0.4 mile to the left is Shadow Oak Park, where Creekside Park can be reached by turning right and biking 0.7 mile. Our reference route on Nogales St. follows another steady uphill which steepens and continues 0.4 mile to Walnut Plaza (shopping center). Pump another 0.2 mile to Amar Rd. (5.5).

Amar Rd. - The Hillside Tour. Turn right (west) on the Class X road with a wide bike shoulder and pedal through shadeless residential territory. There are barren hills to the left and scattered peeks down into the valley on the right. Follow another steady upgrade which steepens and then reaches the crest at (6.6). For the next two miles to Grand Ave., the route transitions from this steady upgrade to a region of rolling hills.

Bike past scattered residential areas and enjoy the periodic views down into the valley. The road passes Lemon Ave. (7.1), then roller coasters through a less populated area before reaching a little valley with a small, tightly packed community. In a short distance, Amar Rd. reaches the Grand Ave. intersection (8.7).

Temple Ave. - The Downgrade. Pass a gas station and continue on the road now named Temple Ave. Pass the Mt. San Antonio College Wildlife Sanctuary, the campus entrance, and follow the steady upgrade alongside the campus. The upgrade continues through more open country, across Bonita Dr., then follows the gut-buster steady uphill to the crest 1.2 miles from Grand Ave. Enjoy the view from the crest, then bike downhill on divided highway through cattle country. Pass on the periphery of California State Polytechnic University campus on tree-lined roadway, cross San Jose Creek and bike to Valley Blvd. (10.8).

Valley Blvd. - Return Segment. There is a small shopping center 1/4 mile further at Pomona Blvd. (included, there is the Country Peddler, a rural style merchandise store). However, our reference route turns right at Valley Blvd. and continues through open and exposed valley country. There are scattered residential pockets along the way with scattered industry and some farmland. There are continuous views of the so-far barren Puente Hills to the left. Pass the gas station 1.5 miles from Temple Ave. and reach Grand Ave. 0.6 mile beyond. Turn left and puff up the workout upgrade 0.7 mile, returning to Snow Creek Park (12.9).

CONNECTING TRIPS: 1) Connection with the Diamond Bar Loop (Trip #42) - at Brea Canyon Rd., bike 1-1/2 miles south to Colima Rd./Golden Springs Rd. and turn left; 2) connection with the Bonelli Regional Park tour (Trip #44) and the Baseline Road tour (Trip #45) - from the Temple Ave./Valley Blvd. intersection, bike north on the latter road 1.7 miles to the first intersection beyond the Corona Expressway (Ganesha Blvd.) and turn left.

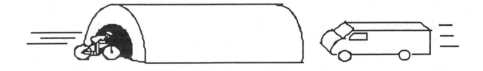

TRIP #44 - BONELLI REGIONAL COUNTY PARK

GENERAL LOCATION: San Dimas, Pomona

LEVEL OF DIFFICULTY: Loop - moderate
                      Distance - 8.9 miles (loop)
                      Elevation gain - periodic moderate grades
                                    (frequent moderate grades on Amar Rd.)

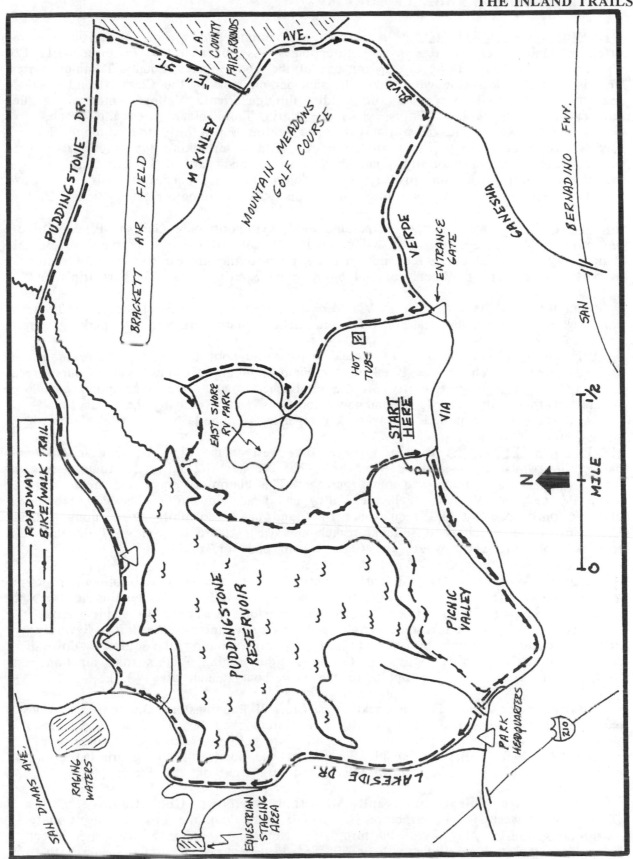

TRIP #44 - BONELLI REGIONAL PARK

GENERAL DESCRIPTION: A pleasant spin around Puddingstone Reservoir, this tour offers a wide variety of terrain and attractions. As our triathlete reviewer Sally Bond notes, it is also part of the course for one of the Los Angeles County Triathlon series. This is a varied class ride with wide bike shoulder on most of the Class III and Class X segments. The route traverses rolling hills through Picnic Valley, winds along the east shoreline by Raging Waters, visits the North Shore picnic area and beach, cruises by Brackett Field on a flat road, and returns for a hilly tour through the scenic East Shore area. There are numerous vistas overlooking the reservoir. The picnic areas are in a naturally scenic and well-groomed part of Bonelli Park. There are several short grades on this tour which "push" this trip out of the *easy* category; however, there is an *easy* two-mile mini loop which circumnavigates Picnic Valley.

TRAILHEAD: From the San Bernardino Fwy., exit north onto Ganesha Blvd. Drive 3/4 mile to Via Verde, turn left and continue 3/4 mile to the east entrance of Bonelli Park. Pay the $3.00 entry fee and drive l/2 mile to the nearest parking. An option is to park in the Raging Waters lot and enjoy some exciting water rides at trip's end.

From the Foothill Fwy., exit at Via Verde and turn east. Drive l/4 mile to the west park entrance. Continue another mile and make a hard left into the parking area.

Bring a light water supply as there's water throughout the park. There is a three mile waterless stretch in the Brackett Air Field-Mountain Meadows Golf Course area. Look out for thorns, particularly off the established roads. Our tour group picked up several of these little devils at unknown locations and eventually had flat tires! (Once the thorns are pulled out, plan on repairing a tube.)

TRIP DESCRIPTION: **Picnic Valley.** Bike west on the Class I path near the parking lot which follows along Via Verde. For the next l/2 mile, the route passes a large pogoda, playgrounds and picnic areas. The charming grass and treed areas along the path are all part of Picnic Valley and heads downhill. The path crosses under a park roadway and then veers right and heads downhill again along Lakeside Dr. Next it passes above a sailboat launch area where there is a view of the lake and reaches a parking entry where the Class I path ends (1.2).

Raging Waters. Pass the parking entry (stay to the left) and follow the Raging Waters sign to the right at the next road junction. (A left at this junction leads to the Equestrian Staging Area.) Bike next to Puddingstone Reservoir to a picturesque overlook with the reservoir to the right and Raging Waters to the left. Several different water rides can be viewed (and visited), including the ultimate downhill ride, the seven-story high "Dropout" (2.0). At the Raging Waters road junction just beyond, turn right and bike uphill to the powerboat launch area (2.6).

Puddingstone Dr. For the next mile, Class II Puddingstone Dr. passes a series of excellent picnic areas and an area with a miniature sand beach. The road crosses Walnut Ave. (3.2) and begins a short uphill just before reaching the outskirts of Brackett Air Field. Bike alongside the airport and admire the longhorn cattle in the hills to the north, pass the control tower, and turn right on "E" Street (4.5).

L.A. County Fairgrounds and Mountain Meadows Golf Course. Follow the Class I path (west side of street only) one-half mile along the Los Angeles County Fairgrounds to McKinley Ave. and turn left. Note that there is a nifty spot directly below the Brackett Field flight path on "E" St. Pedal a Class X stretch 0.3 mile to Ganesha Blvd. and then veer right (5.3).

Bike on the mild Class II road uphill along the golf course for 1/2 mile.   Turn right at Via Verde and follow the steeper upgrade to the Bonelli Park east entry gate.

East Shore.   One option is to continue 1/2 mile back to the parking area. However, this reference ride follows the road right on a steep upgrade which passes the Puddingstone Hot Tubs (public tubs with nice vistas) (6.6); this grade levels in a short distance.   Bike into the East Shore RV Park and turn right at the corner Market.

East Shore, Puddingstone Reservoir

Stay to the right and follow the winding downhill into the lower RV park (7.4), turn left at any of the small streets, and follow the road toward the reservoir.   Bike below the tent camp area, then pass through the bike entry near the lake edge, and join up with the pleasant Class I path along the lake.   In this area is one of the outstanding lake views; this is a particularly nice location from which to watch the powerboats and jet skiers (8.1).   Continue uphill on the path to the inviting East Shore picnic area, following the trail inland to the road (8.5), and then turn left. Bike 0.2 mile to Via Verde, turn right and return to the parking area (8.9).

CONNECTING TRIPS: 1) Connection with the Baseline Road tour (Trip #45) - at Lakeside Dr. and Via Verde, continue west on Via Verde; 2) connection with the Glendora Bikeway (Trip #35) - follow Via Verde west to San Dimas Ave., turn right and bike 2-1/2 miles to Gladstone St., and then turn left.

TRIP #45 - BASELINE ROAD

GENERAL LOCATION: San Dimas, La Verne, Claremont

LEVEL OF DIFFICULTY: Loop - moderate
Distance - 22.3 miles (loop)
Elevation gain - periodic moderate grades

GENERAL DESCRIPTION: This very scenic loop explores Ganesha Park, Bonelli Regional County Park, cruises the foothills of the San Gabriel Mountains, and visits three fine cities to boot. Most of this tour is on Class X roads with relatively light traffic and with wide biking shoulder. There are hill, valley, and mountain vistas scattered throughout this trip. There are numerous interesting diversion trips throughout the loop tour which are identified in the detailed trip writeup.

TRAILHEAD: From the San Bernardino Fwy., exit at Dudley St. in Pomona. Turn north and continue as the street changes name to Via Vista Dr. Follow this winding road one mile into Ganesha Park; continue toward the north end of the park on what is now Paige Dr. and find parking.

Bring a filled water bottle (two on hot and smoggy days). There is water at several parks which are generally reached with short diversions off the main route.

Ganesha Park itself is a pleasant base of operations. There's dense tree cover, hiking trails, picnic areas, swimming pool, children's playgrounds and restrooms.

TRIP DESCRIPTION: **Ganesha Park to Bonelli Regional County Park.** Leave the picnic area near the swimming pool and return to Paige Dr. heading north. Bike uphill about 0.3 mile to McKinley Ave., turn left and continue uphill above the Los Angeles County Fairplex on Class III bikeway. In 0.5 mile on McKinley Ave., the road crests and continues a short distance to Ganesha Blvd. (0.9).

Turn left and bike one-half mile on the mild upgrade on Class III roadway alongside the Mountain Meadows Golf Course. Turn right at Via Verde and follow the steeper upgrade to the Bonelli Park east entrance gate (2.9). Bike in the hills of the large and pleasant park on Via Verde and in 1/2 mile reach a spur leading to a parking area. There are options to stay on Via Verde or to bike the paralleling Class I path through the tree-shaded picnic area known as Picnic Valley. The reference route stays on Via Verde and continues another 0.9 mile on rolling hills before reaching the park's west entrance gate at Lakeside Dr. (4.4). Continue west a short distance, pass under the Foothill Fwy., and reach San Dimas Ave.

Western Trip Segment. Turn right and bike 0.4 flat mile to an area with an exceptional view north into the valley area. Follow this Class X road on the steep downgrade with barren hills to the east. Continue downhill past Avd. Loma Vista (5.5) alongside the Foothill Fwy.; the road curves east and passes under that freeway in 0.4 mile. Continue through the rolling hills in a small canyon and pass the area with a view of Raging Waters. In a short distance, the road curves back to the north and levels, passes Ben's Bait Shop (bait and cold liquid refreshments) and then passes a gas station. The route continues across Arrow Hwy. and reaches Bonita Ave. just beyond (7.2).

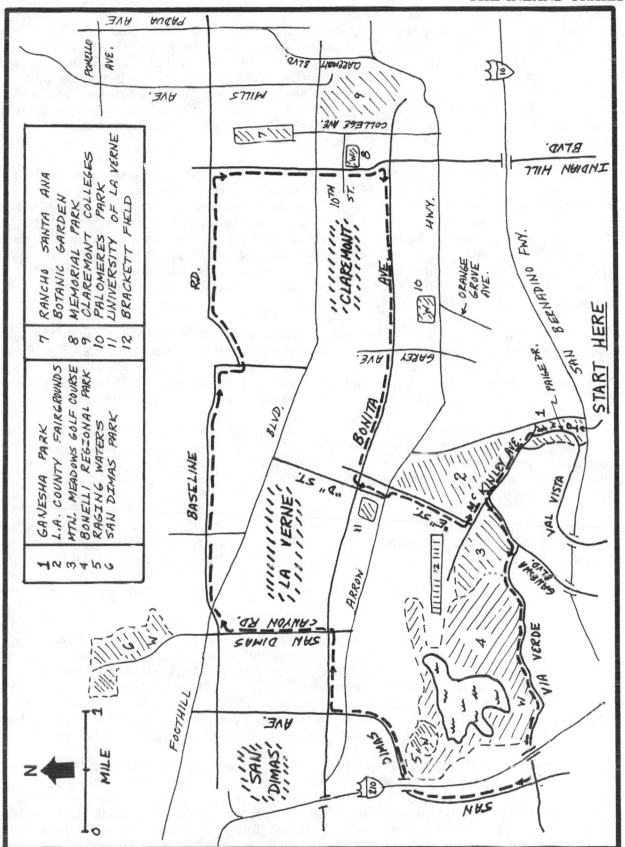

TRIP #45 - BASELINE ROAD

Turn right (east) and pedal 0.8 mile on this palm-lined road, passing several small shopping plazas before reaching San Dimas Canyon Rd. Turn left and bike on another Class X road with wide shoulder. The road heads uphill through an area with a view of the San Gabriel Mountains directly ahead, crests, and returns downhill passing Allen Ave. In a short distance is the State Hwy. 30 undercrossing and a more rural area with Baseline Rd. just beyond (9.0). There is a spur-trip option to continue north 0.4 mile to San Dimas Canyon Park for water, restrooms, shade, recreation fields, picnic areas, and a nature center.

Baseline Road. Our reference route turns right and continues on this Class X road along the base of the San Gabriel Mountains. Bike through the surrounding residential area, pass Wheeler Ave., and continue through rolling hills to Williams Ave. (11.3). Follow the marked Baseline Rd. detour south and turn left in a short distance at College Way. Follow this road along the Live Oak Canyon Wash and return to Baseline Rd. Bike on a light and steady upgrade which levels near Mountain Ave. (14.4); there is a nifty (and steep) diversion trip on this road into the hillside residential area. Our reference tour continues on Baseline Rd. through the residential area 0.5 mile to Indian Hill Blvd.

Indian Hill Blvd. Turn right and follow another Class X road through the quiet and tree-shaded residential area. The refreshing downhill leads past Cahuilla Park (water, shade), Claremont High School, and crosses Foothill Blvd. just beyond (15.9). The road narrows and continues through the treed, rural residential setting past inviting Memorial Park (water, restrooms, shade, grass, and playgrounds).

Bonita Ave. The return west on this road passes through a residential area up to Mountain Ave., then transitions into a more industrially-oriented region up to the La Verne city limit (17.9). The flat, lightly travelled, Class X road returns to the tree-lined residential area and continues to "D" St. (19.9). There is an old fashioned, but well maintained, shopping complex here with a donut shop (Don's weakness!).

The Return Segment. Turn left (south) on "D' St., cruise by the University of La Verne, and continue 0.3 mile to Foothill Blvd. Turn left and right again at the next intersection ("E' St.). Pedal past the Pomona Raceway between Brackett Field and the west side of the Los Angeles County Fairplex to McKinley Ave. Continue 0.3 mile to the Ganesha Blvd. intersection (21.4), then return to Ganesha Park by retracing the outgoing route. The total tour is 22.3 miles.

Diversion Trips. There are several additional interesting areas to explore in the Claremont area. There is an interesting workout in the Mills Rd. - Pomelo Dr. - Padua Ave. region (Mills Rd. becomes Baldy Rd. and can be continued on the gut-wrenching uphill to Mt. Baldy - expert bikers only!!). There is some excellent tour biking available in the area bounded by Foothill Blvd.-Indian Hill Blvd.-Arrow Hwy.-Claremont Blvd.; in this zone are Pomona College, Claremont College, Claremont Men's College, Scripps College, Harvey Mudd College and Pitzer College.

CONNECTING TRIPS: 1) Connection with the Bonelli Regional County Park tour (Trip #44) - at Lakeside Dr. and Via Verde, turn north on the former street; 2) connection with the San Jose Hills ride (Trip #43) and the Diamond Bar Loop (Trip #42) - from the intersection of Ganesha Blvd. and Via Verde, bike south 1-1/2 miles on the former road to Holt Ave. Turn right and follow that street as it becomes Valley Blvd. 1-3/4 miles to Temple Ave. Continue south for the San Jose Hills trip and turn left on Temple Ave. to reach Diamond Bar Blvd. and the Diamond Bar Loop trip.

TRIP #46 - LA MIRADA BIKEWAY SYSTEM

GENERAL LOCATION: La Mirada

LEVEL OF DIFFICULTY: Loop - easy
Distance - 9.8 miles (loop)
Elevation gain - periodic easy-to-moderate grades

GENERAL DESCRIPTION: All too often, those little green spots on our maps wind up being wayside parks with some tumbleweeds and a drinking fountain! Not this tour! This is a well designed route on primarily Class I/Class II bikeways with the trip highlights being Creek Park and La Mirada Park. After cruising a few miles on the city streets, the route follows a natural and refreshing Class I path alongside La Mirada Creek, then visits the green rolling knolls and recreation areas of La Mirada Park. This inviting park has its own network of fine walking/biking trails.

TRAILHEAD: From the Santa Ana Fwy., exit north at Valley View Ave. and continue 1.8 miles to Foster Rd. (just beyond Rosecrans Ave.). Turn right and drive 0.3 mile to Gardenhill Rd., turn left, then continue 0.2 mile to the parking area in front of the Gardenhill Park Community Center. Gardenhill Park has a playground, trees, picnic benches and barbecue facilities, as well as water and restrooms.

Bring a light water supply. There is water at the parks and numerous gas stations along the way.

TRIP DESCRIPTION: **The City Streets.** Exit the park and turn right, biking through the residential area a short distance to Foster Rd. and then turn right again. Continue a short distance and turn left (south) on Valley View Ave. Follow the mild stair-step upgrade on this Class II path 0.5 mile to Rosecrans Ave. (0.8). Turn left and continue through the residential setting past Biola Ave.; a left turn here takes the biker to Biola University.

Our reference route remains on Rosecrans Ave. and continues 0.5 mile to La Mirada Blvd. (1.8). Turn right and cruise by the La Mirada Civic Theater and the La Mirada Mall. In 0.4 mile, turn left at Santa Gertrudes Ave. where there is a small delicatessen, among other businesses at this intersection. Pass Rosecrans Ave. (3.9) on this Class II route and bike the short workout upgrade to the point where there is a clear view of the Los Coyotes Hills.

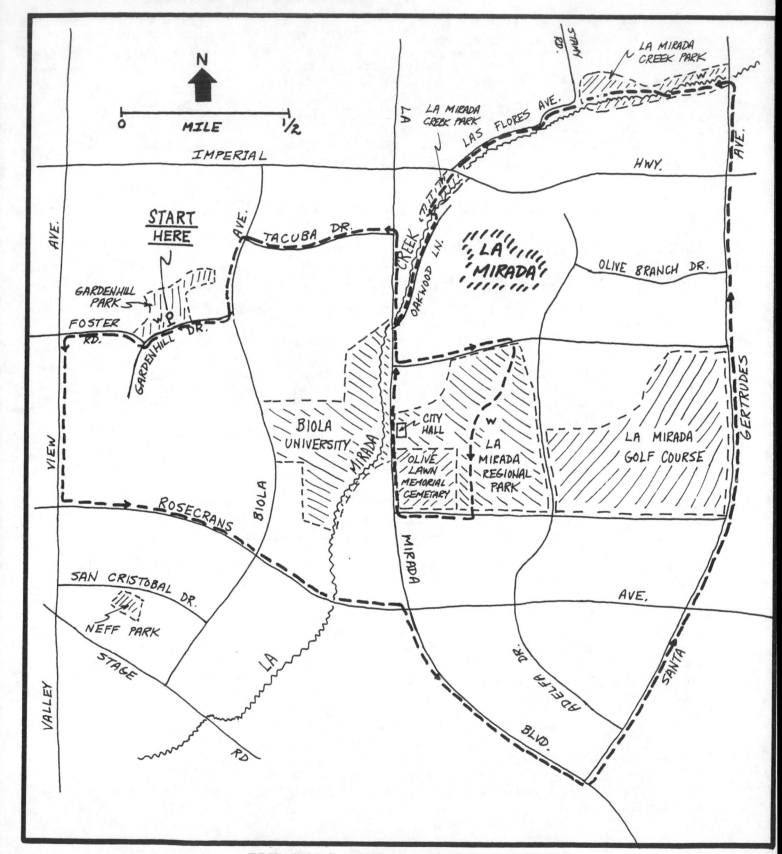

TRIP #46 - LA MIRADA BIKEWAY SYSTEM

Pedal alongside the La Mirada Golf Course through modest rolling hills, pass Foster Rd., and reach Imperial Hwy. (5.1). Bike 0.3 mile on Class X road and, near the bottom of the first grade, cross the street to the Class I bike entry.

Creek Park. Follow the path through grassy Creek Park alongside La Mirada Creek. The path follows the creek a short distance on both north and south sides. Keep a wary eye for rotating sprinklers in this area; Don was thoroughly zapped by one of these gadgets at one of the bridge crossings. (Don never was too bright!) Follow the tree-lined bikeway to the park edge and transition to Los Flores Ave. There are horse corrals, chicken, geese and even rabbits in this area.

Bike to Imperial Hwy. (6.2); just before reaching this street, follow the dirt path back down to the creek and pass through the short tunnel under Imperial Hwy. This is the southern segment of Creek Park. Meander along the creek through this serene environment following the small bridges which cross the creek. At the last creek crossing before reaching the tunnel, follow the path to the left up to the residential area and turn right on Oakwood Ln. Bike to La Mirada Blvd. and cross that busy road.

La Mirada Park. Note that there are many paths throughout the park and only a sample route is described. Turn left (south) and bike 0.2 mile to Foster Rd., turn left and turn right in a short distance into the parking area (7.4). Follow the Class I path that is dead ahead on the short workout upgrade into the La Mirada Park vicinity. There are numerous recreation fields in this green and scenic area. Follow the path until it passes near Adelfa Dr., then take the path junction to the right towards the swimming pool and tennis courts.

Near the lowest set of courts, follow that path to the right, turn left at its terminus, and continue down to the small lake. This is a pleasant rest spot with a wide variety of friendly water fowl. Walk a short distance across the grass to Alicante Rd. and turn right (8.1).

The Return Leg. Bike a short distance past the well-manicured Olive Lawn Cemetary to La Mirada Blvd. Turn right (north) and follow the rolling hills past the water fountain at City Hall, continuing to Tacuba Dr. (9.1). Turn left and bike on the Class III street through the quiet residential area. Continue 0.5 mile to Biola Ave. and turn left; follow that Class II route to Gardenhill Rd. Pedal through well-groomed residential territory past Gardenhill Elementary School and return to the Gardenhill Park Community Center (9.8).

CONNECTING TRIPS: There is an interesting hilly connecting tour of the Los Coyotes Country Club vicinity. The route passes through an area of plush residential estates. Continue east on Rosecrans Ave. past the Santa Gertrudes Ave. intersection, turn right at Beach Blvd. and turn left at the first street, which is Los Coyotes Dr.

POTPOURRI

1st Street Near City Hall

TRIP #47 - SKYSCRAPER TOUR

GENERAL LOCATION: Los Angeles Civic Center

LEVEL OF DIFFICULTY: Loop - moderate
Distance - 10.8 miles
Elevation gain - periodic moderate grades on
Beverly Blvd./1st St.

GENERAL DESCRIPTION: At it's best, this is an early Sunday morning tour. Start between 7:00 am and 8:00 am and plan to spend several hours riding and browsing. Traffic during the week is murderous and our recommendation is, "Save it for Sunday." The tour is on a mix of roads with much of the route on Class II or Class III paths, or unmarked roads with a wide, marked car-parking area.

This little beauty provides a fine morning cross section of the Los Angeles scene. The tour starts at scenic MacArthur Park, then heads into central Los Angeles, visiting the L.A. Convention Center, skyscraperville, and the L.A. Flower Market. Next is a short tour through "Street People's Los Angeles," Koreatown and Little Tokyo, El Peublo De Los Angeles Historic Park, and Union Station. The return leg passes through the Los Angeles Civic Center and returns to the trip origin via the rolling hills of Beverly Blvd.

For the truly adventurous, this is a "can't miss" trip.

TRAILHEAD: From the Santa Monica Fwy., exit north at Vermont Ave. and drive 3/4 mile to Wilshire Blvd. Turn right and continue 3/4 mile (past Lafayette Park) to Park View and turn right. Find parking at the west edge of MacArthur Park subject to the posted laws. (There is no parking time limit Sunday and no meter fees -- there is no posted guideline on the latter rule, but we were not ticketed.)

From the Harbor Fwy., exit west at 6th St. and drive 1-1/4 mile to Park View. Turn left, cross Wilshire Blvd. and park as above. From the Hollywood Fwy., take the Alvarado St. turnoff southbound and drive 1.1 miles to Wilshire Blvd. Turn left at Park View.

Bring a filled water bottle or two if you do not want to rely on the scattered water sources. There are very few public restrooms along the route. The portable restrooms at MacArthur Park were in the worst state that we have ever seen! Plan on showing a credit card at a gas station or use the facilities at landmark spots such as Union Station.

An option to start the tour from a better kept public area is to start from Lafayette Park. This option adds about one mile to the reference tour.

TRIP DESCRIPTION: **MacArthur Park.** Tour the park before leaving on the trip to the Civic Center. There is a small but beautiful man-made lake complete with water fountain. There are bikeways/walkways throughout the treed park which allow easy access to the park's north side. In this grass-laden hilly park are observation and picnic benches, an outdoor theater, and a mixed array of walkers, joggers, sitters, and "overnight campers."

197

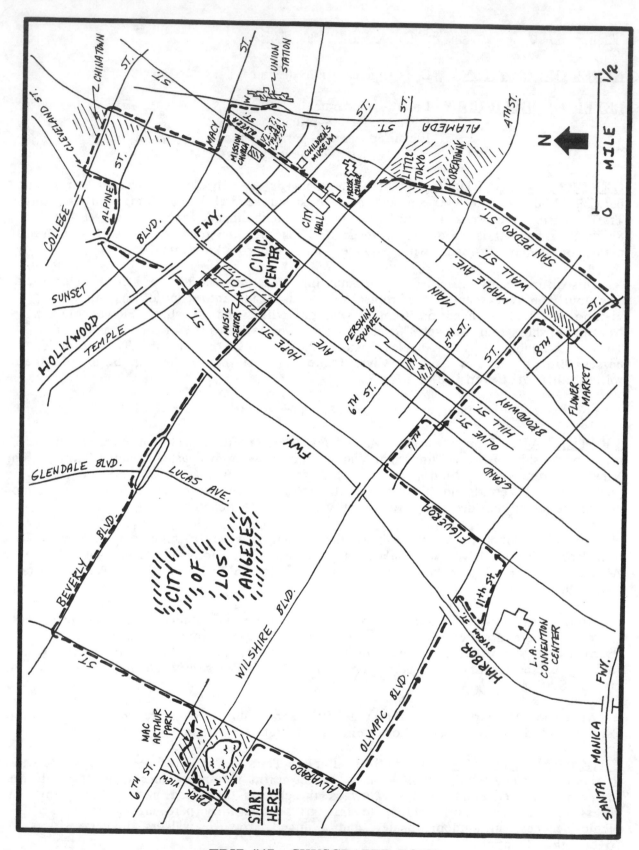

TRIP #47 - SKYSCRAPER TOUR

Eastward into the Big City. Pedal south on Alvarado St. and follow the mild upgrade near 8th St. and continue on Class II-like bikeway to Olympic Blvd. Note that "Class II-like" is used on this tour to mean unsigned roads with a marked lane for car parking and adequate bike space within the lane. Turn left on Olympic Blvd. (0.6) and pedal on flat Class II roadway through a light commercial section with scattered residences. Bike under the Harbor Fwy. and turn right at the first street, Byram St. (1.3).

Convention Center to L.A. Wholesale Flower Terminal. Turn left again at 111th St. and pass in front of the Los Angeles Convention Center. There is a view of the L.A. skyscraper complex to the left in this area. Turn left onto Class II Figueroa St. and pedal to 9th St. where the marked bikepath ends. Continue north into the "teeth" of skyscraper country and follow the short upgrade to Wilshire Blvd. (2.2). Turn right and bike on the road that is almost totally shadowed by the surrounding high-rises.

Pass Hope St. and the First Interstate Bank Building, the scene of the deadly and spectacular 1988 fire. Turn left in a short distance and travel one block north to Pershing Square, listen to a "fire and brimstone" speech from one of the locals (subject is variable), then backtrack to Wilshire Blvd. Continue to the street's end at Grand Ave., turn right, then left again at 7th St.

Follow the continued Class X road past pace-setting Clifton's Cafeteria and continue 0.4 mile to Los Angeles St., where the commercial buildings dwindle in height and the sunshine returns (3.1). Turn right at Maple Ave. and pass the quaint L.A. Wholesale Flower Terminal. This local "flower capitol" bustles at 5:30 am Monday, Wednesday and Friday. Turn left at 8th St., bike a short distance to San Pedro St., and turn left (northeast) (3.3).

"War Zone" to Koreatown. Travelling north on San Pedro St. provides a study of poverty and filth (we are providing the "full" L.A. tour!). There is trash everywhere and a large number of folks milling around, many of whom are street people. In 0.6 mile is 4th St. and the southern terminus of Koreatown. The environment transitions to one of cleanliness and order from the south side of 4th St. to the north side. At 2nd St. in Little Tokyo, cross the street and follow the diagonal bikeway/walkway through the nifty little shopping center. Stop and observe L.A. City Hall which is framed by the buildings in the mall.

Northward to Union Station. Cross 1st St. and bike northwest on Class II bikeway with Parker Center to the right. Turn right on Main St., pass under the City Hall-City Hall East walkway, and continue to the Temple St. intersection (4.4). On the west side is the interesting U.S. Courthouse and to the east, the Los Angeles Mall and pleasant Fletcher Boman Square. Just beyond is the L.A. Children's Museum.

Cross over the Santa Ana Fwy. and enter the birthplace of Los Angeles. Directly ahead is the expansive El Pueblo De Los Angeles Historic Park which includes the old Mission Church to the left and the charming L. A. Plaza to the right (4.6). Just north of the plaza, paralleling Main St., is renowned Olvera St. Pedal north on Main St. and turn right on Sunset Blvd./Macy St., then right again on Alameda St. Bike a short distance to the classic Union Station railroad passenger terminal. Return to Macy St. and bike west.

199

Mac Arthur Park

Chinatown and the Los Angeles Civic Center. Continue west 0.2 mile to Broadway and turn right. Bike through Chinatown on the busy Class X road with two lanes and no bike shoulder -- bike in the middle of the right lane in this stretch all the way to College St. (5.9). Turn left on the Class II bike route and pedal a moderate upgrade 0.2 mile to Alpine St. Turn right and bike the testy upgrade which crests and heads downhill to Figueroa St.

Turn left and stare into the L.A. Civic Center, and bike downhill under the Hollywood Fwy. Turn left at Temple St., bike uphill to the crest at Grand Ave., then cruise by the Music Center complex. Continue downhill to Hill St. (7.1) and turn right. Then bike further downhill over the top of the L.A. subway to 1st St. Turn right again.

The Return Segment. Bike a short distance on this Class II street and begin the short workout upgrade to a point with views of the L.A. area skyline both east and west. Pass the north side of the L.A. Music Center and bike downhill under the Harbor Fwy. (7.9).

Different from most of our tours, we saved the most testy hills until last. This is a great opportunity to work off all those goodies which were consumed at the landmark sites along the way. Follow the short uphill to the crest from which there is a grand view of three more hills. Just before reaching the Glendale Blvd. overpass, turn right and bike down the paralleling road to Glendale Blvd., cross that street and bike back up to Beverly Blvd. (previously 1st St.) -- trust us, its easier! Bike the steep upgrade which crests at Belmont Ave. Continue up another shorter upgrade, then pedal downhill to Alvarado St. (8.9).

200

Turn left (southwest) and bike on Class II-like roadway through the commercial/industrial area. Continue through light rolling hills past 3rd St. and continue another 1/2 mile to 6th St. and the edge of MacArthur Park. Bike northwest through the park, pass the outdoor theater, and pedal through the tunnel to the park's south side. Follow the path up to Park View and the starting point (9.8).

CONNECTING TRIPS: Connection with the Exposition Park/USC Campus Tour (Trip #48) - at the intersection of Olympic Blvd. and Figueroa St., turn southwest on the latter street and bike 1-3/4 mile.

TRIP #48 - INNER CITY BIKEWAY SYSTEM

GENERAL LOCATION: Central Los Angeles, Exposition Park, USC Campus

LEVEL OF DIFFICULTY: Exposition Park-USC Campus: Loop - easy
Distance - 3.8 miles
Elevation gain - flat

GENERAL DESCRIPTION: Central Los Angeles. There is a system of predominantly Class III bikeways spread throughout the central city area, as is shown in the accompanying tour map. The problem is that these routes are so little used by bikers that drivers appear oblivious to the fact that these are shared roadways. This was particularly true on the north-south Hoover St. and Broadway routes. Also, most routes are on busy, fast moving roadways.

We have only biked selected segments of this system, but will generalize: For bikers who are uncomfortable biking with heavy traffic on roadways with limited biking room, use these routes only as connectors to other rides, but not as primary routes. We have included the "Inner City Bikeway System" for completeness.

Exposition Park-USC Campus. There is an interesting and scenic tour available in the Exposition Park-University of Southern California area. The area is shown in the mini-tour map below. Take this tour any time when there is <u>not</u> a major event at either the Coliseum or the Sports Arena. Allow extra time beyond that needed for biking to visit the following: Science and Industry Museum, Museum of Natural History, and the Rose Garden in Exposition Park and the USC Campus.

TRAILHEAD: **Exposition Park-USC Campus.** From the Harbor Fwy., exit west at Martin Luther King Jr. Blvd. and turn right (north) in 0.6 miles at Vermont Ave. Drive 0.3 mile to N. Coliseum Dr. and turn right. Find parking subject to posted laws.

Water is plentiful on this tour.

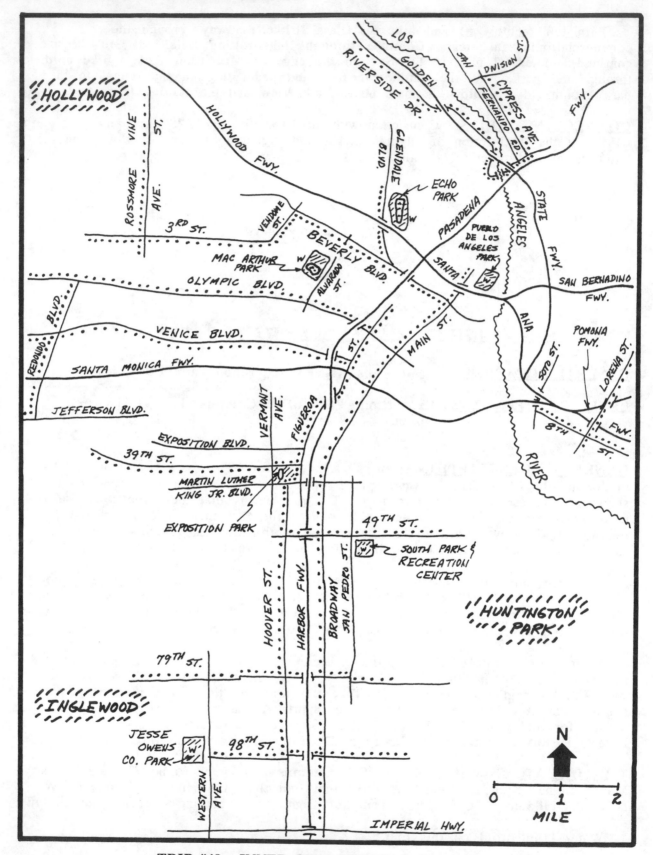

TRIP #48 - INNER CITY BIKEWAY SYSTEM

TRIP DESCRIPTION: Exposition Park-U.S.C. Campus. A sample Class I peripheral route is shown in the mini-tour map below. However, we recommend a free-form tour which includes many of the scenic interior bikeways/walkways.

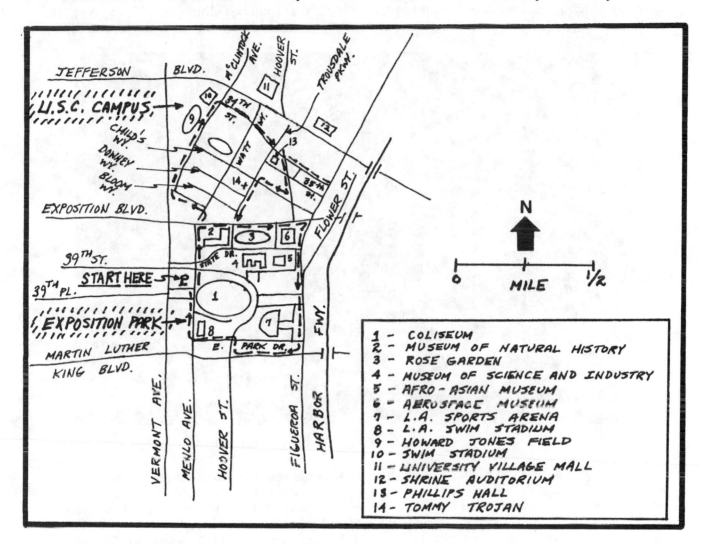

1 - COLISEUM
2 - MUSEUM OF NATURAL HISTORY
3 - ROSE GARDEN
4 - MUSEUM OF SCIENCE AND INDUSTRY
5 - AFRO-ASIAN MUSEUM
6 - AEROSPACE MUSEUM
7 - L.A. SPORTS ARENA
8 - L.A. SWIM STADIUM
9 - HOWARD JONES FIELD
10 - SWIM STADIUM
11 - UNIVERSITY VILLAGE MALL
12 - SHRINE AUDITORIUM
13 - PHILLIPS HALL
14 - TOMMY TROJAN

Exposition Park. Bike north on Menlo Ave. 0.2 mile and turn right on Exposition Blvd. Bike past one of several treed rest/picnic areas and pass the striking main entrance to the Museum of Natural History. Follow the wide walkway past the north edge of the exquisite Rose Garden (0.4), then continue a short distance to the aircraft displays behind the Aerospace Museum.

Turn right at Figueroa St. and bike on the walkway passing Julie's Trojan Barrel (across the street), the Mitsubishi IMAX theater, and the main entry into the Museum of Science and Industry and the Afro-American Museum. Bike past the Sports Arena to Martin Luther King Jr. Blvd. (1.0) and turn right. Follow the wide sidewalk to Hoover St. and turn right, left at the next street (E. Park Dr.), and bike alongside the classic Los Angeles Swim Stadium. Cruise along the periphery of the gigantic Coliseum and return to the trip origin (1.6).

   USC Campus. Cross Exposition Blvd. at Hoover St. and turn left immediately (1.8), pass the Computer Science Center, then turn right at McClintock Ave. Enjoy the varied architectures which are found throughout the entire campus while biking past the Andrus Gerontology Center, Bloom Wy., the tennis stadium at Child's Wy., the track stadium, Howard Jones' Field, and the swim stadium, complete with jacuzzi (2.2).

Rose Garden

   Turn right at 34th St., pedal past the Carson Motion Picture Studio, the water fountain at Trousdale Pkwy., and continue to the end of the street (2.7). Backtrack a short distance and turn sharply left onto Hoover Way. Pass towering Phillips Hall and follow the picturesque roadway to Child's Wy. (3.2). Turn right and bike through the stately common with its lovely water fountain, then turn left again at Trousdale Pkwy. In a short distance is the popular USC (and UCLA) landmark, Tommy Trojan.

   Continue pedaling to Exposition Blvd. Cross this road and turn right, then bike just beyond the Rose Garden and turn left. Turn right again at State Dr. and bike a short distance to the trip origin (3.8). NOTE: Don is a UCLA graduate, so inclusion of this tour should be considred "beyond the call of duty."

CONNECTING TRIPS: Connection with Tour de Los Angeles (Trip #49) - at the intersection of Trousdale Pkwy. and Jefferson Blvd. (near the water fountain), bike east on Jefferson Blvd., then turn north on Figueroa St. Continue to Venice Blvd.

?

TRIP #49 - TOUR de LOS ANGELES

GENERAL LOCATION: Ballona Creek, Central Los Angeles, L.A. River, Long Beach, San Pedro, Palos Verdes, South Bay

LEVEL OF DIFFICULTY: Loop - strenuous
Distance - 71.7 miles
Elevation gain - periodic moderate-to-steep grades in San Pedro and the Palos Verdes Peninsula; flat elsewhere

GENERAL DESCRIPTION: This nifty seventy mile plus "looper" cruises Ballona Creek, travels inland into the heart of the City of Los Angeles, then follows the Los Angeles River to Long Beach. Next, the tour visits the scenic Palos Verdes Peninsula before heading north on the South Bay Bike Trail, returning to the origin at Fisherman's Village in Marina Del Rey. If the biker wants a true slice of the Los Angeles area, do this tour. Most of the route is on Class I or Class II path. Because of heavy traffic in the Central Los Angeles area, this trip is best saved for weekends.

TRAILHEAD: Follow the Marina Fwy. to its terminus and continue west to Lincoln Blvd. Turn left (south) on Lincoln Blvd. and continue about 1/2 mile to Fiji Wy. Take Fiji Wy. to the parking area at Fisherman's Village or use the overflow parking lot between the village and Lincoln Blvd.

Bring a couple of bottles of water to minimize water stops even though there is water at several parks along the way. Also bring an automobile roadmap as a backup, should the biker stray from the described route.

TRIP DESCRIPTION: **Ballona Creek - Central Los Angeles.** The trip description will detail only the new or confusing portions of this loop. This tour starts at Fisherman's Village and continues northeast along Ballona Creek to McManus Park (Trip #4) (6.6). Bike east on National Blvd. which fuses in a short distance with Class III Jefferson Blvd. In 0.9 mile, turn left at Redondo Blvd. and bike on Class III bikeway with a wide shoulder under the Santa Monica Fwy. Continue past Washington Blvd. to Venice Blvd. (gas station) and turn right (8.9).

Pedal on Class II roadway through a mixed commercial/residential area, follow the short, mild upgrade and pass under West Blvd. At Crenshaw Blvd. the path transitions to Class III and the bike shoulder varies from skimpy to modest from this juncture to downtown Los Angeles. (This was our least favorite segment of the trip.)

Continue through varied areas of residential, commercial, and limited industrial development past Normandie Ave. (11.7). On the northeast corner is Normandie Recreation Center (water, recreation fields). Nearby is the Rosedale Cemetary and Loyola High School---this area is definitely the highlight of the Venice Blvd. segment. Pedal past Vermont Ave., pass under the Harbor Fwy., and continue through the run-down commercial district to Figueroa St. (13.6).

Central Los Angeles to Los Angeles River. Follow Class X roadway through another 1.8 miles of an old commercial area to Hooper Blvd. The route is Venice Blvd. to Broadway, left to 16th St., 0.5 mile to San Pedro St., left to 15th St., 0.3 mile to Griffith, left to 14th Pl., 0.3 mile to Central Ave., right to 15th St. and 0.3 mile to Hooper Blvd.

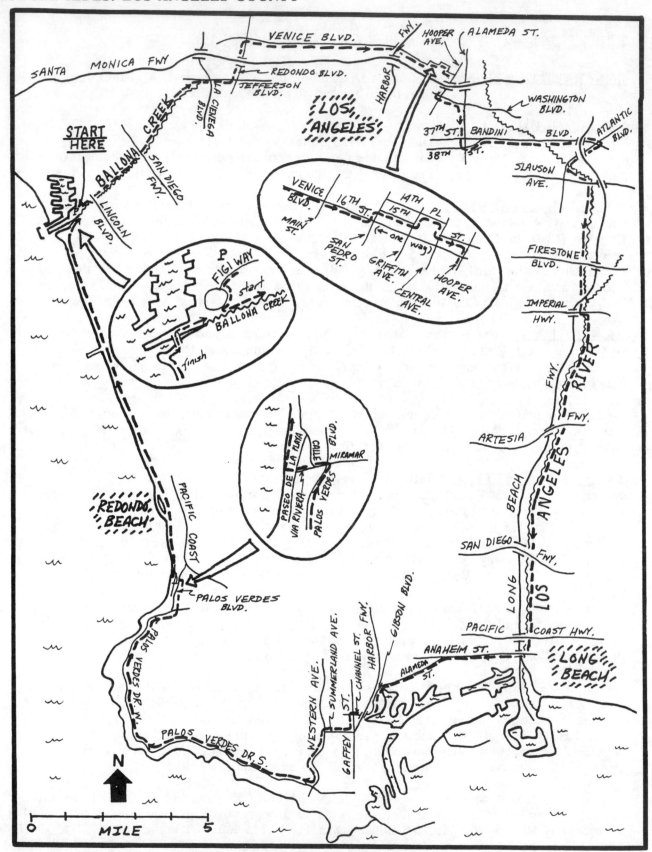

TRIP #49 - TOUR de LOS ANGELES

Turn right, pass under the Santa Monica Fwy., and turn left (east) at Washington Blvd. in 0.2 mile. In 0.4 mile at Alameda St., the road passes "truck city" where there are hundreds of trucks clustered near the local railway complex. In another 1/2 mile, turn right at Santa Fe Ave. (16.5) and continue south for 0.7 mile. Turn left at 38th St. which fuses into Bandini Blvd. in a short distance. This is a fine wide road which crosses Soto St. and a gas station in 0.4 mile, passes the Farmer John plant (P.U.!), and then crosses the Los Angeles River. The road parallels the river, continues another three miles to the Long Beach Fwy. undercrossing, and reaches Atlantic Blvd. just beyond (20.7). Recross the Los Angeles River and bike to the bicycle entry point on the southeast side of the bridge.

Los Angeles River. Follow the Los Angeles River 5.3 miles south to Imperial Blvd. (Trip #21), cross over the river to the east levee, and continue 10.0 miles further south to Anaheim St. (Trip #20B) (36.0).

San Pedro. (See Trip #9 map.) Cross the river and bike 2-1/2 miles west on Class X Anaheim St. to Alameda St.; the region is effectively early 20th-century industrial. Turn left and bike one mile until the road reaches the Los Angeles Harbor area. The street becomes "B" St., continues another 1-1/4 mile to the Harbor Fwy., then turns sharply south on what is now Gibson Blvd. (A Class I path is on the harbor side of the street.) Bike 1-3/4 miles to Channel St. and turn right, leaving the harbor area (42.5).

Follow Channel St. a short distance to Gaffey St. and turn left. Bike a steady 1/2-mile upgrade to Class III Summerland Ave. Turn right and bike a series of testy upgrades to Western Ave. There is water at Peck Park to the right. Our route, however, turns left and continues through rolling hills to 25th St. (46.0).

Palos Verdes Peninsula. Turn right and follow 25th St., which becomes Palos Verdes Dr. South, and bike the southern part of the peninsula (see Trip #6C). Follow the road as it turns north and becomes Palos Verdes Dr. West, continuing to Malaga Cove Plaza (Trip #6B) (57.8).

South Bay Bike Trail. (See Trip #1A map.) Bike east to Palos Verdes Blvd., turn left and bike 0.9 mile to Calle Miramar. Turn left toward the beach, veer left on Via Rivera, and continue about 0.1 mile across Paseo De La Playa to the beach parking lot. Coast down the bikeway/walkway to the South Bay Bike Trail origin. Continue north 12.7 miles to the trip starting point at Fisherman's Village (Trips #1A and #1B). The total tour is 71.7 miles.

<u>CONNECTING TRIPS</u>: See individual trip write-ups.

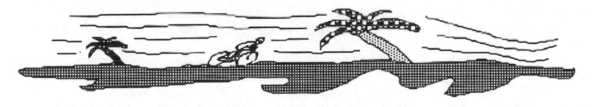

TRIP #50 - AVALON, SANTA CATALINA ISLAND

<u>GENERAL LOCATION</u>: Avalon, Santa Catalina

BICYCLE RIDES: LOS ANGELES COUNTY

LEVEL OF DIFFICULTY: Round trip - strenuous
Distance - 9.7 miles (loop)
Elevation gain - steady, strenuous upgrades on
Wrigley Terrace Dr. and Chimes Tower Rd. area

GENERAL DESCRIPTION: We visited Catalina for this fantastic tour on our wedding anniversary--very romantic! We strongly recommend that you make the trip just for the sake of biking the Avalon area. Visit Santa Catalina Island, bike this scenic route, and return the same day; however, a more relaxing option is to stay overnight and spend the next day telling the locals how you "smoked" the tourist golf-cart crowd with your bikes!

The described tour leaves the channel boat landing and tracks scenic Pebbly Beach Dr. along the coast, then follows an inland road to Mt. Ada, cresting just above the Inn on Mt. Ada (former Wrigley residence). Next is a tour of Avalon proper, a visit to Avalon's Casino, a workout pedal to the Chimes Tower, and a traverse of the hills to Avalon Canyon Rd. From this point is a nifty uphill ride to the Wrigley Memorial and Botanical Gardens and a restful return to the Cabrillo Mole.

TRAILHEAD: Avalon can be reached by several channel boat carriers from San Pedro, Long Beach or Newport Beach, and a couple of air carriers from San Pedro or Long Beach. During summer or holiday periods, make round trip reservations at least one or two weeks in advance. Bikers can transport bikes on Catalina Cruise Lines for a small fee; check with the line of your choice if interested in this option. Another possibility is to rent a multi-speed bike at Brown's Bikes on Pebbly Beach Rd. near the Cabrillo Mole or a beach cruiser (one-speed bike for flat area biking only) at Catalina Auto Rentals at Crescent Ave. and Metropole Ave. (This information is current as of December 1988.) Visitors planning overnight trips to Catalina during peak season should not arrive in Avalon without confirmed reservations.

Bring a filled water bottle. There are abundant public water sources in the flats of Avalon (where it is not needed) and _no_ water in the hillside mountainous areas (where it _is_ needed).

TRIP DESCRIPTION: Pebbly Beach Rd. From the Cabrillo Mole, turn left on Pebbly Beach Rd. and bike on the flat road with the ocean immediately to the left and the cliffs to the right. Pass the cruise ship anchorage (Mexican-bound cruise ships visit Santa Catalina Island weekly), the Amphibian Air Terminal (stop and watch the amphibians make their ocean landings), and the Buffalo Nickel Restaurant at Pebbly Beach.

This is a 0.9 mile stretch of continuous ocean viewing. Continue 0.2 mile to the small residential-industrial complex and, just beyond, branch to the roadway which heads inland and uphill.

The Inn at Mt. Ada (Former Wrigley Residence). Turn right and shift into the "granny gears" on this one-way highway stretch (keep an eye peeled for kamikazee rental golf carters going the wrong way!). The small road progresses on a series of switchbacks through a treed, semi-arid canyon area, follows an uphill, traverses the side of Mt. Ada, then reaches one of several scenic viewpoints in about 1/2 mile. In about one mile from the initial branch point, the road reaches a crest with a spectacular overlook of Avalon and the harbor (2.3).

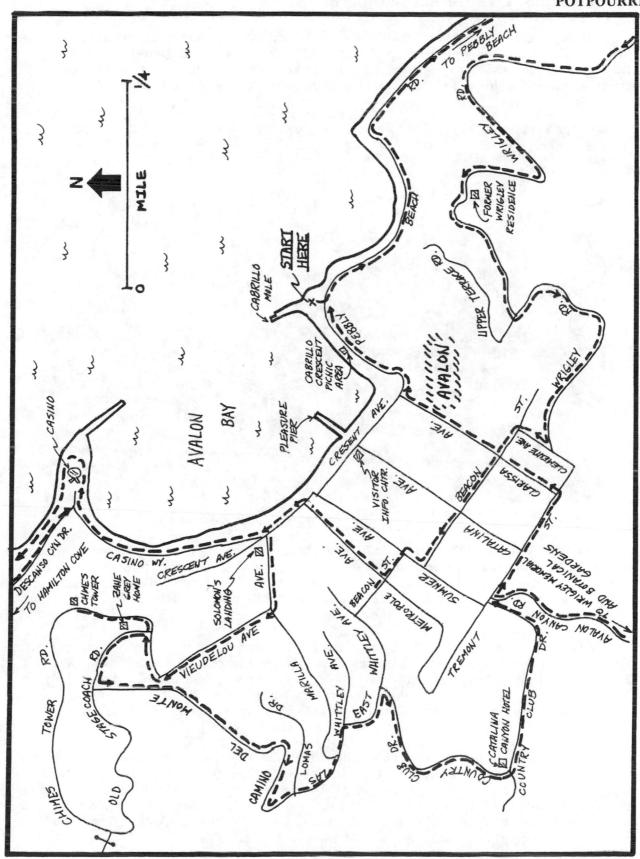

TRIP #50 - AVALON, SANTA CATALINA ISLAND

Just beyond is the <u>private</u> road entry to the Inn at Mt. Ada. The majestic former Wrigley Residence is visible at different angles from the road, now named Wrigley Rd. There are additional spectacular harbor views as the narrow (now two-way) street switchbacks down to the City of Avalon at Clemente Ave. (3.2).

Avalon Harbor From Mount Ada

City of Avalon. Turn right and in a short distance turn left at Beacon St. Continue 1/4 mile on this residential street to Metropole Ave. and turn right. Follow the mixed commercial/residential road to the Metropole Market Place and turn left (3.7). To the right is the Busy Bee Restaurant, with some delightful outdoor dining under umbrellas and alongside the harbor.

However, our route goes left and passes Solomon's Landing (one of our dinnertime favorites, with a bakery and deli), then proceeds on Crescent Ave. to Casino Way. Follow this road below the cliffs past the Casino Landing and the Catalina Island Yacht Center. Just beyond is the landmark Casino of Avalon. Turn right and tour the Casino periphery, passing the Catalina Island Museum entrance, the Casino Dock Cafe, and reach the Scuba dive area at Casino Point.

Continue around the Casino and follow the beach pathway to developed Descanso Beach. (4.1). Bike the short uphill to Descanso Canyon Dr., turn right and follow the testy upgrade through lovely tree-covered Descanso Canyon. We followed the road for a half mile and turned around, although more adventurous bikers can follow the road another 1/2 mile to the deadend at condo city in Hamilton Cove. Return to Solomon's Landing and turn right at Marilla Ave. (5.2).

Chimes Tower. Turn right and pump 0.1 mile up steep Marilla Ave. The reward is a right turn at Vieudelou Ave. and another steep upgrade for 0.2 mile. Continue past Old Stagecoach Rd. and bike on continued steep uphill to a fine viewpoint just below the Zane Grey Hotel (original home of Zane Grey).

Bike a short distance on continued steep uphill on one-way road (against the traffic) to the Chimes Tower and yet another scenic viewpoint. (Note that more ambitious bikers can take the one-way Old Stagecoach Rd.-Chimes Tower Rd. loop and bike downhill to the tower) (5.5).

The Traverse to Avalon Canyon Rd. Backtrack to Old Stagecoach Rd. and turn onto that street. In 0.1 mile at the junction, turn left onto Camino Del Monte. Follow the short workout upgrade, then enjoy a steep downgrade on a tree-lined street with impressive residences. At the next intersection, stay to the right (as with each succeeding intersection through Avalon Canyon Rd.) and proceed on Las Lomas Dr. Pedal downhill past Marilla Ave. and turn right at East Whittley Ave.

Just beyond, turn hard right onto Country Club Dr., follow the downhill on tree-lined roadway, and enjoy the view of the canyon area. At the Catalina Canyon Hotel, follow the road as it proceeds past the spur road to the right (also named Country Club Dr.) and veers to the left (east). Follow the fun downhill past Picture Point (a golfer viewpoint/meeting point), the Catalina Clubhouse, and continue to Tremont St. (6.8). Turn right and in a short distance turn right again at Avalon Canyon Rd.

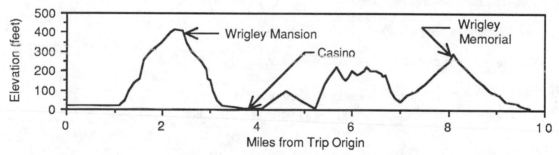

Wrigley Memorial and Botanical Garden. Follow the tree-lined uphill road past the north edge of the Catalina Island Golf Course; the 1.2 mile route to the Wrigley Memorial is on steady uphill varying from moderate to testy. This rural road passes the Sand Trap at Falls Canyon Rd. (lemonade, "firewater", and snacks), the Catalina Stables, Bird Park Campground (water, restrooms), and continues past the southern edge of the golf course (7.4).

In 0.2 mile pass the Avalon Canyon Campground (water, restrooms), and follow the steady workout grade to the pay entrance to the stately Wrigley Memorial. Bike riding is prohibited beyond this point. Note that every type of plant life indiginous to the area and a few imported varieties are all classified in the general area (7.9).

The Finale. Backtrack to Tremont Ave. and turn right, biking 0.2 mile to Clarissa Ave. (9.2). Turn left and continue through residential area to the street's end at Crescent Ave. Turn left for the Avalon Shopping Mall (no biking between Clarissa Ave. and Metropole Ave.). However, the reference route turns right, proceeds past the Cabrillo Crescent Picnic Area and returns to the trip origin at Cabrillo Mole (9.7).

CONNECTING TRIPS: There are no current connector routes. Bicycling into the island interior beyond the gate above Old Stagecoach Rd. is currently prohibited.

OTHER BICYCLING INFORMATION SOURCES

Our experience has been that new bike route options can be found using a variety of sources. Our condensed recommendation list for information sources for Los Angeles County is as follows:

1. **CALTRANS: District 07 - L.A., Orange, and Ventura Counties**
   Address: State of California
   Department of Transportation
   P.O. Box 2304
   Terminal Annex
   L.A., Ca. 90051
   or
   California Department of Transportation
   120 S. Spring St.
   L.A., Ca. 90012

CALTRANS provides a fine "starter kit" publication which includes bicycling laws and safety tips, sources of additional information, Park and Ride locations, bike facilities at beaches and coastal parks, and selected bike routes.

2. **Department of Water Resources**
   Address: Southern District
   P. O. Box 6598
   L.A., Ca. 90055

   California Aqueduct Information (213) 620-5667

3. **City of L.A. and County Government**
   Addresses: L.A. City Department of Transportation
   200 N. Spring St.
   L.A., Ca. 90012

   L.A. County Road Department
   1540 Alcazar St.
   L.A., Ca. 90033

   Bikeways Unit (City of L.A. information) (213) 485-3051

4. **City Government**
   Address: Write to individual City Hall, Public Works, or Park and Recreation Departments for the city of interest.

5. **National Forest, State and Local Parks**
   Addresses: U.S. Department of Agriculture
   U.S. Forest Service: Angeles National Forest
   150 S. Los Robles
   Pasadena, Ca. 91101

6. **Bicycling Organizations** (examples)
   Address: California Association of Bicycle Organizations
   P.O. Box 2684
   Dublin, Ca. 94566

   American Youth Hostels
   357 W. 7th St.
   San Pedro, Ca. 90731

   Downey Cyclists
   11430 Paramount Blvd.
   Downey, Ca. 90241

   Los Angeles Wheelmen
   1220 Fonthill Ave.
   Torrance, Ca. 90503

   Malibu Beach and Bike Club
   Box 116
   Malibu, Ca. 90265

   Palos Verdes Cyclists
   5023 Pacific Coast Hwy.
   Torrance, Ca. 90505

   Pedali Allez, LA
   515 San Vicente Blvd. (#D)
   Santa Monica, Ca. 90402

   Sierra Club Bicycle Touring (back country emphasis)
   3550 W. 5th St. (Room 321)
   L.A., Ca. 90020

7. **American Automobile Club** (membership required)
   Address: Bicycling Tour Counselor
   L.A. District Office
   Automobile Club of Southern California
   2601 S. Figueroa St.
   L.A., Ca. 90007

8. **Other Sources**
   Addresses: Bicycling and sports shops, bicycle magazines available free at bicycle shops (e.g. *California Bicyclist, City Sports, Competitor,* and *Southwest Cycling*), fellow bikers, and (God forbid) other bicycling books.

INDEX

214

BICYCLE RIDES: LOS ANGELES COUNTY